Learn the subject...
Study right...
Master your classes...

Are you **REA**dy? It all starts here.
Master high school Physics with
REA's comprehensive study guide.

Visit us online at
www.rea.com

The *High School* TUTOR®

PHYSICS

Staff of Research & Education Association

Special Chapter Reviews by
Joseph J. Molitoris, Ph.D.
Department of Physics
Muhlenberg College, Allentown, PA

Research & Education Association
Visit our website at
www.rea.com

Research & Education Association
61 Ethel Road West
Piscataway, New Jersey 08854
E-mail: info@rea.com

THE HIGH SCHOOL TUTOR®
PHYSICS

Printed in the United States of America

Library of Congress Control Number 2006932110

International Standard Book Number 0-87891-597-4

THE HIGH SCHOOL TUTOR® and REA® are registered
trademarks of Research & Education Association, Inc.

REA's HIGH SCHOOL TUTOR® SERIES
Designed with You in Mind

REA's High School Tutor® series gives you everything you need to excel in your high school classes, especially on midterms, finals, and even pop quizzes.

Think of this book as access to your own private tutor. Here, right at your fingertips, in a handy Q & A format, is a great companion to your textbook. You'll also find that the High School Tutor® lends greater depth to classroom lectures. You've heard all about the theorems, the timelines, the big ideas, and the key principles; this book equips you to break it all down into bite-size chunks.

To obtain maximum benefit from the book, students should familiarize themselves with the tips below.

Larry Kling
High School Tutor Program Director

HOW TO USE THIS BOOK

Physics students will find this book to be an invaluable supplement to their textbooks. The book is divided into 19 chapters, each dealing with a separate topic. The information is presented in problem-and-solution format to match the format of the tests and quizzes teachers are likely to use. By reviewing the questions and the provided answers, students can prepare themselves for actual test situations.

HOW TO GRASP A TOPIC FULLY

1.   Refer to your class text and read the section pertaining to the topic. You should become acquainted with the themes discussed there.

2.   Locate the topic you are looking for by referring to the Table of Contents in the front of this book.

To learn and understand a topic thoroughly and retain its contents, it will generally be necessary for you to review the problems several times. Repeated review is essential to gain experience in recognizing the themes that are most relevant and selecting the best solution techniques.

HOW TO FIND A QUESTION TYPE

To locate one or more questions related to particular subject matter, refer to the index. The numbers in the index refer to *question* numbers, not to page numbers. This arrangement is intended to facilitate finding a question rapidly, since two or more questions may appear on a page.

If a particular type of question cannot be found readily, it is recommended that you refer to the Table of Contents in the front pages and then turn to the chapter that is applicable to the question being sought.

In preparing for an exam, it is useful to find the topics to be covered on the exam in the Table of Contents, and then review the questions under those topics several times. This should equip you with what might be needed for the exam.

ABOUT RESEARCH & EDUCATION ASSOCIATION

Founded in 1959, Research & Education Association is dedicated to publishing the finest and most effective educational materials—including software, study guides, and test preps—for students in middle school, high school, graduate school, and beyond. Today, REA's wide-ranging catalog is a leading resource for teachers, students, and professionals.

We invite you to visit us at *www.rea.com* to find out how "REA is making the world smarter."

STAFF ACKNOWLEDGMENTS

We would like to thank **Pam Weston**, Vice President, Publishing, for setting the quality standards for production integrity and managing the publication to completion; **Molly Solanki**, Associate Editor, for post-production quality assurance; **Anne Winthrop Esposito**, Senior Editor, for coordination of revisions; **Rachel DiMatteo**, Graphic Designer, for typesetting revisions; and **Christine Saul**, Senior Graphic Artist, for cover design.

CONTENTS

UNITS CONVERSION FACTORS

This section includes a particularly useful and comprehensive table to aid students and teachers in converting between systems of units.

The problems and their solutions in this book use **SI** (**International System**) as well as English units. Both of these units are in extensive use throughout the world, and therefore students should develop a good facility to work with both sets of units until a single standard of units has been found acceptable internationally.

In working out or solving a problem in one system of units or the other, essentially only the numbers change. Also, the conversion from one unit system to another is easily achieved through the use of conversion factors that are given in the subsequent table. Accordingly, the units are one of the least important aspects of a problem. For these reasons, a student should not be concerned mainly with which units are used in any particular problem. Instead, a student should obtain from that problem and its solution an understanding of the underlying principles and solution techniques that are illustrated there.

To convert	To	Multiply by	For the reverse, multiply by
acres	square feet	4.356×10^4	2.296×10^{-5}
acres	square meters	4047	2.471×10^{-4}
ampere-hours	coulombs	3600	2.778×10^{-4}
ampere-turns	gilberts	1.257	0.7958
ampere-turns per cm. ..	ampere-turns per inch	2.54	0.3937
angstrom units	inches	3.937×10^{-9}	2.54×10^8
angstrom units	meters	10^{-10}	10^{10}
atmospheres	feet of water	33.90	0.02950
atmospheres	inch of mercury at 0°C	29.92	3.342×10^{-2}
atmospheres	kilogram per square meter	1.033×10^4	9.678×10^{-5}
atmospheres	millimeter of mercury at 0°C	760	1.316×10^{-3}
atmospheres	pascals	1.0133×10^5	0.9869×10^{-5}
atmospheres	pounds per square inch	14.70	0.06804
bars	atmospheres	9.870×10^{-7}	1.0133
bars	dynes per square cm.	10^6	10^{-6}
bars	pascals	10^5	10^{-5}
bars	pounds per square inch	14.504	6.8947×10^{-2}
Btu	ergs	1.0548×10^{10}	9.486×10^{-11}
Btu	foot-pounds	778.3	1.285×10^{-3}
Btu	joules	1054.8	9.480×10^{-4}
Btu	kilogram-calories	0.252	3.969
calories, gram	Btu	3.968×10^{-3}	252
calories, gram	foot-pounds	3.087	0.324
calories, gram	joules	4.185	0.2389
Celsius	Fahrenheit	$(°C \times 9/5) + 32 = °F$	$(°F - 32) \times 5/9 = °C$

To convert	To	Multiply	For the reverse, multiply by
Celsius	kelvin	°C + 273.1 = K	K − 273.1 = °C
centimeters	angstrom units	1×10^8	1×10^{-8}
centimeters	feet	0.03281	30.479
centistokes	square meters per second	1×10^{-6}	1×10^6
circular mils	square centimeters	5.067×10^{-6}	1.973×10^5
circular mils	square mils	0.7854	1.273
cubic feet	gallons (liquid U.S.)	7.481	0.1337
cubic feet	liters	28.32	3.531×10^{-2}
cubic inches	cubic centimeters	16.39	6.102×10^{-2}
cubic inches	cubic feet	5.787×10^{-4}	1728
cubic inches	cubic meters	1.639×10^{-5}	6.102×10^4
cubic inches	gallons (liquid U.S.)	4.329×10^{-3}	231
cubic meters	cubic feet	35.31	2.832×10^{-2}
cubic meters	cubic yards	1.308	0.7646
curies	coulombs per minute	1.1×10^{12}	0.91×10^{-12}
cycles per second	hertz	1	1
degrees (angle)	mils	17.45	5.73×10^{-2}
degrees (angle)	radians	1.745×10^{-2}	57.3
dynes	pounds	2.248×10^{-6}	4.448×10^5
electron volts	joules	1.602×10^{-19}	0.624×10^{18}
ergs	foot-pounds	7.376×10^{-8}	1.356×10^7
ergs	joules	10^{-7}	10^7
ergs per second	watts	10^{-7}	10^7
ergs per square cm.	watts per square cm.	10^{-3}	10^3
Fahrenheit	kelvin	(°F + 459.67)/1.8	1.8K − 459.67
Fahrenheit	Rankine	°F + 459.67 = °R	°R − 459.67 = °F
faradays	ampere-hours	26.8	3.731×10^{-2}
feet	centimeters	30.48	3.281×10^{-2}
feet	meters	0.3048	3.281
feet	mils	1.2×10^4	8.333×10^{-5}
fermis	meters	10^{-15}	10^{15}
foot candles	lux	10.764	0.0929
foot lamberts	candelas per square meter	3.4263	0.2918
foot-pounds	gram-centimeters	1.383×10^4	1.235×10^{-5}
foot-pounds	horsepower-hours	5.05×10^{-7}	1.98×10^6
foot-pounds	kilogram-meters	0.1383	7.233
foot-pounds	kilowatt-hours	3.766×10^{-7}	2.655×10^6
foot-pounds	ounce-inches	192	5.208×10^{-3}
gallons (liquid U.S.)	cubic meters	3.785×10^{-3}	264.2
gallons (liquid U.S.)	gallons (liquid British Imperial)	0.8327	1.201
gammas	teslas	10^{-9}	10^9
gausses	lines per square cm.	1.0	1.0
gausses	lines per square inch	6.452	0.155
gausses	teslas	10^{-4}	10^4
gausses	webers per square inch	6.452×10^{-8}	1.55×10^7
gilberts	amperes	0.7958	1.257
grads	radians	1.571×10^{-2}	63.65
grains	grams	0.06480	15.432
grains	pounds	$1/_{7000}$	7000
grams	dynes	980.7	1.02×10^{-3}
grams	grains	15.43	6.481×10^{-2}

To convert	To	Multiply	For the reverse, multiply by
grams	ounces (avdp)	3.527×10^{-2}	28.35
grams	poundals	7.093×10^{-2}	14.1
hectares	acres	2.471	0.4047
horsepower	Btu per minute	42.418	2.357×10^{-2}
horsepower	foot-pounds per minute	3.3×10^4	3.03×10^{-5}
horsepower	foot-pounds per second	550	1.182×10^{-3}
horsepower	horsepower (metric)	1.014	0.9863
horsepower	kilowatts	0.746	1.341
inches	centimeters	2.54	0.3937
inches	feet	8.333×10^{-2}	12
inches	meters	2.54×10^{-2}	39.37
inches	miles	1.578×10^{-5}	6.336×10^4
inches	mils	10^3	10^{-3}
inches	yards	2.778×10^{-2}	36
joules	foot-pounds	0.7376	1.356
joules	watt-hours	2.778×10^{-4}	3600
kilograms	tons (long)	9.842×10^{-4}	1016
kilograms	tons (short)	1.102×10^{-3}	907.2
kilograms	pounds (avdp)	2.205	0.4536
kilometers	feet	3281	3.408×10^{-4}
kilometers	inches	3.937×10^4	2.54×10^{-5}
kilometers per hour	feet per minute	54.68	1.829×10^{-2}
kilowatt-hours	Btu	3413	2.93×10^{-4}
kilowatt-hours	foot-pounds	2.655×10^6	3.766×10^{-7}
kilowatt-hours	horsepower-hours	1.341	0.7457
kilowatt-hours	joules	3.6×10^6	2.778×10^{-7}
knots	feet per second	1.688	0.5925
knots	miles per hour	1.1508	0.869
lamberts	candles per square cm.	0.3183	3.142
lamberts	candles per square inch	2.054	0.4869
liters	cubic centimeters	10^3	10^{-3}
liters	cubic inches	61.02	1.639×10^{-2}
liters	gallons (liquid U.S.)	0.2642	3.785
liters	pints (liquid U.S.)	2.113	0.4732
lumens per square foot	foot-candles	1	1
lumens per square meter	foot-candles	0.0929	10.764
lux	foot-candles	0.0929	10.764
maxwells	kilolines	10^{-3}	10^3
maxwells	webers	10^{-8}	10^8
meters	feet	3.28	30.48×10^{-2}
meters	inches	39.37	2.54×10^{-2}
meters	miles	6.214×10^{-4}	1609.35
meters	yards	1.094	0.9144
miles (nautical)	feet	6076.1	1.646×10^{-4}
miles (nautical)	meters	1852	5.4×10^{-4}
miles (statute)	feet	5280	1.894×10^{-4}
miles (statute)	kilometers	1.609	0.6214
miles (statute)	miles (nautical)	0.869	1.1508
miles per hour	feet per second	1.467	0.6818
miles per hour	knots	0.8684	1.152
millimeters	microns	10^3	10^{-3}

To convert	To	Multiply	For the reverse, multiply by
mils	meters	2.54×10^{-5}	3.94×10^4
mils	minutes	3.438	0.2909
minutes (angle)	degrees	1.666×10^{-2}	60
minutes (angle)	radians	2.909×10^{-4}	3484
newtons	dynes	10^5	10^{-5}
newtons	kilograms	0.1020	9.807
newtons per sq. meter	pascals	1	1
newtons	pounds (avdp)	0.2248	4.448
oersteds	amperes per meter	7.9577×10	1.257×10^{-2}
ounces (fluid)	quarts	3.125×10^{-2}	32
ounces (avdp)	pounds	6.25×10^{-2}	16
pints	quarts (liquid U.S.)	0.50	2
poundals	dynes	1.383×10^4	7.233×10^{-5}
poundals	pounds (avdp)	3.108×10^{-2}	32.17
pounds	grams	453.6	2.205×10^{-3}
pounds (force)	newtons	4.4482	0.2288
pounds per square inch	dynes per square cm.	6.8946×10^4	1.450×10^{-5}
pounds per square inch	pascals	6.895×10^3	1.45×10^{-4}
quarts (U.S. liquid)	cubic centimeters	946.4	1.057×10^{-3}
radians	mils	10^3	10^{-3}
radians	minutes of arc	3.438×10^3	2.909×10^{-4}
radians	seconds of arc	2.06265×10^5	4.848×10^{-6}
revolutions per minute	radians per second	0.1047	9.549
roentgens	coulombs per kilogram	2.58×10^{-4}	3.876×10^3
slugs	kilograms	1.459	0.6854
slugs	pounds (avdp)	32.174	3.108×10^{-2}
square feet	square centimeters	929.034	1.076×10^{-3}
square feet	square inches	144	6.944×10^{-3}
square feet	square miles	3.587×10^{-8}	27.88×10^6
square inches	square centimeters	6.452	0.155
square kilometers	square miles	0.3861	2.59
stokes	square meter per second	10^{-4}	10^{-4}
tons (metric)	kilograms	10^3	10^{-3}
tons (short)	pounds	2000	5×10^{-4}
torrs	newtons per square meter	133.32	7.5×10^{-3}
watts	Btu per hour	3.413	0.293
watts	foot-pounds per minute	44.26	2.26×10^{-2}
watts	horsepower	1.341×10^{-3}	746
watt-seconds	joules	1	1
webers	maxwells	10^8	10^{-8}
webers per square meter	gausses	10^4	10^{-4}

CHAPTER 1

VECTORS

┌───┐
Basic Attacks and Strategies for
Solving Problems in this Chapter
└───┘

Physics deals with many geometric objects such as scalars and vectors. A scalar is a quantity which has only a magnitude such as length, temperature, and speed. A vector (see Figure 1) is a quantity which has both magnitude and direction such as displacement, velocity, and force. The magnitude is given by the length of the vector and a suitable scale, and the direction by the arrow in the figure. Except in relativity, in physics vectors have two (in two dimensions) or three (in three dimensions) components.

Consider two displacement vectors represented in Cartesian coordinates as

$$\vec{A} = A_x\hat{x} + A_y\hat{y} = (A_x, A_y), \text{ and } \vec{B} = B_x\hat{x} + B_y\hat{y} = (B_x, B_y).$$

The first notation is called unit vector notation. *The second is called* coordinate, *or* point notation. *The magnitude of either vector (see Figure 2) may be found by the theorem of Pythagoras*

$$A = |\vec{A}| = \sqrt{A_x^2 + A_y^2}$$

and the direction by the tangent rule $\tan\theta = A_y/A_x$. *Equivalently, one may use* $\sin\theta = A_y/A$ *or* $\cos\theta = A_x/A$.

The two vectors $\vec{A}$ *and* $\vec{B}$ *may be added (See Figure 3) to get the resultant, or sum*

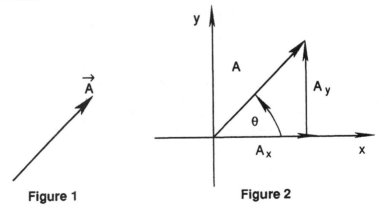

Figure 1   Figure 2

$$\vec{R} = (R_x, R_y) = (A_x + B_x, A_y + B_y).$$

The direction is again given by finding $\theta = $ Arctan (R_y / R_x) such that tan $\theta = R_y / R_x$. A similar rule applies for finding the difference. Note that this is equivalent to walking first along vector $\vec{A}$ and then along vector $\vec{B}$ to get to the resultant location $\vec{R}$. This method of adding the components and using the Pythagorean theorem and trigonometry is called the component method. It can easily be generalized to adding more than two vectors or dealing with higher dimensions. For example, in three dimensions, one would get

$$\vec{R} = (A_x + B_x + C_x)\hat{x} + (A_y + B_y + C_y)\hat{y} + (A_z + B_z + C_z)\hat{z}$$

in unit vector notation.

The other equivalent way to add vectors is by Newton's parallelogram rule. One connects the vectors head to tail, just as in the component method. One could then find the magnitude of $\vec{R}$ and the direction angle θ graphically using a ruler and protractor as in a force table laboratory exercise. Analytically, one can use geometry and the laws of cosines and sines. From geometry and Figure 3, $\angle R = \theta_A + 180° - \theta_B$. The law of cosines then gives

$$R = \sqrt{A^2 + B^2 + - 2AB \cos \angle R}.$$

The law of sines states that sin $\angle R/R = $ sin $\angle B/B$. One may thus find $\angle B$ and from it get the direction of the resultant $\theta = \theta_A + \angle B$.

Vectors cannot be multiplied or divided as scalars can. However, there are two special products: the dot product and the cross product. The dot product, or two vectors $\vec{A}$ and $\vec{B}$, is a scalar $C = \vec{A} \cdot \vec{B} = AB \cos \theta = A_x B_x + A_y B_y + A_z B_z$. The dot product may be used to find the work done by a force exerted over a certain distance, for example. The cross product is more complicated and is given by $\vec{C} = \vec{A} \times \vec{B}$ where

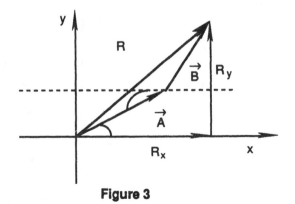

Figure 3

$$\vec{C} = (A_y B_z - A_z B_y)\hat{x} + (A_z B_x - A_x B_z)\hat{y} + (A_x B_y - A_y B_x)\hat{z}$$

For example, if A points in the x–direction and B in the y–direction, then $\vec{C} = A_x B_y \hat{z} = AB\,\hat{z}$. More conveniently, the cross product has a magnitude given by C = AB sin θ, θ being the angle from A to B, and a direction given by the right hand rule. Coil the fingers of your right hand from $\vec{A}$ to $\vec{B}$ and stick out the thumb; your thumb then points in the direction of C. For example, if $\vec{A}$ and $\vec{B}$ are in the xy plane (Figure 4), then the cross product points in the z–direction. The cross product is used in physics to find the torque exerted by a force acting at a certain position.

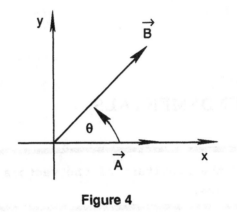

Figure 4

CHAPTER 1

VECTORS

VECTOR FUNDAMENTALS

● PROBLEM 1-1

Find the resultant of the vectors $\vec{S}_1$ and $\vec{S}_2$ specified in the figure.

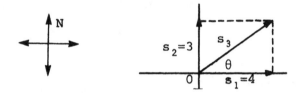

Solution. From the Pythagorean theorem, $S_1^2 + S_2^2 = S_3^2$, or $4^2 + 3^2 = S_3^2$, and so we get $S_3 = 5$ units. The direction of S_3 may be specified by the angle θ which it makes with S_1.

$$\sin \theta = \frac{S_2}{S_3} = 0.60 \quad \text{gives } \theta = 37°.$$

Resultant $\vec{S}_3$ therefore represents a displacement of 5 units from 0 in the direction 37° north of east.

● PROBLEM 1-2

Three forces acting at a point are $\vec{F}_1 = 2\hat{i} - \hat{j} + 3\hat{k}$, $\vec{F}_2 = -\hat{i} + 3\hat{j} + 2\hat{k}$, and $\vec{F}_3 = -\hat{i} + 2\hat{j} - \hat{k}$. Find the directions and magnitudes of $\vec{F}_1 + \vec{F}_2 + \vec{F}_3$, $\vec{F}_1 - \vec{F}_2 + \vec{F}_3$, and $\vec{F}_1 + \vec{F}_2 - \vec{F}_3$.

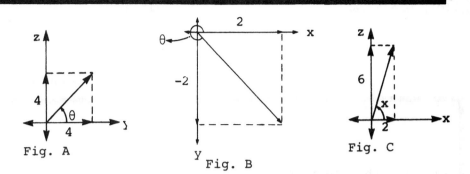

Fig. A   Fig. B   Fig. C

Solution: When vectors are added (or subtracted), their components in the directions of the unit vectors add (or subtract) algebraically. Thus since

$$\vec{F}_1 = 2\hat{i} - \hat{j} + 3\hat{k}, \quad \vec{F}_2 = - \hat{i} + 3\hat{j} + 2\hat{k}, \quad \vec{F}_3 = - \hat{i} + 2\hat{j} - \hat{k},$$

then it follows that

$$\vec{F}_1 + \vec{F}_2 + \vec{F}_3 = (2 - 1 - 1)\hat{i} + (- 1 + 3 + 2)\hat{j}$$
$$+ (3 + 2 - 1)\hat{k}$$
$$= 0\hat{i} + 4\hat{j} + 4\hat{k}.$$

Similarly,

$$\vec{F}_1 - \vec{F}_2 + \vec{F}_3 = \left[2 - (- 1) - 1\right]\hat{i} + \left[- 1 - (3) + 2\right]\hat{j}$$
$$+ \left[3 - (2) - 1\right]\hat{k}$$
$$= 2\hat{i} - 2\hat{j} + 0\hat{k}$$

and $\vec{F}_1 + \vec{F}_2 - \vec{F}_3 = \left[2 - 1 - (- 1)\right]\hat{i} + \left[- 1 + 3 - (2)\right]\hat{j}$
$$+ \left[3 + 2 - (- 1)\right]\hat{k}$$
$$= 2\hat{i} + 0\hat{j} + 6\hat{k}$$

The vector $\vec{F}_1 + \vec{F}_2 + \vec{F}_3$ thus has no component in the x-direction, one of 4 units in the y-direction, and one of 4 units in the z-direction. It therefore has a magnitude of $\sqrt{4^2 + 4^2}$ units = 4 $\sqrt{2}$ units = 5.66 units, and lies in the y- z plane, making an angle θ with the y - axis, as shown in figure (a), where tan θ = 4/4 = 1. Thus θ = 45°.

Similarly, $\vec{F}_1 - \vec{F}_2 + \vec{F}_3$ has a magnitude of 2 $\sqrt{2}$ units = 2.82 units, and lies in the x - y plane, making an angle ϕ with the x-axis, as shown in figure (b), where tan ϕ = + 2/-2 = - 1. Thus ϕ = 315°.

2

Also, $\vec{F_1} + \vec{F_2} - \vec{F_3}$ has a magnitude of $\sqrt{2^2 + 6^2}$ units $= 2\sqrt{10}$ units $= 6.32$ units, and lies in the x - z plane at an angle χ to the x-axis, as shown in figure (c), where $\tan\chi = 6/2 = 3$. Thus $\chi = 71°34'$.

• **PROBLEM** 1-3

We consider the vector

$$\vec{A} = 3\hat{x} + \hat{y} + 2\hat{z}$$

(a) Find the length of $\vec{A}$.

(b) What is the length of the projection of $\vec{A}$ on the xy plane?

(c) Construct a vector in the xy plane and perpendicular to $\vec{A}$.

(d) Construct the unit vector $\hat{B}$.

(e) Find the scalar product with $\vec{A}$ of the vector $\vec{C} = 2\hat{x}$.

(f) Find the form of $\vec{A}$ and $\vec{C}$ in a reference frame obtained from the old reference frame by a rotation of $\pi/2$ clockwise looking along the positive z axis.

(g) Find the scalar product $\vec{A} \cdot \vec{C}$ in the primed coordinate system.

(h) Find the vector product $\vec{A} \times \vec{C}$.

(i) Form the vector $\vec{A} - \vec{C}$.

Fig. 1

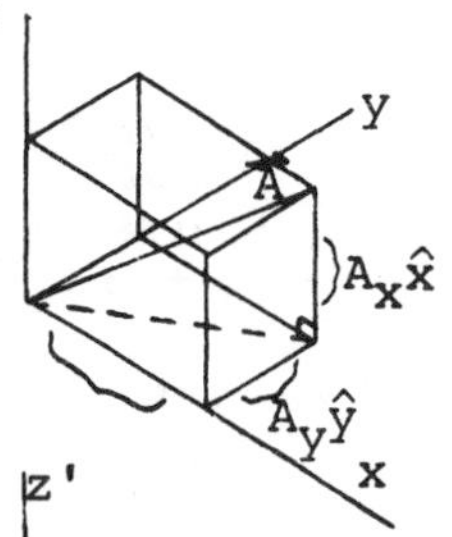

Fig. 2

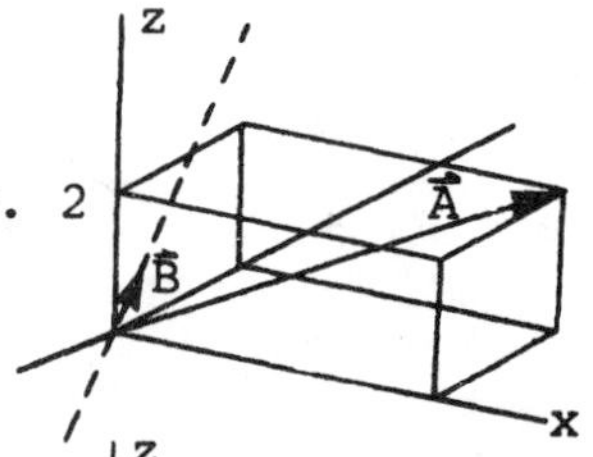

Fig. 3

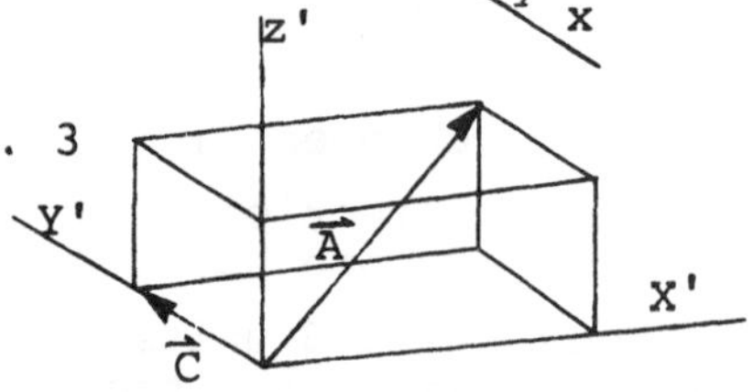

Fig. 4

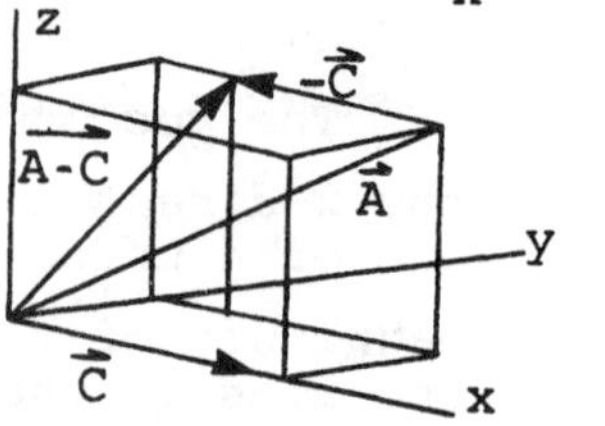

The primed reference frame x', y', z', is generated from the unprimed system x, y, z, by a rotation of $+\pi/2$ about the z axis.

<u>Solution:</u> (a) When a vector is given in the form $A_x\hat{x} + A_y\hat{y} + A_z\hat{z}$, its length is given by $\sqrt{A_x^2 + A_y^2 + A_z^2}$.

This can be seen from diagram 1. Vector $\vec{A}$ has components in the x, y and z directions. The x and y components form the legs of a right triangle. By the Pythagorean theorem the length of the hypotenuse of this triangle is $\sqrt{A_x{}^2 + A_y{}^2}$. But this line segment whose length is $\sqrt{A_x{}^2 + A_y{}^2}$ is one leg in a right triangle whose other leg is $A_z\hat{z}$ and whose hypotenuse is vector $\vec{A}$. Applying the Pythagorean theorem again, we find that the length of $\vec{A}$ is $\sqrt{A_x{}^2 + A_y{}^2 + A_z{}^2}$. Substituting our values we have $\sqrt{3^2 + 1^2 + 2^2} = \sqrt{14}$.

(b) We refer again to diagram 1. The projection of $\vec{A}$ on the xy plane is simply the dotted line which is the vector $A_x\hat{x} + A_y\hat{y}$. Its length is $\sqrt{A_x{}^2 + A_y{}^2}$ by the Pythagorean theorem. In our problem, the length is $\sqrt{3^2 + 1^2} = \sqrt{10}$.

(c) Construct a vector in the xy plane and perpendicular to A. We want a vector of the form

$$B = B_x\hat{x} + B_y\hat{y}$$

with the property $A \cdot B = 0$ (since $\vec{A} \cdot \vec{B} = |\vec{A}||\vec{B}| \cos \phi$ where ϕ is the angle between $\vec{A}$ and $\vec{B}$). Hence

$$(3\hat{x} + \hat{y} + 2\hat{z}) \cdot (B_x\hat{x} + B_y\hat{y}) = 0.$$

On taking the scalar product we find

$$3B_x + B_y = 0,$$

or

$$\frac{B_y}{B_x} = -3.$$

The length of the vector B is not determined by the specification of the problem. We have therefore determined just the slope of vector B, not its magnitude. See diagram 2.

(d) The unit vector B is the vector in the B direction but with the magnitude 1. It lies in the xy plane, and its slope (B_y/B_x) is equal to -3. Therefore, $\hat{B}$ must satisfy the following two equations:

$$\hat{B}_x{}^2 + \hat{B}_y{}^2 = 1$$

$$\frac{\hat{B}_y}{\hat{B}_x} = -3$$

Solving simultaneously we have: $\hat{B}_x{}^2 + (-3\hat{B}_x)^2 = 1$ or $\hat{B}_x = 1/\sqrt{10}$ and $\hat{B}_y = -3/\sqrt{10}$.

The vector B is then:

$$\hat{B} = (1/\sqrt{10})\hat{x} - (3/\sqrt{10})\hat{y}$$

4

(e) Converting the vectors into coordinate form and computing the dot product (scalar product):

$$(3\hat{x} + \hat{y} + 2\hat{z}) \cdot (2\hat{x} + 0\hat{y} + 0\hat{z}) =$$

$$6 + 0 + 0 = 6$$

(f) Find the form of $\vec{A}$ and $\vec{C}$ in a reference frame obtained from the old reference frame by a rotation of $\pi/2$ clockwise looking along the positive z axis. The new unit vectors $\hat{x}'$, $\hat{y}'$, $\hat{z}'$ are related to the old $\hat{x}$, $\hat{y}$, $\hat{z}$ by (see fig. 3)

$$\hat{x}' = \hat{y}; \quad \hat{y}' = -\hat{x}; \quad \hat{z}' = \hat{z}.$$

Where $\hat{x}$ appeared we now have $-\hat{y}'$; where $\hat{y}$ appeared, we now have $\hat{x}'$, so that

$$A = \hat{x}' - 3\hat{y}' + 2\hat{z}'; \quad C = -2\hat{y}'.$$

(g) Using the results of part (f), we convert the vectors $\vec{A}$ and $\vec{C}$ into coordinate form in the primed coordinate system, giving us the following dot product:

$$\vec{A} \cdot \vec{C} = (\hat{x}' - 3\hat{y}' + 2\hat{z}') \cdot (0\hat{x}' - 2\hat{y}' + 0\hat{z}') =$$

$$0 + 6 + 0 = 6$$

This is exactly the result obtained in the unprimed system.

(h) Find the vector product $\vec{A} \times \vec{C}$. In the unprimed system $\vec{A} \times \vec{C}$ is defined as

$$\begin{vmatrix} \hat{x} & \hat{y} & \hat{z} \\ 3 & 1 & 2 \\ 2 & 0 & 0 \end{vmatrix} = 4\hat{y} - 2\hat{z}.$$

(i) Form the vector $\vec{A} - \vec{C}$. We have
$$\vec{A} - \vec{C} = (3 - 2)\hat{x} + \hat{y} + 2\hat{z} = \hat{x} + \hat{y} + 2\hat{z}.$$

DISPLACEMENT VECTORS

● PROBLEM 1-4

Two hikers set off in an eastward direction. Hiker 1 travels 3 km while hiker 2 travels 6 times the distance covered by hiker 1. What is the displacement of hiker 2?

Solution: From the information given the displacement vector is directed east. The magnitude of the displacement vector for hiker 2 is 6 times the magnitude of the displacement vector for hiker 1. Therefore, its magnitude is

$$6 \times (3 \text{ km}) = 18 \text{ km}$$

● **PROBLEM 1-5**

Two wires are attached to a corner fence post with the wires making an angle of 90° with each other. If each wire pulls on the post with a force of 50 pounds, what is the resultant force acting on the post? See Figure.

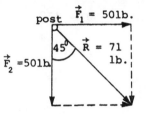

Solution: As shown in the figure, we complete the parallelogram. If we measure R and scale it, we find it is equal to about 71 pounds. The angle of the resultant is 45° from either of the component vectors.

If we use the fact that the component vectors are at right angles to each other, we can write

$$R^2 = 50^2 + 50^2$$

whence

R = 71 pounds approximately at 45° to each wire.

● **PROBLEM 1-6**

If a person walks 1 km north, 5 km west, 3 km south, and 7 km east, find the resultant displacement vector.

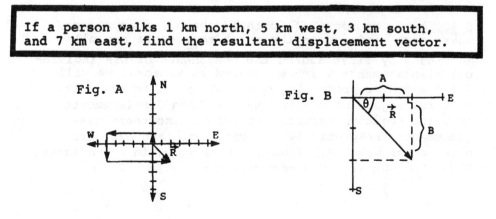

<u>Solution:</u>   The vector diagram is shown in figure (a).
The resultant displacement vector is labelled $\vec{R}$. The
magnitude of this vector is 2.8 km. The direction, as
measured with a protractor, is 45° south of east, or
the tangent may be used to find the direction, since
a right triangle is formed.

We shall also compute the solution analytically.

In figure (b) a closeup of the resultant vector $\vec{R}$
is shown. We can see from the graph that side A and
side B each equal 2 km. Thus, by the Pythagorean
theorem:

$$R^2 = A^2 + B^2 = (2 \text{ km})^2 + (2 \text{ km})^2 = 8 \text{ km}^2$$

$$R = 2 \sqrt{2} \text{ km} = 2(1.4)\text{km} = 2.8 \text{ km}$$

$$\tan \theta = \frac{2 \text{ km}}{2 \text{ km}} = 1, \qquad \theta = 45°$$

$$\vec{R} = 2.8 \text{ km, } 45° \text{ south of east.}$$

● **PROBLEM 1-7**

An army recruit on a training exercise is instructed to
walk due west for 5 mi, then in a northeasterly direction
for 4 mi, and finally due north for 3 mi. When he
completes his exercise, what is his resultant displacement $\vec{R}$? How far will he be from where he started?

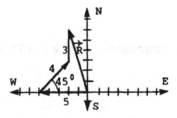

<u>Solution:</u>   The recruit's path is shown in the figure,
where each division on the graph represents one mile.

We find $\vec{R}$ by first adding the components of his individual displacements which we regard as vectors. We will
let $\vec{E}$ and $\vec{N}$, representing east and north, be our unit
vectors, regarding western and southern displacements
as being negative eastern and negative northern displacements, respectively.   Assume north and east are
given equal weights.   Then $\vec{NE}$ is as shown in the diagram.
Thus, the sum of the components is:

7

$\vec{E}$	$\vec{N}$
− 5 mi	0 mi
4 cos 45° mi	4 sin 45° mi
0 mi	3 mi
(4 cos 45° − 5)mi	(4 sin 45° + 3)mi

$$\vec{R} = \left[4 \left(\frac{1}{\sqrt{2}} \right) - 5 \right] \text{mi } \vec{E} + \left[4 \left(\frac{1}{\sqrt{2}} \right) + 3 \right] \vec{N}$$

$$= (2.8 - 5)\text{mi } \vec{E} + (2.8 + 3)\text{mi } \vec{N}$$

$$= - 2.2 \text{ mi } \vec{E} + 5.8 \text{ mi } \vec{N}$$

The recruit's final distance from the starting point will be the magnitude of $\vec{R}$:

$$R = \sqrt{(- 2.2 \text{ mi})^2 + (5.8 \text{ mi})^2} = 6.20 \text{ mi}$$

● PROBLEM 1-8

A ship leaving its port sails due north for 30 miles and then 50 miles in a direction 60° east of north. See the Figure. At the end of this time where is the ship relative to its port?

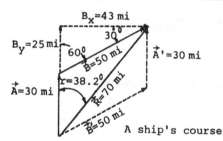

A ship's course

Solution by Parallelogram Method:

The figure shows the parallelogram completed by the dashed vectors $\vec{A}'$ and $\vec{B}'$. Also shown is the resultant $\vec{R}$ which is found to represent about 70 miles. Angle r is found to be about 38.2° east of north.

Solution by Component Method:

The figure also shows the vector $\vec{B}$ resolved into the components $\vec{B}_x$ and $\vec{B}_y$, which are found to be 43 miles and 25 miles, respectively. (By trigonometry $\vec{B}_x = 50$ miles × cos 30° = 43 miles, and

$\vec{B}_y = 50$ miles $\times$ sin $30° = 25$ miles).Since $\vec{A}$ and $\vec{B}$ lie along the same direction in this problem, we add them directly to get 30 miles + 25 miles, or 55 miles. We then have a right triangle with one side equal to 55 miles and the other side equal to 43 miles. From these data we find the resultant R according to the equation:

$$R^2 = 55^2 + 43^2$$

whence   R = about 70 miles

Solution by the Cosine Law:

In solving this problem by means of the cosine law, we write

$$R^2 = A^2 + B^2 + 2 \; AB \; \cos \theta$$

$$R^2 = 30^2 + 50^2 + 2 \times 30 \times 50 \times 0.5000$$

$$= 4900$$

whence the magnitude of R is

R = 70 miles

$$\tan r = \frac{B \; \sin \theta}{A + B \; \cos \theta} = \frac{50 \times 0.866}{30 + 50 \times 0.500}$$

$$= 0.788$$

whence   r = 38.2° approximately.

VELOCITY VECTORS

● **PROBLEM 1-9**

An aircraft is climbing with a steady speed of 200 m/sec at an angle of $20°$ to the horizontal (see figure). What are the horizontal and vertical components of its velocity?

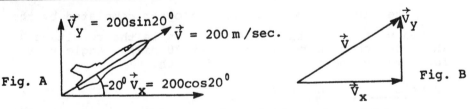

Fig. A

Fig. B

Solution: Using trigonometric relations for right triangles, the velocity can be broken down into two components perpendicular to each other.
Horizontal component = 200 cos 20°

Vertical component   = 200 sin 20°.

Trigonometric tables tell us that

cos 20° = 0.9397 and sin 20° = 0.3420

Therefore, horizontal component = 200 × 0.9397
                                = 187.94 m/sec

Vertical component = 200 × 0.3420
                   = 68.40 m/sec.

Notice that the sum of 187.94 and 68.40 is not 200, but you can check that $(187.94)^2 + (68.40)^2 = (200)^2$. This occurs because the horizontal and vertical components, $\vec{V}_x$ and $\vec{V}_y$, of the velocity are vectors and must be added accordingly. Since they are pernependicular to each other, forming a right triangle with $\vec{V}$ as the hypotenuse,

$$V_x^2 + V_y^2 = V^2$$

● **PROBLEM 1-10**

An automobile driver, A, traveling relative to the earth at 65 mi/hr on a straight, level road, is ahead of motorcycle officer B, traveling in the same direction at 80 mi/hr. What is the velocity of B relative to A? Find the same quantity if B is ahead of A.

Solution: The velocity of B relative to A is equal to the velocity of B relative to the earth minus the velocity of A relative to the earth, or

$$V_{BA} = V_{BE} - V_{AE} = 80 \text{ mi/hr} - 65 \text{ mi/hr} = 15 \text{ mi/hr}$$

If B is ahead of A, the velocity of B relative to A is still the velocity of B relative to the earth minus the velocity of A relative to the earth or 15 mi/hr.

In the first case, B is overtaking A, and, in the second, B is pulling ahead of A.

● **PROBLEM 1-11**

City A is 100 miles north and 200 miles west of city B. An airplane flies in a direct line between the cities in a time of one hour. What are the vectors that describe the distance of A from B, and the velocity of the airplane?

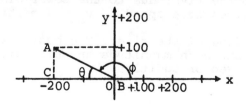

10

Solution: We will define first a coordinate system with B at the origin (see the figure below). The x-direction is east and the y-direction is north. The vector BA is specified by its coordinates

$$x = -200 \text{ mi}$$
$$y = 100 \text{ mi}$$

or by its magnitude and direction

$$(BA)^2 = x^2 + y^2$$
$$= \left((-200)^2 + (100)^2 \right) \text{mi}^2$$

$$BA = 100\sqrt{5} \text{ mi}$$
$$\sin \theta = \frac{CA}{BA} = \frac{100}{100} \sqrt{5} = \frac{1}{\sqrt{5}}$$

$$\theta = 26.5°$$
$$\phi = 180° - \theta = 153.5°$$

The velocities are given in a similar way. Since they are constant

$$V_x = \frac{x}{1 \text{ hr}} = \frac{-200 \text{ mi}}{1 \text{ hr}} = -200 \text{ mi/hr}$$

$$V_y = \frac{y}{1 \text{ hr}} = \frac{100 \text{ mi}}{1 \text{ hr}} = 100 \text{ mi/hr}$$

$$V^2 = V_x^2 + V_y^2 = \left((-200)^2 + (100)^2 \right) \text{mi}^2/\text{hr}^2$$

$$V = 100 \sqrt{5} \text{ mi/hr}$$

$$\phi = 153.5°$$

● PROBLEM 1-12

A certain boat can move at a speed of 10 mi/hr in still water. The helmsman steers straight across a river in which the current is 4 mi/hr. What is the velocity of the boat?

Solution: The boat has a speed of v_b = 10 mi/hr perpendicular to the river due to the power of the boat. The current gives it a speed of v_c = 4 mi/hr in the direction of flow of the river. The boat's resultant velocity (having both magnitude and direction) can be found through vector addition.

$$\vec{v} = \vec{v}_b + \vec{v}_c$$

The magnitude of the velocity which is the speed of the boat is found using the Pythagorean theorem (see figure).

$$v = \sqrt{v_b^2 + v_c^2}$$

$$= \sqrt{(10)^2 + (4)^2} = \sqrt{116}$$

$$= 10.8 \text{ mi/hr.}$$

The angle θ, which determines the direction of the velocity is,

$$\theta = \tan^{-1}\left(\frac{v_c}{v_b}\right)$$

$$= \tan^{-1}\left(\frac{4}{10}\right)$$

$$= 22°$$

● **PROBLEM** 1-13

A boy can throw a baseball horizontally with a speed of 20 m/sec. If he performs this feat in a convertible that is moving at 30 m/sec in a direction perpendicular to the direction in which he is throwing (see figure), what will be the actual speed and direction of motion of the baseball?

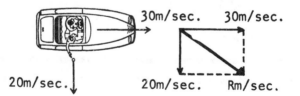

30m/sec.   30m/sec.

20m/sec.   20m/sec.   Rm/sec.

Solution: Since the baseball is originally travelling with the convertible, it has the speed of 30 m/sec in the direction the car is travelling. When the boy throws the ball perpendicular to the car's path, he imparts an additional velocity of 20 m/sec in that direction. The ball's velocity is then 30 m/sec in the direction the convertible is moving and 20 m/sec perpendicular to this movement. Its resultant velocity can be found through adding vectors as shown in the diagram.

If the resultant velocity is R m/sec at an angle θ to the direction in which the convertible is moving, then

$$R^2 = (20)^2 + (30)^2 = 1300$$
$$R = \sqrt{1300} = 36.06 \text{ m/sec}$$

12

Also, $\tan \theta = \frac{20}{30} = 0.666$

From tables of tangents, $\theta = 33.69°$. Therefore, the ball has a speed of 36.06 m/sec in a direction at an angle of 33.69° to the direction in which the convertible is travelling.

● PROBLEM 1-14

An airplane, whose ground speed in still air is 200 mi/hr, is flying with its nose pointed due north. If there is a cross wind of 50 mi/hr in an easterly direction, what is the ground speed of the airplane?

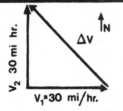

Solution: The cross wind causes the plane to travel 50 mi/hr to the east in addition to its speed of 200 mi/hr to the north. To find its speed with respect to ground, use vector addition. Vectors are quantities that have both magnitude and direction; and velocity fits this specification. Using the Pythagorean theorem, we can find the magnitude of the resultant velocity v. This magnitude is the plane's speed. Speed does not have direction (note that speed is not a vector).

$$v = \sqrt{v_{airplane}^2 + v_{wind}^2}$$
$$= \sqrt{(200)^2 + (50)^2}$$
$$= \sqrt{42,500}$$
$$= 206 \text{ mi/hr}.$$

● PROBLEM 1-15

At $t_1 = 0$ an automobile is moving eastward with a velocity of 30 mi/hr. At $t_2 = 1$ min the automobile is moving northward at the same velocity. What average acceleration has the automobile experienced?

Solution: Since velocity is a vector quantity, vector addition must be used to solve this problem. Geometrically, when two vectors are added, the tail of the second vector is placed at the head of the first and the re-

13

sultant vector is drawn from the tail of the first to the head of the second. To find the difference between the two velocities, we write

$$\vec{v}_2 - \vec{v}_1 = \Delta\vec{v}$$

Changing the expression above into one including only addition:

$$\vec{v}_2 = \Delta\vec{v} + \vec{v}_1$$

This is shown in the accompanying vector diagram.

The magnitude of Δv is (refer to the figure and use the Pythagorean theorem)

$$\Delta v = \sqrt{(30 \text{ mi/hr})^2 + (30 \text{ mi/hr})^2}$$

$$= \sqrt{1800 \ (\text{mi/hr})^2}$$

$$= 42.4 \text{ mi/hr}$$

The magnitude of the average acceleration is

$$\bar{a} = \frac{\Delta v}{\Delta t}$$

$$= \frac{42.4 \text{ mi/hr}}{60 \text{ sec}}$$

$$= 0.71 \ (\text{mi/hr})/\text{sec}$$

The direction of Δv, and hence the direction of a is, from the figure, in the direction northwest.

● PROBLEM 1-16

The compass of an aircraft indicates that it is headed due north, and its airspeed indicator shows that it is moving through the air at 120 mi/hr. If there is a wind of 50 mi/hr from west to east, what is the velocity of the aircraft relative to the earth?

Solution: Let subscript A refer to the aircraft, and subscript F to the moving air. Subscript E refers to the earth. We have given

$$v_{AF} = 120 \text{ mi/hr, due north}$$

$$\vec{v}_{FE} = 50 \text{ mi/hr, due east,}$$

and we wish to find the magnitude and direction of $\vec{v}_{AE}$. By the law of addition of velocities

$$\vec{v}_{AE} = \vec{v}_{AF} + \vec{v}_{FE} .$$

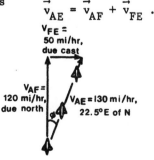

14

The three relative velocities are shown in the figure. It follows from this diagram that

$$|\vec{v}_{AE}| = 130 \text{ mi/hr.}$$

Furthermore,

$$\tan \varphi = \frac{50 \text{ mi/hr}}{120 \text{ mi/hr}}$$

and

$$\tan \varphi = .4167$$

$$\varphi = 22.5^{\circ}$$

The airplane travels at a speed of 130 mi/hr at an angle of 22.5° east of due north.

CHAPTER 2

STATICS

**Basic Attacks and Strategies for
Solving Problems in this Chapter**

*Statics is the study of the condition of objects (usually at rest) with
especial regard to the forces involved. Fundamental to physics is the
concept of a* force. *Intuitively, a force is a push or a pull acting on some
object. More precisely, Newton's laws help us to define a force. Newton's
first law states that an object at rest remains at rest and an object in
motion remains in motion with constant velocity in the absence of external
forces. Newton's second law is the basis of dynamics, but one consequence
of it is that the* weight *force of any mass is* W = mg, *where g is the
gravitational acceleration = 9.8 m/s² near the surface of the Earth.
Newton's third law says that for every action force there is an equal and
opposite reaction force.*

*Other than weight, several important forces are tension (the force in
a string or cable), the normal force N acting perpendicular to a surface,
the force of static friction* ($F_s \leq \mu_s N$), *the force of kinetic friction* ($F_k = \mu_k N$),
*and a pivot or reaction force R acting at an angle θ with respect to the
surface. For example, in standing on the floor, you exert a force of
magnitude W on the floor; the floor responds by exerting a force N = R on
you. The reaction force of the floor prevents you from falling through the
floor.*

*In order to solve a statics (or any) physics problem, first write down the
information in terms of numbers and symbols. Then draw a figure
showing the relevant objects and angles. Next, choose points in the system*

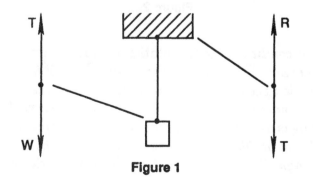

Figure 1

and draw free body diagrams for those points. For example, in Figure 1, two important free body diagrams are shown for the case of a mass suspended by a cord from a ceiling.

In statics, we now apply the two conditions of equilibrium. The first condition is that the sum of the forces in each direction is zero: $\Sigma \vec{F} = 0$. The equilibrium is said to be static if also the velocity $\vec{v} = 0$. For example, in Figure 1, choosing the positive direction as down, we get

$$\Sigma F_y = W - T = 0 \ and \ T - R = 0.$$

Hence, $T = W$ and $R = T$; the weight determines both the tension in the string and the reaction force of the ceiling. In Figure 2, a force F pulls an object of mass m on a flat but rough surface with coefficient of static friction μ_s and coefficient of kinetic friction μ_k. Resolving F into its x and y components, we find $F_x = F \cos \theta$ and $F_y = F \sin \theta$. Static equilibrium in the y–direction gives

$$\Sigma F_y = F_y + N - W = 0 \quad or \quad N = mg - F \sin \theta$$

to find the normal force. Note that the normal force is not always equal to mg! If the object starts out at rest, then it will begin to move when

$$\Sigma F_x = F_x - F_s = 0 \quad or \quad F \cos \theta = \mu_s N.$$

If the object is moving at constant velocity, then

$$\Sigma F_x = F_x - F_k = 0 \quad or \quad \mu_k N = F \cos \theta.$$

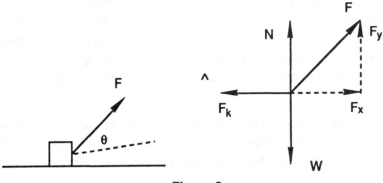

Figure 2

The second condition, that of rotational equilibrium, is that the sum of all torques is zero: $\Sigma \vec{\tau} = 0$ where the torque $\vec{\tau} = \vec{r} \times \vec{F}$ is a cross product. Note that position vector $\vec{r}$ where the force acts and the force $\vec{F}$ must be drawn with a common origin of find the angle θ between them; then the right hand rule is used to find the direction of the torque. Figure 3 shows a standard boom problem, where the boom has weight $B = m_b g$ and the person has weight $W = mg$. The first equilibrium condition gives

$$\Sigma\,F_x = R_x - T_x = 0; \text{ hence } R_x = T\cos\theta.$$

Also,

$$\Sigma\,F_y = R_y + T_y - W - B = 0 \text{ or } R_y = W + B - T\sin\theta.$$

If R and T are unknown, one cannot find them just from these two equations. Hence, choose the point where the boom contacts the wall as the origin for calculating torques. Rotational equilibrium then implies

$$\Sigma\,\tau = \Sigma\,rF\sin\theta$$

$$= (0)\,(R) - xW\sin 90 - d/2\,B\sin 90 + dT\sin(180 - \theta)$$

$$= 0$$

or solving for the tension T = (xW + Bd/2) / (d sin θ). The positive and negative directions come from the right hand rule. The angles come from moving the position vector such that it and the force have a common origin (Figure 4).

The concept of rotational equilibrium can also be used to locate the center of gravity or gravitational center of a system of objects. This is just the pivot point where the system balances as in the childhood seesaw. More importantly, the center of gravity often coincides with the center of mass of an object where $\vec{r}_{cm} = \Sigma\,m\vec{r}\,/\,\Sigma\,m$. In the beam problem, Figure 3, we assumed the weight of the beam acted at the center of mass of the beam d/2.

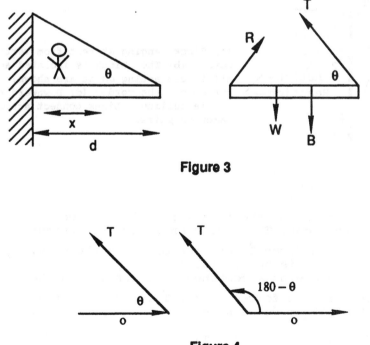

Figure 3

Figure 4

CHAPTER 2

STATICS

FORCE SYSTEMS IN EQUILIBRIUM

● **PROBLEM** 2-1

A block hangs at rest from the ceiling by a vertical cord. Find the forces acting on the block and on the cord.

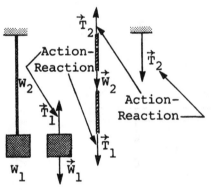

(a) Block hanging at rest from vertical cord. (b) The block is isolated and all forces acting *on* it are shown. (c) Forces on the cord. (d) Downward force on the ceiling. Lines connect action-reaction pairs.

(a)   (b)   (c)   (d)

<u>Solution:</u> Part (b) of the figure is the free-body diagram for the body. The forces on it are its weight $\vec{w}_1$ and the upward force $\vec{T}_1$ exerted on it by the cord. If we take the x-axis horizontal and the y-axis vertical, there are no x-components of force, and the y-components are the forces $\vec{w}_1$ and $\vec{T}_1$. Then, from the condition that $\Sigma F_y = 0$, we have

$$\Sigma F_y = T_1 - w_1 = 0, \qquad T_1 = w_1$$

from Newton's first law.

In order that both forces have the same line
of action, the center of gravity of the body must
lie vertically below the point of attachment of the
cord.

Let us emphasize again that the forces $\vec{w}_1$ and $\vec{T}_1$
are not an action-reaction pair, although they are
equal in magnitude, opposite in direction, and have
the same line of action. The weight $\vec{w}_1$ is a force of
attraction exerted on the body by the earth. Its
reaction is an equal and opposite force of attraction
exerted on the earth by the body. The reaction is one
of the set of forces acting on the earth, and therefore
it does not appear in the free-body diagram of the
suspended block.

The reaction to the force $\vec{T}_1$ is an equal downward force, $\vec{T}_1'$, exerted on the cord by the suspended
body.

$T_1 = T_1'$ (from Newton's third law).

The force $\vec{T}_1'$ is shown in part (c), which is the
free-body diagram of the cord. The other forces on
the cord are its own weight $\vec{w}_2$ and the upward force
$\vec{T}_2$ exerted on its upper end by the ceiling. Since
the cord is also in equilibrium,

$\Sigma F_y = T_2 - w_2 - T_1' = 0$

$T_2 = w_2 + T_1'$.   (1st law)

The reaction to $\vec{T}_2$ is the downward force $\vec{T}_2'$ in
part (d), exerted on the ceiling by the cord.

$T_2 = T_2'$ (3rd law)

As a numerical example, let the body weight 20 lb
and the cord weigh 1 lb. Then

$T_1 = w_1 = 20$ lb,

$T_1' = T_1 = 20$ lb,

$T_2 = w_2 + T_1' = 1$ lb $+ 20$ lb $= 21$ lb,

$T_2' = T_2 = 21$ lb.

● PROBLEM 2-2

Three forces acting on a particle and keeping it in
equilibrium must be coplanar and concurrent. Show that
the vectors representing the forces, when added in
order, form a closed triangle; and further show that
the magnitude of any force divided by the sine of the

17

angle between the lines of action of the other two is a constant quantity.

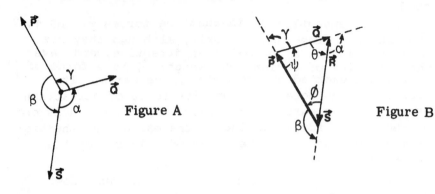

Figure A

Figure B

<u>Solution</u>: Let the three forces be $\vec{P}$, $\vec{Q}$, and $\vec{S}$, at angles α, β, and γ to one another as shown in figure (a). In order that the three forces shall be in equilibrium, the resultant $\vec{R}$ of $\vec{P}$ and $\vec{Q}$ must be equal and opposite to $\vec{S}$. The vectors $\vec{P}$, $\vec{Q}$, and $\vec{S}$ are concurrent and, since the vector $\vec{R}$ is in the same plane as $\vec{P}$ and $\vec{Q}$, they are coplanar.

But the resultant of $\vec{P}$ and $\vec{Q}$ is obtained by vector addition, as in figure (b). That is, $\vec{R}$ is the third side of the triangle formed by placing the tail of $\vec{Q}$ at the head of $\vec{P}$. The force $\vec{S}$ is equal and opposite to $\vec{R}$ and thus will occupy the same space as $\vec{R}$, the third side of the triangle, but will be opposite in direction to $\vec{R}$. Thus $\vec{P} + \vec{Q} + \vec{S}$ taken in order, form a closed triangle and their sum is of necessity zero. Applying the law of sines to the triangle of figure (b)

$$\frac{P}{\sin\theta} = \frac{Q}{\sin\phi} = \frac{S}{\sin\psi}$$

$$\therefore \frac{P}{\sin(180-\alpha)} = \frac{Q}{\sin(180-\beta)} = \frac{S}{\sin(180-\gamma)}$$

$$\therefore \frac{P}{\sin\alpha} = \frac{Q}{\sin\beta} = \frac{S}{\sin\gamma} = \text{const.}$$

● PROBLEM 2-3

A 200 lb man hangs from the middle of a tightly stretched rope so that the angle between the rope and the horizontal direction is 5°, as shown in Figure A. Calculate the tension in the rope. (Figure B).

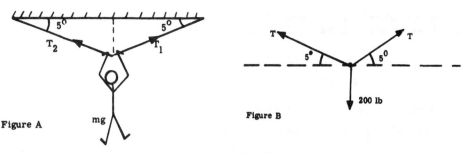

Figure A   mg

Figure B

Solution: Since the two sections of the rope are symmetrical with
respect to the man, the tensions in them must have the same magnitude,
(Fig. B.) This can be arrived at by summing the forces in the horizontal direction and setting them equal to zero since the system is in
equilibrium. Then

$$\Sigma F_x = T_1 \cos 5° - T_2 \cos 5° = 0$$

and

$$T_1 = T_2 = T$$

Considering the forces in the vertical direction,

$$\Sigma F_y = T \sin 5° + T \sin 5° - 200 \text{ lb} = 0$$

$$200 \text{ lb} = 2T \sin 5° = 2T(0.0871)$$

$$T = \frac{(200)}{(2)(0.0871)} = 1150 \text{ lbs.}$$

Note the significant force that can be exerted on objects
at either end of the rope by this arrangement. The tension
in the rope is over five times the weight of the man. Had
the angle been as small as 1°, the tension would have been

$$T = \frac{200}{2 \sin 1°} = \frac{200}{(2)(0.0174)} = 5730 \text{ lbs.}$$

This technique for exerting a large force would only be useful to move
something a very small distance, since any motion of one end of the
rope would change the small angle considerably and the tension would decrease accordingly.

● **PROBLEM 2-4**

Find the tension in the cable shown in Figure A. Neglect the
weight of the wooden boom.

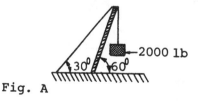

Fig. A

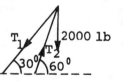

Fig. B: Force Diagram

Solution: Take the directions of the tensions in the cable and
the boom to be as shown in the force diagram(fig.B). We assume
at this point, that the given directions are correct. However,
the forces may turn out to point in the opposite direction. If
this is the case, our solutions for the tensions will be negative.

We can thus correct ourselves at the end of the problem. The first condition of equilibrium yields

$$\Sigma F_x = T_2 \cos 60° - T_1 \cos 30° = 0 \qquad (1)$$

$$\Sigma F_y = T_2 \sin 60° - T_1 \sin 30° - 2000 = 0 \qquad (2)$$

We wish to find T_1, the tension in the cable. Solving for T_2 in terms of T_1 in equation (1) gives

$$T_2 = \frac{T_1 \cos 30°}{\cos 60°}$$

Substituting this in equation (2),

$$\left(\frac{T_1 \cos 30°}{\cos 60°} \right) \sin 60° - T_1 \sin 30° = 2000$$

Solving for T_1:

$$T_1 (\cos 30° \tan 60° - \sin 30°) = 2000$$

$$T_1 = \frac{2000}{\cos 30° \tan 60° - \sin 30°} = \frac{2000}{(0.8660)(1.7321) - (0.5000)}$$

$$= \frac{2000}{1.5 - 0.5} = 2000 \text{ lb}$$

Since our answer is positive, the force acts in the direction assumed in the beginning.

● **PROBLEM 2-5**

In figure A, a block of weight w hangs from a cord which is knotted at O to two other cords fastened to the ceiling. Find the tensions in these three cords. Let w = 50 lb, $\theta_2 = 30°$, and $\theta_3 = 60°$. The weights of the cords are negligible.

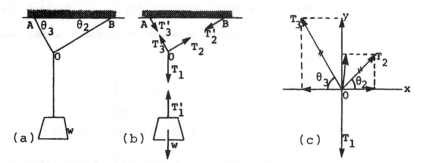

(a) A block hanging in equilibrium.   (b) Forces acting on the block, on the knot, and and the ceiling.   (c) Forces on the knot O resolved into x- and y- components.

Solution: In order to use the conditions of
equilibrium to compute an unknown force, we must
consider some body which is in equilibrium and on
which the desired force acts. The hanging block is
one such body and the tension in the vertical cord
supporting the block is equal to the weight of the
block. The inclined cords do not exert forces on
the block, but they do act on the knot at O. Hence,
we consider the knot as a small body in equilibrium,
whose own weight is negligible.

The free body diagrams for the block and the knot
are shown in figure B, where $\vec{T}_1$, $\vec{T}_2$, and $\vec{T}_3$ represent
the forces exerted on the knot by the three cords and
$\vec{T}_1'$, $\vec{T}_2'$, and $\vec{T}_3'$ are the reactions to these forces.

Consider first the hanging block. Since it is in
equilibrium,

T_1' = w = 50 lb

Since $\vec{T}_1$ and $\vec{T}_1'$ form an action-reaction pair,

$T_1' = T_1$

Hence T_1 = 50 lb.

To find the forces $\vec{T}_2$ and $\vec{T}_3$, we resolve these
forces (see fig. C) into rectangular components. Then,
from Newton's second law,

$\Sigma F_x = T_2 \cos \theta_2 - T_3 \cos \theta_3 = 0,$

$\Sigma F_y = T_2 \sin \theta_2 + T_3 \sin \theta_3 - T_1 = 0$

We have $T_2 \cos 30° - T_3 \cos 60° = 0$

$T_2 \sin 30° + T_3 \sin 60° = 50$

or $0.866 \, T_2 - 0.500 \, T_3 = 0$

$0.500 \, T_2 + 0.866 \, T_3 = 0$

Solving these equations simultaneously, we find
the tensions to be

T_2 = 25 lb, T_3 = 43.3 lb.

Finally, we know from Newton's third law that the
inclined cords exert on the ceiling the forces $\vec{T}_2'$ and
$\vec{T}_3'$, equal and opposite to $\vec{T}_2$ and $\vec{T}_3$, respectively.

21

EQUILIBRIUM CONDITIONS FOR FORCES AND MOMENTS

● **PROBLEM 2-6**

A light horizontal bar is 4.0 ft long. A 3.0-lb force acts vertically upward on it 1.0 ft from the right-hand end. Find the torque about each end.

```
|←————————— 4 ft. —————————→|
(                                    )   Force on Bar
        F = 3 lb.↑   |← 1 ft.→|
```

Solution: Since the force is perpendicular to the bar, the moment arms are measured along the bar.

About the right-hand end

$$L_r = 3.0 \text{ lb} \times 1.0 \text{ ft} = 3.0 \text{ lb-ft} \qquad \text{clockwise}$$

About the right-hand end

$$L_1 = 3.0 \text{ lb} \times 3.0 \text{ ft} = 9.0 \text{ lb-ft counterclockwise}$$

The torques produced by this single force about the two axes differ in both magnitude and direction. This causes the bar to twist through an angle θ which is proportional to the torque.

● **PROBLEM 2-7**

A rigid rod whose own weight is negligible (see figure) is pivoted at point O and carries a body of weight w_1 at end A. Find the weight w_2 of a second body which must be attached at end B if the rod is to be in equilibrium, and find the force exerted on the rod by the pivot at O.

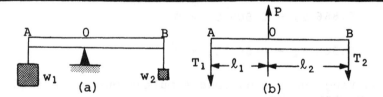

Solution: The question states that the rod is in equilibrium. In this case, the net force on the rod must be zero, and the net torque on the rod about the pivot must also be zero.

The forces on the rod are $\vec{T}_1$ and $\vec{T}_2$, the weights of masses 1 and 2, respectively, and $\vec{P}$, the force of the pivot on the rod. Hence

$$T_1 + T_2 - P = 0$$

or $$T_1 + T_2 = P \qquad (1)$$

The torque about a point O is

$$\vec{\tau} = r \times F$$

where $\vec{r}$ is the vector from O locating the point of application of $\vec{F}$. The net torque about O is

$$T_2 \ell_2 - T_1 \ell_1 = 0$$

since the torque due to T_2 is opposite in direction to the torque due to T_1. Then

$$T_2 \ell_2 = T_1 \ell_1 \qquad (2)$$

Substituting (2) in (1)

$$T_1 + \frac{T_1 \ell_1}{\ell_2} = P$$

$$P = T_1 \left(1 + \frac{\ell_1}{\ell_2} \right)$$

But $T_1 = w_1$, and

$$P = w_1 \left(1 + \frac{\ell_1}{\ell_2} \right)$$

If $\ell_1 = 3$ ft, $\ell_2 = 4$ ft and $w_1 = 4$ lb

$$P = 4 \text{ lb} \left(1 + \frac{3}{4} \right) = 7 \text{ lb}$$

Furthermore, $T_2 = \dfrac{T_1 \ell_1}{\ell_2}$.

Since $T_2 = w_2$, and $T_1 = w_1$

$$w_2 = \frac{w_1 \ell_1}{\ell_2} = (4 \text{ lb}) \left(\frac{3}{4} \right) = 3 \text{ lb}$$

● **PROBLEM 2-8**

What scale readings would you predict when a uniform 120-lb plank 6.0 ft long is placed on two balances as shown in the figure, with 1.0 ft extending beyond the left support and 2.0 ft extending beyond the right support?

23

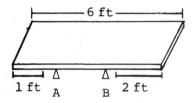

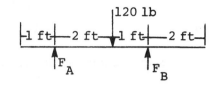

a) Beam with Supports   b) Diagram of Forces

Solution: From the first condition for equilibrium, the forces upward must equal the forces downward,

$F_A + F_B - 120 \text{ lb} = 0$

The plank is uniform, meaning that the center of mass is at the center of the beam, three feet from each end. This is the point at which the 120 lb gravitational force can be considered to act.

Torque about a point is defined as the tendency of a force to cause rotation about the point. The magnitude of the torque is given by the product of the magnitude of the force and the perpendicular distance of the line of action of the force (the line along which the force acts) from the point of rotation. The direction of the torque can be found using the right hand rule. Place the fingers of the right hand in the direction of the distance vector. Rotate the distance vector into the direction of the force vector. If this rotation is in the clockwise direction, the torque is negative. For counterclockwise rotation, the torque is positive. For equilibrium, the sum of all the torques about any point in the body must equal zero.

To apply this second condition for equilibrium, we may choose to write torques about an axis through A, noting that the center of mass of the plank is 2.0 ft from A.

$- 120 \text{ lb} \times 2.0 \text{ ft} + F_B(3.0 \text{ ft}) = 0$ or $F_B = 80 \text{ lb}$

Substitution of 80 lb for F_B in the first equation gives $F_A = 40$ lb. Alternatively, we may write a second torque equation, this time about an axis through B.

$+ 120 \text{ lb} \times 1.0 \text{ ft} - F_A(3.0 \text{ ft}) = 0$ or $F_A = 40 \text{ lb}$.

● **PROBLEM 2-9**

(a) At what point should a uniform board 100 cm long be supported so that it balances a 10 gram mass placed at one end, a 60 gram mass on the other end, and a 40 gram mass 30 cm from the 10 gram mass (see figure). (b) What is the magnitude of the supporting force $\vec{F}$?

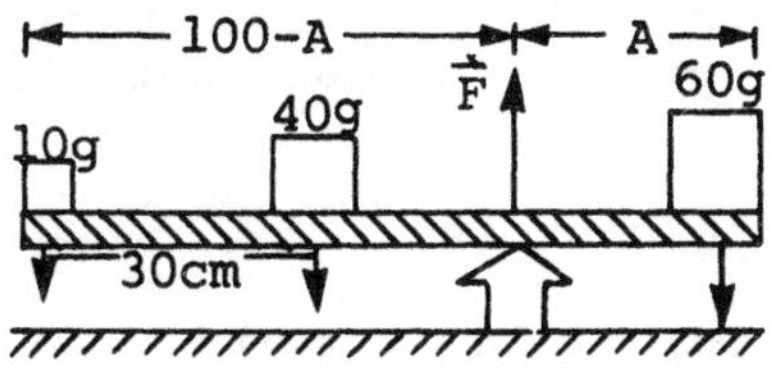

Solution: If the board is to balance, the sum of the moment about any point along the board must equal zero. A torque τ with respect to the point is defined as

$$\vec{\tau} = \vec{r} \times \vec{F}$$

where the direction of the torque is given by the right hand rule for the vector product of two vectors. For a two dimensional problem, such as this one, we note whether each torque produced is clockwise or counterclockwise; with clockwise torques taken as negative. This is done by noting the direction in which the fingers of the right hand must curl in order to swing $\vec{r}$ into $\vec{F}$ through the smaller angle θ between them. The magnitude of the torque is given by

$$\tau = rF \sin \theta .$$

For this problem, $\vec{r}$ and $\vec{F}$ are perpendicular so that the magnitudes of the torques are just rF. Since the force $\vec{F}$ produced at the support is unknown, we take moments about this point. In this case, $\vec{F}$ does not contribute to the net torque since its displacement vect is zero. We have

$$(10)(g)(100\text{-}A) + (40)(g)(100\text{-}A\text{-}30) - (60)(g)(A) = 0$$

where g is the acceleration due to gravity. We solve for A, the distance of point of support from the 60gm mass:

$$1000 - 10A + 4000 - 40A - 1200 - 60A = 0$$

$$110A = 3800$$

$$A = 34.5 \text{ cm}$$

(b) The force $\vec{F}$ can be found by applying the first condition of equilibrium in the vertical direction.

$$\Sigma F_y = 0 = F - (10)(g) - (40)(g) - (60)(g)$$

$$F = (110)(g) = (110 \text{ gm})(980 \text{ cm/sec}^2) = 1.078 \times 10^5 \text{ dynes} = 1.078 \text{ Newtons}$$

• PROBLEM 2-10

Locate the center of mass of the machine part in the figure consisting of a disk 2 in. in diameter and 1 in. long, and a rod 1 in. in diameter and 6 in. long, constructed of a homogeneous material.

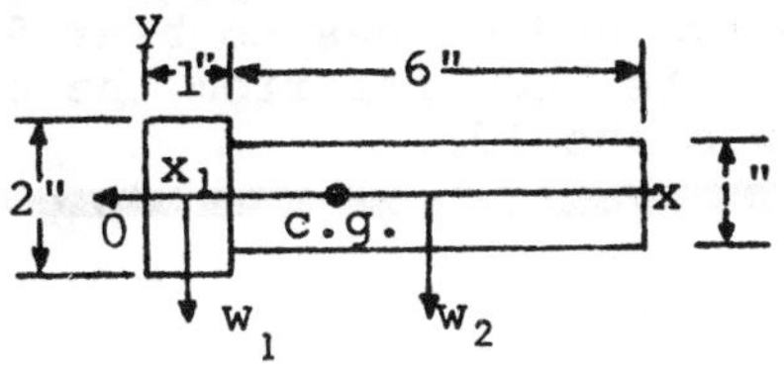

Solution: By symmetry, the center of mass lies on the axis and the center of mass of each part is midway between its ends.

The volume of the disk is:

$$v_d = \pi r^2 h = \pi (1 \text{ in})^2 (1 \text{ in}) = \pi \text{ in}^3.$$

The volume of the rod is:

$$v_r = \pi r^2 h = \pi (\tfrac{1}{2} \text{ in})^2 (6 \text{ in}) = \tfrac{3}{2} \pi \text{ in}^3$$

Since the disk and the rod are both constructed of the same homogeneous material, the ratio of their masses will equal the ratio of their volumes:

$$\frac{\text{mass of disk}}{\text{mass of rod}} = \frac{m_d}{m_r} = \frac{\rho v_d}{\rho v_r} = \frac{\pi \text{ in}^3}{\tfrac{3}{2} \pi \text{ in}^3} = \frac{2}{3}$$

where ρ is their common density.

The formula for the distance of the center of mass from a given origin 0 is:

$$\bar{x} \quad \frac{m_d x_d + m_r x_r}{m_d + m_r}$$

where x_d and x_r are the distances of the centers of mass of m_d and m_r respectively from 0.

Take the origin 0 at the left face of the disk, on the axis. Then $x_d = \tfrac{1}{2}$ in., and $x_r = 4$ in. Since $m_d = 2/3 \, m_r$

$$\bar{x} = \frac{\tfrac{2}{3} m_r (\tfrac{1}{2} \text{ in}) + m_r (4 \text{ in})}{\tfrac{2}{3} m_r + m_r} = 2.6 \text{ in.}$$

The center of gravity is on the axis, 2.6 in. to the right of 0.

● PROBLEM 2-11

Two men lift the ends of a 20 ft beam weighing 200 lb onto their shoulders. Both men are of the same height so that the beam is carried horizontally, but one is much the stronger of the two and wishes to bear 50% more of the weight than his mate. How far from the end of the beam should he put his shoulder?

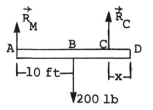

Solution: The beam exerts downward forces on the shoulders of the 2 men. This total downward force is just the weight of the beam and, since the beam is uniform, the weight acts through its center (see figure). The 2 men exert upward forces $\vec{R}_c$ and $\vec{R}_m$, the former at distance x from one end and the latter at the other end. The beam is in equilibrium vertically since it experiences no motion in that direction. Therefore we can apply the first condition of equilibrium in the vertical direction.

$$\sum F_y = R_m + R_c - 200 \text{ lb} = 0$$
$$R_m + R_c = 200 \text{ lb.} \qquad (1)$$

But we were given in the problem that one man, (the one on the right end) carries 50% more of the weight than his mate. Therefore

$$R_c = \frac{150}{100} R_m$$

or $R_m = \frac{2}{3} R_c \qquad (2)$

Substituting equation (2) in (1), we find

$$\frac{2}{3} R_c + R_c = 200 \text{ lb}$$

$$\frac{5}{3} R_c = 200 \text{ lb}$$

$$R_c = 120 \text{ lb}$$

Note that we solved for $\vec{R}_c$ since it is this force's distance from end D that we wish to know. Since the beam is in equilibrium rotationally, the second condition of equilibrium can be applied. Taking moments about end A, the magnitude of the force $\vec{R}_m$ is not needed. We have

$$\sum T_A = \left(R_m\right)(0) + R_c (20 \text{ ft} - x) - (200 \text{ lb})(10 \text{ ft}) = 0$$

$$20 \text{ ft} - x = \frac{2000 \text{ ft-lb}}{R_c} = \frac{2000 \text{ ft-lb}}{120 \text{ lb}} = 16 \frac{2}{3} \text{ ft.}$$

27

$$x = 20 \text{ ft} - 16\tfrac{2}{3} \text{ ft} = 3\tfrac{1}{3} \text{ ft}$$

A uniform wooden beam, of length 20 ft and weight 200 lb, is lying on a horizontal floor. A carpenter raises one end of it until the beam is inclined at 30° to the horizontal. He maintains it in this position by exerting a force at right angles to the beam while he waits for his mate to arrive to lift the other end. What is the magnitude of the force he exerts?

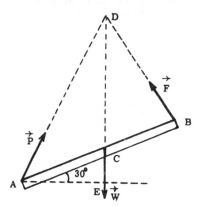

Solution: Consult the diagram: AB is the beam and C its midpoint. The weight W acts through C, since the beam is uniform and the two other forces acting on the beam are the force $\vec{F}$ exerted by the carpenter at B at right angles to AB and a total force $\vec{P}$ exerted by the floor at A in an unspecified direction.

Since the beam is acted on by three forces which maintain it in equilibrium, the lines of action of the three forces must be concurrent. Thus, the direction of force $\vec{P}$ is from A to the point D at which $\vec{F}$ and $\vec{W}$ meet.

Since the board is not in motion, the second condition of equilibrium can be applied. Taking moments about point A, we have

$$\sum T_A = P \times 0 + F \times AB - W \times AE = 0$$

$$F = W \frac{AE}{AB} = W \frac{AC \cos 30}{AB} = \frac{1}{2} W \cos 30 = \frac{\sqrt{3}}{4} W.$$

$\therefore$ F = 86.6 lb.

STATIC AND KINETIC FRICTION

The force required to start a mass of 50 kilograms moving over a rough surface is 343 Nt. What is the coefficient of starting friction?

Solution: The coefficient of starting friction is given by the relation

$$F = \mu_{st} N$$

where F is the force of friction, μ_{st} is the coefficient of starting friction, and N is the force normal to the direction of travel. Since we assume the object is travelling on a horizontal plane, the normal force is simply the force of gravity, by Newton's Second Law. This force is

$$N = mg$$

$$N = 50 \text{ kg} (9.80 \text{ m/s}^2) = 490 \text{ Newton}$$

Therefore

$$343 \text{ nt} = \mu_{st} \times 490 \text{ nt}$$

$$\mu_{st} = 0.70.$$

A box is dragged up and down a concrete slope of 15° to the horizontal. To get the box started up the slope, it is necessary to exert six times the force needed to get it started down the slope. If the force is always parallel to the slope, what is the coefficient of static friction between the box and the concrete?

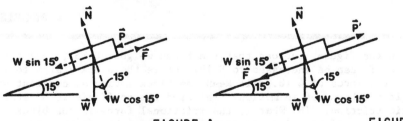

FIGURE A   FIGURE B

Solution: When the box is about to slide down the slope, the forces acting on it are as shown in (figure (a)). The weight of the box W acts vertically downward, the frictional force which attempts to prevent the motion acts up the slope, and the concrete exerts a normal force at right angles to the slope. When the box is just on the point of moving, $F = \mu_s N$, where μ_s is the coefficient of static friction required.

Let us resolve the force $\vec{W}$ into its components along, and at right angles to, the slope. Since the angle between the slope and the horizontal is 15°, this is also the angle between the normal to the slope and the normal to the horizontal (i.e., the vertical). Thus $\vec{W}$ has components W cos 15° at right angles to the plane and W sin 15° down the plane.

The box is just in equilibrium. From the conditions for equilibrium, we know that

N = W cos 15°.

and $P + W \sin 15° = F = \mu_s N = \mu_s W \cos 15°$.

∴ $P = \mu_s W \cos 15 - W \sin 15°$.

Figure (b) shows that, when the box is about to slide up the slope, the situation is very similar. The box is in equilibrium once more, so that

N = W cos 15°

and $P' = W \sin 15° + F = W \sin 15° + \mu_s N$

= $W \sin 15° + \mu_s W \cos 15°$.

But we know that the force P' = 6P.

∴ $W \sin 15° + \mu_s W \cos 15° = 6 (\mu_s W \cos 15° - W \sin 15°)$.

∴ $5\mu_s W \cos 15° = 7 W \sin 15°$.

∴ $\mu_s = \frac{7}{5} \tan 15° = \frac{7}{5} \times 0.268 = 0.375$.

● **PROBLEM 2-15**

In the figure, suppose that the block weighs 20 lb., that the tension T can be increased to 8 lb. before the block starts to slide, and that a force of 4 lb. will keep the block moving at constant speed once it has been set in motion. (a) Find the coefficients of static and kinetic friction. (b) What is the frictional force if the block is at rest on the surface and a horizontal force of 5 lb. is exerted on it?

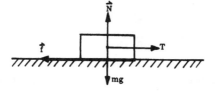

Solution: a) There are 2 forces of friction which can act on a body. These are the forces of kinetic and static friction. If a body, such as that in the figure, is initially at rest and we begin pulling on it with a variable force T, the block will remain at rest. This means that no matter what force T we apply to the body, the frictional force f always balances it. However, at some value of T, the frictional force no longer balances it, and the block begins translating. We may describe this static frictional force by

$$f_s \le \mu_s N \qquad (1)$$

where μ_s is the coefficient of static friction and N is the normal force of the table on the block. (The equality holds when the block begins translating). Once the block begins translating, the static frictional force stops acting and the kinetic frictional force takes over. This force is

$$f_k = \mu_k N \qquad (2)$$

It is also found that $f_k < f_{s\ max}$, and that once the block starts moving, we may reduce T and the block will still move. Applying the Second Law to the block of mass m

$$N - mg = ma_y$$
$$T - f = ma_x$$

Here a_x and a_y are the x and y components of the block's acceleration. Because the block coesn't leave the surface of the table, $a_y = 0$. Hence

$$N = mg \qquad (3)$$
$$T - f = ma_x \qquad (4)$$

The block is initially at rest, and just begins to slip when T = 8 lb. If we examine the block just before it moves, $a_x = 0$, and f is the maximum force of static friction. Then, using (1)

$$T - f_{s\ max} = 0$$

$$T = \mu_s N$$

$$8\ lb = \mu_s N$$

Using (3)

$$\mu_s = \frac{8\ lb}{mg} = \frac{8\ lb}{20\ lb} = .4$$

Once translation at constant velocity begins, T = 4 lb, $a_x = 0$ and f in (4) is $f_k = \mu_k N$. Hence

$$T - f_k = 0$$

31

$$T = \mu_k N$$

$$\mu_k = \frac{4 \text{ lb}}{20 \text{ lb}} = .20$$

b) Note that, if the block is initially at rest, a force of 8 lb is needed to start the motion of the block. Hence, if we pull the block with a force of 5 lb., $a_x = 0$ and, the force of static friction is acting. Then, from (4)

$$T - f_s = 0$$

$$T = f_s = 5 \text{ lb.}$$

● PROBLEM 2-16

If the coefficient of sliding friction for steel on ice is 0.05, what force is required to keep a man weighing 150 pounds moving at constant speed along the ice?

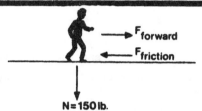

N = 150 lb.

Solution: To keep the man moving at constant velocity, we must oppose the force of friction tending to retard his motion with an equal but opposite force (see diagram).

The force of friction is given by:

$$F = \mu_{kinetic} N$$

By Newton's Third Law

$$F_{forward} = F_{friction}$$

Therefore

$$F_{forward} = \mu_{kinetic} N$$

$$F_{forward} = (.05)(150 \text{ lb}) = 7.5 \text{ lb.}$$

● PROBLEM 2-17

A 1200-lb sled is pulled along a horizontal surface at uniform speed by means of a rope that makes an angle of 30° above the horizontal (see figure (a)). If the tension in the rope is 100 lb, what is the coefficient of friction?

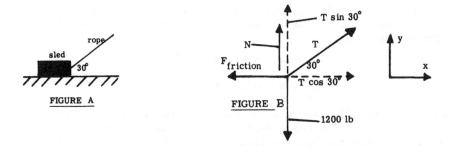

FIGURE A

FIGURE B

Solution. Since the sled is being pulled at constant velocity, there are no unbalanced forces. We break up the tension in the rope into components parallel and perpendicular to the horizontal (see figure (a)). By Newton's second law

$$\sum F_x = 0 \text{ therefore } F_{friction} = \mu N = T \cos 30° \qquad (1)$$

$$\sum F_y = 0 \text{ therefore } N + T \sin 30° = 1200$$

$$N = 1200 \text{ lb} - T \sin 30° \qquad (2)$$

From (1), $\mu = \dfrac{T \cos 30°}{N}$

Substituting (2) into this expression,

$$\mu = \frac{T \cos 30°}{1200 \text{ lb} - T \sin 30°} = \frac{(100 \text{ lb})(.866)}{1200 \text{ lb} - (100)\left(\frac{1}{2}\right)\text{lb}}$$

$$= \frac{86.6}{1150} = 0.0753.$$

● **PROBLEM 2-18**

In the figure, a block has been placed on an inclined plane and the slope angle θ of the plane has been adjusted until the block slides down the plane at constant speed, once it has been set in motion. Find the angle θ.

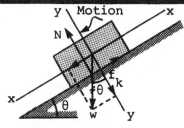

Solution: The forces on the block are its weight w and the normal and frictional components of the force exerted by the plane. The angle θ of the inclined plane is adjusted until the block slides down the plane. Since motion exists, the friction force is $f_k = \mu_k N$. Take axes perpendicular and parallel to the surface of the plane. Then, applying Newton's Second Law to the x and y components of the block's motion, we obtain (see figure)

$$\Sigma F_x = \mu_k N - w \sin \theta = 0$$

$$\Sigma F_y = N - w \cos \theta = 0 .$$

where ΣF_x and ΣF_y are the x and y components of the net force on the block. Both of these equations are equal to zero because the block accelerates neither parallel nor perpendicular to the plane. Hence

$$\mu_k N = w \sin \theta ,$$

$$N = w \cos \theta .$$

Dividing the former by the latter, we get

$$\mu_k = \tan \theta .$$

It follows that a block, regardless of its weight, slides down an inclined plane with constant speed if the tangent of the slope angle of the plane equals the coefficient of kinetic friction. Measurement of this angle then provides a simple experimental method of determining the coefficient of kinetic friction.

CHAPTER 3

KINEMATICS

Basic Attacks and Strategies for
Solving Problems in this Chapter

Kinematics is the study of motion using mathematics and the concepts of space and time, without regard to forces. The displacement of a particle $\vec{r}$, the instantaneous velocity $\vec{v}$, and the instantaneous acceleration $\vec{a}$ are the important physical quantities.

Consider the special case of constant or uniform acceleration $\vec{a}$ = rate of change in velocity/time = constant. *In one dimension, the statement would be that a = constant and the acceleration-time curve is given by Figure 1a. The average acceleration would be $\langle \vec{a} \rangle = \Delta\vec{v}/\Delta t = (\vec{v} - \vec{v_0})/(t - 0)$. The meaning of this physics problem-solving technique is that the area under the acceleration-time curve is the change in velocity (hatched area in Figure 1a).*

In one dimension the first important kinematic equation would be v = v$_0$ + at. *Hence, if one knows the change and velocity and the time, the acceleration can be found. This means that the slope of the velocity-time curve (Figure 2a) is the acceleration.*

Now, the definition of velocity is $\vec{v}$ = rate of change in direction/time. *The average velocity is $\langle \vec{v} \rangle = \Delta\vec{r}/\Delta t = (\vec{r} - \vec{r_0})/(t - 0)$. Hence, if one knows the distance covered and the time taken, one can find the average velocity. For the special case of uniform acceleration only, $\langle \vec{v} \rangle = (\vec{v} + \vec{v_0})/2$, as one would expect for an average value.*

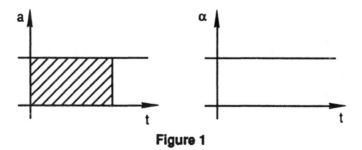

Figure 1

In one dimension, the second important kinematic equation is that x $= x_0 + v_0 t + 1/2\, at^2$. *(See Figure 3a for the position-time curve.) Note that the slope of the position-time curve at any time is the instantaneous velocity.*

A third important kinematic formula is obtained by solving for the time $t = (v - v_0)\,/\,a$ *and substituting into* $x - x_0 = <v>\,t$ *to get*

$$v^2 = v^2_0 + 2a\,(x - x_0).$$

This formula is useful if the time is not part of the given information in the problem.

Angular kinematics is very similar to the above case of translational motion. The important observables are angular acceleration $\alpha = \Delta\omega/t$, *angular velocity* $\omega = \Delta\theta/t$ *or* $2\pi F$, *and angular displacement* θ *in radians. The important formulae are*

$$\omega = \omega_0 + \alpha t$$

$$\theta = \theta_0 + \omega_0\, t + 1/2\, \alpha t^2$$

$$\omega^2 - \omega^2_0 = 2\alpha\,(\theta - \theta_0).$$

The angular acceleration-time, angular velocity-time, and angle-time, curves are shown in Figures 1b, 2b, and 3b, respectively. The way to attack the problem is to write down the given information using appropriate symbols, draw a picture, and then choose from the small number of kinematic formulae to find the solution. Each formula involves only three

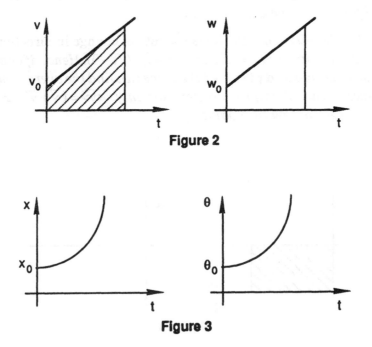

Figure 2

Figure 3

variables; hence the numerical value of two of these must be known to find the answer.

Free fall in one dimension is a special case of constant acceleration translational kinematics. If the direction downward is taken as negative, then $a = -g = -9.8 \text{ m/s}^2$, and the first two formulae become $v = v_0 - gt$ and $y = y_0 + v_0 t - 1/2\, gt^2$. The displacement-time curve is thus a parabola. If an object is projected upwards with a positive initial velocity, the time to reach the apex where $v = 0$ is just $t = v_0/g$.

Projectile motion in two dimensions follows from keeping track of the components in the first two kinematic formulae

$$v_y = v_{oy} - gt \quad \text{and} \quad y = y_0 + v_{oy} t - 1/2\, gt^2$$

$$v_x = v_{ox} = \text{constant} \quad \text{and} \quad x = x_0 + v_{ox} t.$$

The y versus x curve may be shown to be parabolic. Note that because velocity is a vector, $v_{ox} = v_0 \cos \theta$ and $v_{oy} = v_0 \sin \theta$, where θ is the initial angle of projection (see Figure 4). The time to reach the apex of the path is again $t = v_{oy} / g$, and the height may be found by substituting into the $y = y(t)$ equation. Also, the range is found by substituting $t_R = 2t$ into the equation $x = x_0 + v_x t$.

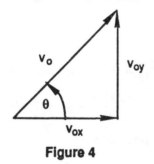

Figure 4

CHAPTER 3

KINEMATICS

FUNDAMENTALS OF VELOCITY AND ACCELERATION, FREE FALL

● PROBLEM 3-1

A car covers a distance of 30 miles in ½ hour. What is its speed in miles per hour and in feet per second?

Solution:

$$v_{average} = \frac{s}{t} = \frac{30 \text{ mi}}{\frac{1}{2} \text{ hr}} = 60 \text{ mi per hr}$$

$$= \frac{60 \text{ mi}}{\text{hr}} \times \frac{5280 \text{ ft}}{\text{mi}} \times \frac{1 \text{ hr}}{3600 \text{ sec}}$$

$$= 88 \text{ ft per sec}$$

This useful relation, that 60 miles per hour equals 88 feet per second, is one you should commit to memory.

● PROBLEM 3-2

An eastbound car travels a distance of 40 m in 5 s. Determine the speed of the car.

Solution: The observables of distance, d = 40 m, and time interval, t = 5 s, are given. We know that, since the velocity v of the car is constant,

$$v = \frac{d}{t} = \frac{40 \text{ m}}{5 \text{ s}} = 8 \frac{m}{s}$$

Here, d is the distance travelled in time t. The speed
of the car is 8 m/s.

A car starts from rest and reaches a speed of 30 miles per
hour in 8 seconds. What is its acceleration?

Solution: v = at for constant acceleration. We
shall convert the velocity in miles per hour into feet
per second. A useful conversion factor to remember is
that 60 mph is about 88 ft. per second. Therefore,
30 mph is about 44 ft. per second. Substituting we have:

$$a = \frac{v_{final}}{t} = \frac{44 \text{ ft}}{\text{sec} \times 8 \text{ sec}}$$
$$= 5.5 \text{ ft per sec per sec.}$$

A car starts from rest and reaches a speed of 88 feet per
second in 16 seconds. How far does it travel during this
time?

Solution 1: In this problem we assume constant
acceleration.

The acceleration of the car is

$$a = \frac{88 \text{ ft}}{16 \text{ sec} \times \text{sec}} = 5.5 \text{ ft per sec}^2$$

Then

$$s = \frac{1}{2} at^2 = \frac{1}{2} \times 5.5 \frac{\text{ft}}{\text{sec}^2} \times (16 \text{ sec})^2 = 704 \text{ ft.}$$

Solution 2:

The average velocity of the car is

$$v_{average} = \frac{v_{final} - v_{initial}}{2}$$

$$= \frac{88 \text{ ft/sec} - 0 \text{ ft/sec}}{2} = 44 \text{ ft per sec.}$$

Then

$$s = v_{average} \times \text{time} = 44 \text{ ft per sec} \times 16 \text{ sec}$$

$$= 704 \text{ ft}$$

An object, starting from rest, is given an acceleration of 16 feet per second^2 for 3 seconds. What is its speed at the end of 3 seconds?

Solution: Since the acceleration is constant, we have

$$a = \frac{v_{final} - v_{initial}}{t}$$

or $v_{final} = v_{initial} + at$

But $v_{initial} = 0$ for the object started from rest. Therefore

$$v_{final} = a \times t = \frac{16 \text{ ft}}{\text{sec}^2} \times 3 \text{ sec} = 48 \text{ ft per sec.}$$

Suppose that the first half of the distance between two points is covered at a speed v_1 = 10 mi/hr and, that during the second half, the speed is v_2 = 40 mi/hr. What is the average speed for the entire trip?

Solution: The average speed is the total distance traveled divided by the total traveling time. The average speed is not

$$\bar{v} = \frac{10 \text{ mi/hr} + 40 \text{ mi/hr}}{2} = 25 \text{ mi/hr.}$$

Let $2x$ be the total distance traveled and let t_1 and t_2 denote the times necessary for the two parts of the trip. Then,

$$\bar{v} = \frac{2x}{t_1 + t_2}$$

Since only the velocities are known, the average velocity must be expressed in terms of these variables. In order to eliminate unknown variables, we see that

$$t_1 = \frac{x}{v_1}; \quad t_2 = \frac{x}{v_2}.$$

$$t_1 + t_2 = \frac{x}{v_1} + \frac{x}{v_2} = \frac{x(v_1 + v_2)}{v_1 v_2}.$$

Therefore,

$$\bar{v} = \frac{2x}{\dfrac{x(v_1 + v_2)}{v_1 v_2}} = \frac{2v_1 v_2}{v_1 + v_2}$$

$$= \frac{2(10 \text{ mi/hr})(40 \text{ mi/hr})}{10 \text{ mi/hr} + 40 \text{ mi/hr}} = \frac{800}{50} \text{ mi/hr}$$

$$= 16 \text{ mi/hr.}$$

• **PROBLEM 3-7**

A car travels at the constant speed of 30 mph for 20 miles, at a speed of 40 mph for the next 20 miles, and then travels the final 20 miles at 50 mph. What was the average speed for the trip?

Solution: For situations in which the speed is variable, the rate at which distance d is traveled as a function of time, t, can be described by the average speed. The average speed $\bar{v}$ is equal to that constant speed which would be required for an object to travel the same distance d in the same time t. Therefore

$$\bar{v} = \frac{d}{t} .$$

The total time the car travels is the sum of the times for each segment of the trip.

$$t = t_1 + t_2 + t_3 = \frac{d_1}{v_1} + \frac{d_2}{v_2} + \frac{d_3}{v_3}$$

$$t = \frac{20 \text{ mi}}{30 \text{ mph}} + \frac{20 \text{ mi}}{40 \text{ mph}} + \frac{20 \text{ mi}}{50 \text{ mph}} = (0.67 + 0.50 + 0.40)\text{hr} = 1.57 \text{ hr}$$

The total distance is

$$d = d_1 + d_2 + d_3 = (20 + 20 + 20)\text{mi} = 60 \text{ mi}$$

Therefore, the average speed is

$$\bar{v} = \frac{d}{t} = \frac{60 \text{ mi}}{1.57 \text{ hr}} = 38.2 \text{ mph}$$

• **PROBLEM 3-8**

An automobile accelerates at a constant rate from 15 mi/hr to 45 mi/hr in 10 sec while traveling in a straight line. What is the average acceleration?

Solution. The magnitude of the average acceleration, or the rate of change of speed in this case, is the change in speed divided by the time in which it took place, or

$$\bar{a} = \frac{45 \text{ mi/hr} - 15 \text{ mi/hr}}{10 \text{ sec} - 0} = \frac{30 \text{ mi/hr}}{10 \text{ sec}}.$$

Changing units so as to be consistent,

$$\bar{a} = \frac{\left(\frac{30 \text{ mi}}{\text{hr}}\right) \times \left(\frac{5280 \text{ ft}}{\text{mi}}\right) \times \left(\frac{\text{hr}}{3600 \text{ sec}}\right)}{10 \text{ sec}} = \frac{44 \text{ ft/sec}}{10 \text{ sec}} = 4.4 \text{ ft/sec}^2$$

This statement means simply that the speed increases 4.4 ft/sec during each second, or 4.4 ft/sec^2.

● **PROBLEM** 3-9

An automobile traveling at a speed of 30 mi/hr accelerates uniformly to a speed of 60 mi/hr in 10 sec. How far does the automobile travel during the time of acceleration?

<u>Solution.</u> Converting to ft-sec units,

$$30\frac{mi}{hr} = 30\frac{mi}{hr} \times \frac{5280 \text{ ft}}{1 \text{ mi}} \times \frac{1 \text{ hr}}{3600 \text{ sec}} = 44 \text{ ft/sec}$$

$$60\frac{mi}{hr} = 88 \text{ ft/sec.}$$

Uniform acceleration can be found from the change in velocity divided by the time elapsed during the change.

$$a = \frac{\Delta v}{\Delta t} = \frac{88 \text{ ft/sec} - 44 \text{ ft/sec}}{10 \text{ sec}} = 4.4 \text{ ft/sec}^2$$

$$x = v_0 t + \frac{1}{2}at^2$$

$$= (44 \text{ ft/sec}) \times (10 \text{ sec}) + \frac{1}{2} \times (4.4 \text{ ft/sec}^2) \times (10 \text{ sec})^2.$$

$$= 440 \text{ ft} + 220 \text{ ft}$$

$$= 660 \text{ ft.}$$

Suppose next that the automobile, traveling at 60 mi/hr, slows to 20 mi/hr in a period of 20 sec. What was the acceleration?

$$a = \frac{v_2 - v_1}{\Delta t} = \frac{20 \text{ mi/hr} - 60 \text{ mi/hr}}{20 \text{ sec}}$$

$$= -2 (\text{mi/hr})/\text{sec.}$$

The automobile was slowing down during this period so the acceleration is negative.

● **PROBLEM** 3-10

The graph shows a displacement-time curve for a motion along a straight line. What are the average velocities from A to B and from A to C?

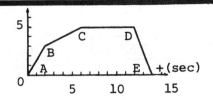

Solution: The average velocity of an object in motion is the distance d it travels divided by the time t it takes in transit.

$$v_{av} = \frac{d}{t}$$

Looking at the figure:

from A to B $v_{av} = \dfrac{d_{AB}}{t_{AB}} = \dfrac{3 \text{ m}}{2 \text{ s}} = 1.5$ m/sec

from A to C $v_{av} = \dfrac{d_{AC}}{t_{AC}} = \dfrac{5 \text{ m}}{6 \text{ s}} = 0.83$ m/sec.

● **PROBLEM 3-11**

Using the given d-t curve calculate the velocity-time curve.

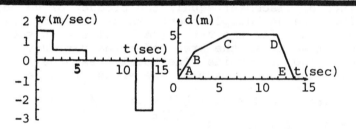

Solution: A velocity-time curve is found from a displacement-time curve by plotting the slope of the d-t curve versus time. Our task in this particular case is made easier by the fact that the velocity in each segment of the trip is constant.

From A to B $v_{AB} = \dfrac{d_{AB}}{t_{AB}} = \dfrac{(3-0)\text{m}}{(2-0)\text{ sec}} = 1.5$ m/sec

From D to E $v_{DE} = \dfrac{d_{DE}}{t_{DE}} = \dfrac{(0-5)\text{ m}}{(14-12)\text{ sec}} = -2.5$ m/sec.

The corresponding segments on the v-t curve are represented by horizontal lines. The rest of the curve is found similarly. Note that the area under the v-t curve at each time gives the displacement. That is,

at t = 6 sec, area = (1.5 × 2 + 0.5 × 4)m = 5 m

at t = 14 sec, area = (1.5 × 2 + 0.5 × 4 − 2.5 × 2)m = 0 m

● **PROBLEM 3-12**

A motion, starting from rest, has the acceleration-time graph shown in figure (a). Draw the v-t graph and calculate the net displacement.

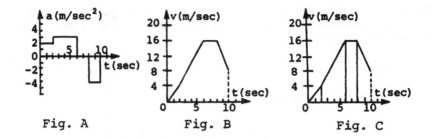

Fig. A   Fig. B   Fig. C

<u>Solution:</u> Between t = 0 and t = 2 sec, a = 2 m/sec². Thus Δ**v** = aΔt = 4 m/sec. Thus at t = 2, **v** = 4 m/sec. Between t = 2 and t = 6, a = 3 m/sec²; thus Δ**v** = 3 × (6 - 2) = 12 m/sec. At t = 6, 4 + 12 =, 16 m/sec and so forth.

Having found the velocities at various times and plotting the **points** as in figure (b), we can connect them with straight lines, since, as we can see from the acceleration-time **graph,** all accelerations are constant (therefore velocity is a linear function of t).

Since displacement equals the product of velocity and time, the net displacement can be found by calculating the area under the v-t curve until t = 10 sec. In figure (c), we break the area under the v-t curve into triangles and trapezoids. The total area under the curve is equal to the sum of the areas of these figures:

d = area = ½(4 × 2) + ½(4 + 16) × 4 + 16 × 2
+ ½(16 + 8) × 2
= 4 + 40 + 32 + 24
= 100 m

● **PROBLEM 3-13**

Two motorcycles are at rest and separated by 24.5 ft. They start at the same time in the same direction, the one in the back having an acceleration of 3 ft/sec², the one in the front going slower at an acceleration of 2 ft/sec². (a) How long does it take for the faster cycle to overtake the slower. (b) How far does the faster machine go before it catches up? (c) How fast is each cycle going at this time?

<u>Solution:</u> (a) Both cycles travel for the same length of time t. At the instant the two machines pass each other, the faster one has traveled exactly 24.5 ft more than the slower one. With the subscripts 1 and 2 representing the faster and slower cycles respectively, we have

$$d_1 = v_{01}t + \tfrac{1}{2}a_1 t^2 = \tfrac{1}{2}a_1 t^2$$

$$d_2 = v_{02}t + \tfrac{1}{2}a_2 t^2 = \tfrac{1}{2}a_2 t^2$$

since the initial velocities v_{01} and v_{02} are both zero. Now

$$d_1 = d_2 + 24.5 \text{ ft.}$$

41

or

$$\tfrac{1}{2}a_1 t^2 = \tfrac{1}{2}a_2 t^2 + 24.5 \text{ ft.}$$

Substituting values, we find the time t at which the two cycles pass each other.

$$\tfrac{1}{2}(3 \text{ ft/sec}^2)(t^2) = \tfrac{1}{2}(2 \text{ ft/sec}^2)(t^2) + 24.5 \text{ ft}$$

$$t^2 = 49 \text{ sec}^2$$

$$t = 7 \text{ sec}$$

(b) The distance d_1 traveled by the faster cycle when it passes the slower one is

$$d_1 = \tfrac{1}{2}a_1 t^2 = \tfrac{1}{2}(3 \text{ ft/sec})(7 \text{ sec})^2 = 73.5 \text{ ft.}$$

(c) The velocities of the two cycles can be found from

$$v = v_0 + at$$

Then, as they pass each other, their velocities are

$$v_1 = a_1 t = (3 \text{ ft/sec}^2)(7 \text{ sec}) = 21 \text{ ft/sec}$$

$$v_2 = a_2 t = (2 \text{ ft/sec}^2)(7 \text{ sec}) = 14 \text{ ft/sec} .$$

● **PROBLEM 3-14**

A skier is filmed by a motion-picture photographer who notices him traveling down a ski run. The skier travels 36 ft during the fourth second of the filming and 48 ft during the sixth second. What distance did he cover in the eight seconds of filming? Assume that the acceleration is uniform throughout.

Solution: The fact that the acceleration is uniform gives us a big advantage since, in this case, the instantaneous acceleration is equivalent to the average acceleration:

$$\vec{a} = \frac{\Delta \vec{v}}{\Delta t} = \frac{\vec{v}_f - \vec{v}_0}{t_f - t_0}$$

where $\vec{v}_f$ and $\vec{v}_0$ are the velocities at times t_f and t_0 respectively. To solve for $\vec{a}$ we use the kinematic equation

$$s = v_0 t + \tfrac{1}{2}at^2$$

where s is the distance covered in time t.

$$36 = v_0(1) + \tfrac{1}{2} a(1) = v_0 + \tfrac{1}{2}a$$

$$48 = v_f(1) + \tfrac{1}{2} a(1) = v_f + \tfrac{1}{2}a$$

where v_0 and v_f are the velocities at the beginning of the fourth and sixth seconds respectively, and both time intervals are one second long.

$$\tfrac{1}{2}a = 36 - v_0 = 48 - v_f$$

$$v_f = v_0 + 12$$

Since there is a two second interval between the times when the skier has velocities v_0 and v_f:

$$a = \frac{v_f - v_0}{\Delta t} = \frac{(v_0 + 12) - v_0}{2} = \frac{12}{2} = 6 \text{ ft/sec}^2$$

Knowing the acceleration, we can now solve for the skier's velocity v_0 at the beginning of the 4th second:

$$36 = v_0(1) + \tfrac{1}{2}(6)(1)$$

$$v_0 = 36 - 3 = 33 \text{ ft/sec}$$

Now, we may solve for v_0', the velocity at the beginning of the filming

$$v_0 = v_0' + at, \qquad\qquad v_0' = v_0 - at$$

$$v_0' = 33 - (6)(3) = 15 \text{ ft/sec}$$

Thus the distance covered in the eigth seconds of filming is:

$$s = v_0't + \tfrac{1}{2}at^2$$

$$= (15 \text{ ft/sec})(8 \text{ sec}) + \tfrac{1}{2}(6 \text{ ft/sec}^2)(8 \text{ sec})^2$$

$$= 312 \text{ ft.}$$

● PROBLEM 3-15

During the takeoff roll, a Boeing 747 jumbo jet is accelerating at 4 m/sec^2. If it requires 40 sec to reach takeoff speed, determine the takeoff speed and how far the jet travels on the ground.

Solution: The initial speed, $v_0 = 0$, the acceleration $a = 4$ m/sec^2, and the time interval of the takeoff, $t = 40$ sec are given. The unknown observables are the final speed, v, and the distance the plane traveled, d. From the laws of kinematics for constant acceleration

$$v_f = v_0 + at, \quad v_0 = 0 \text{ and } v_f \text{ is the plane's final velocity.}$$

Therefore, $v_f = at = (4 \text{ m/sec}^2)(40 \text{ sec}) = 160 \text{ m/sec}$

The plane's takeoff velocity is 160 m/sec in the same direction as the acceleration.

The distance s an object with constant acceleration travels in time t is:

$$s = v_0 t + \tfrac{1}{2} at^2, \qquad\qquad v_0 = 0$$

Hence, $s = \tfrac{1}{2}(4 \text{ m/sec}^2)(40 \text{ sec})^2 = 3,200 \text{ m}$

The plane travels a distance of 3.2 km during the takeoff.

● **PROBLEM** 3-16

The turntable of a record player is accelerated from rest to a speed of 33.3 rpm in 2 sec. What is the angular acceleration?

<u>Solution:</u> The angular kinematics equation for constant acceleration

$$\omega = \omega_0 + \alpha t$$

can be used. The initial velocity ω_0 is zero. The final angular velocity after t = 2 sec is

$$\omega = 2\pi f = 2\pi \times \frac{33.3 \text{ rev/min}}{60 \text{ sec/min}}$$
$$= 2\pi \times 0.556 \text{ sec}^{-1} = 3.48 \text{ sec}^{-1}$$

The angular acceleration is then

$$\alpha = \frac{\omega - \omega_0}{t} = \frac{3.48 \text{ sec}^{-1} - 0 \text{ sec}^{-1}}{2 \text{ sec}} = 1.74 \text{ sec}^{-2}$$

● **PROBLEM** 3-17

In a drag race, a dragster reaches the quarter-mile (402 m) marker with a speed of 80 m/s. What is his acceleration and how long did the run take?

<u>Solution:</u> The initial velocity, $v_0 = 0$, the final velocity, v = 80 m/s, and the distance traveled, d = 402 m, are given. The acceleration a and the time interval t are the unknown observables.

From the kinematics equations,

$$a = \frac{v^2 - v_0^2}{2d} = \frac{(80 \text{ m/s})^2 - (0)}{(2)(402 \text{ m})} = 7.96 \text{ m/s}^2$$

$$t = \frac{v - v_0}{a} = \frac{(80 \text{ m/s}) - (0)}{7.96 \text{ m/s}^2} = 10.1 \text{ s}$$

A ball is released from rest at a certain height. What is its velocity after falling 256 ft?

Solution: Since the initial velocity is zero, we use

$$y = v_0 t + \tfrac{1}{2}at^2 = \tfrac{1}{2}\,gt^2$$

taking 'down' as the positive y-direction.
   Solving for the time to fall 256 ft, we have

$$t = \sqrt{\frac{2y}{g}} = \sqrt{\frac{2 \times 256 \text{ ft}}{(32 \text{ ft/sec}^2)}} = \sqrt{16 \text{ sec}^2} = 4 \text{ sec}$$

The velocity after 4 sec fall is

$$v = v_0 + at = gt = (32 \text{ ft/sec}^2) \times (4 \text{ sec})$$

$$= 128 \text{ ft/sec}.$$

On a long straight road a car accelerates uniformly from rest, reaching a speed of 45 mph in 11 s. It has to maintain that speed for 1½ mi behind a truck until a suitable opportunity for passing the truck arises. The car then accelerates uniformly to 75 mph in a further 11 s. After maintaining that speed for 3 min, the car is brought to a halt by a uniform deceleration of 11 ft/s².
   Illustrate the motion on a suitable diagram, and calculate (a) the total distance traveled, (b) the total time taken, (c) the average speed, and (d) the average acceleration in the first 142 s.

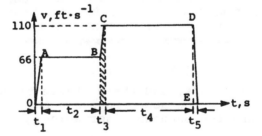

Solution: A velocity-time diagram should be drawn. During the first 11 s the car accelerates uniformly to a speed of 45 mph = 66 ft/s. This part of the diagram is therefore a straight line OA inclined to the t-axis at an angle whose tangent is 66/11. The distance traveled, s_1, is the area under this portion of the graph. Thus

$$s_1 = \tfrac{1}{2} \times 11 \text{ s} \times 66 \text{ ft/s} = 363 \text{ ft.}$$

In the second portion of the motion, the car travels

for 1 ½ mi at a constant speed of 45 mph. This part of the graph, AB, is a straight line parallel to the t-axis, its length being

$$t_2 = \frac{1\frac{1}{2}\ mi}{45\ mi/hr} \times 60\ min/hr \times 60\ s/min = 120\ s.$$

In the third portion of the motion, the car increases its speed by 30 mph = 44 ft · s⁻¹ at uniform acceleration in 11 s. This part of the graph is thus a straight line BC of slope 44/11. The distance traveled in this 11 s, s_3, is the area under this part of the graph, i.e., the shaded portion.

$$s_3 = \frac{1}{2} \times 11\ s \times 44\ ft/s + 11\ s \times 66\ ft/s = 968\ ft.$$

The next portion of the graph is again a straight line parallel to the t-axis. The time t_4 is 3 min = 180 s, and thus

$$s_4 = 75\ mi/hr \times \frac{3}{60}\ hr = 3.75\ mi.$$

In the final part of the motion, the car is brought to rest from a speed of 110 ft · s⁻¹ by a uniform deceleration of 11 ft/s². This portion of the graph, DE, is thus a straight line with a negative slope of 110/11. The time taken to come to rest, t_5, and the distance traversed, s_5, are

$$t_5 = \frac{110\ ft/s}{11\ ft/s} = 10\ s \quad and \quad s_5 = \frac{1}{2} \times 10s \times 110\ ft/s$$
$$= 550\ ft.$$

(a) The total distance traveled is

$$s = s_1 + s_2 + s_3 + s_4 + s_5$$

$$= 363\ ft + 1\frac{1}{2}\ mi + 968\ ft + 3\frac{3}{4}\ mi + 550\ ft$$

$$= 5\frac{1}{4}\ mi + 1881\ ft = 5\ mi\ 3201\ ft = 5\ mi\ 1067\ yd.$$

(b) The total time taken is

$$t = t_1 + t_2 + t_3 + t_4 + t_5$$

$$= (11 + 120 + 11 + 180 + 10)s = 332\ s = 5\ min\ 32\ s.$$

(c) The average speed, $\bar{v}$, is the total distance traveled divided by the total time taken. Thus

$$\bar{v} = \frac{5\ mi\ 1067\ yd}{332\ s} = \frac{29,601}{332}\ ft/s$$

$$= 89.16\ ft/s \times \frac{60\ mph}{88\ ft/s} = 60.8\ mph.$$

(d) The average acceleration in the first 142 s, $\bar{a}$, is
the final speed achieved divided by the total time taken.
Thus

$$\bar{a} = \frac{110 \text{ ft/s}}{142 \text{ s}} = 0.78 \text{ ft/s}^2.$$

● PROBLEM 3-20

A body is released from rest and falls freely. Compute
its position and velocity after 1, 2, 3, and 4 seconds.
Take the origin O at the elevation of the starting point,
the y-axis vertical, and the upward direction as positive.

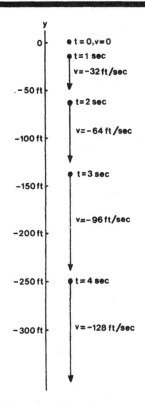

Solution: The initial coordinate y_0 and the initial velocity v_0 are both zero (see figure). The acceleration is
downward, in the negative y-direction, so a = -g =
= - 32 ft/sec^2.

Since the acceleration is constant, we may use the
kinematical equations for constant acceleration, or

$$y = v_0 t + \frac{1}{2}at^2 = 0 - \frac{1}{2}gt^2 = -16\frac{\text{ft}}{\text{sec}^2} \times t^2,$$

$$v = v_0 + at = 0 - gt = -32\frac{\text{ft}}{\text{sec}^2} \times t.$$

When t = 1 sec,

$$y_1 = -16\frac{ft}{sec^2} \times 1 \ sec^2 = -16 \ ft,$$

$$v_1 = -32\frac{ft}{sec^2} \times 1 \ sec = -32\frac{ft}{sec} \ .$$

The body is therefore 16 ft below the origin (y is negative) and has a downward velocity (v is negative) of magnitude 32 ft/sec.

The position and velocity at 2, 3, and 4 sec are found in the same way.

$$y_2 = -16\frac{ft}{sec^2} \times (2 \ sec)^2 = -16\frac{ft}{sec^2} \times 4 \ sec^2 = -64 \ ft$$

$$v_2 = -32\frac{ft}{sec^2} \times 2 \ sec = -64 \ ft/sec$$

$$y_3 = -16\frac{ft}{sec^2} \times (3 \ sec)^2 = -16\frac{ft}{sec^2} \times 9 \ sec^2 = -144 \ ft$$

$$v_3 = -32\frac{ft}{sec^2} \times 3 \ sec = -96 \ ft/sec$$

$$y_4 = -16\frac{ft}{sec^2} \times (4 \ sec)^2 = -16\frac{ft}{sec^2} \times 16 \ sec^2 = -256 \ ft$$

$$v_4 = -32\frac{ft}{sec^2} \times 4 \ sec = -128 \ ft/sec$$

The results are illustrated in the diagram.

● **PROBLEM 3-21**

A ball is thrown upward with an initial speed of 80 ft/sec. How high does it go? What is its speed at the end of 3.0 sec? How high is it at that time?

Solution. Since both upward and downward quantities are involved, upward will be called positive. At the highest point the ball stops, and hence at that point $v_1 = 0$. The only force acting on the ball is the gravitational force which gives a constany acceleration of g = -32 ft/sec². For constant acceleration and unidirectioal motion,

$$2as = v_1^2 - v_0^2$$

$$2(-32 \ ft/sec^2)s_1 = 0 - (80 \ ft/sec)^2$$

48

$$s_1 = \frac{-(80 \text{ ft/sec})^2}{2(-32 \text{ ft/sec}^2)} \approx 100 \text{ ft.}$$

s_1 is the highest point the ball reaches. To find the speed of the ball after 3 seconds,

$$v_2 = v_0 + at$$

$$= 80 \text{ ft/sec} + (-32 \text{ ft/sec}^2)(3.0 \text{ sec})$$

$$= 80 \text{ ft/sec} - 96 \text{ ft/sec} = -16 \text{ ft/sec.}$$

After 3 seconds, the speed of the ball is $v_2 = 16 \text{ ft/sec}$ downward. The height of the ball after 3 seconds can be found from

$$s_2 = v_0 t + \frac{1}{2}at^2$$

$$= (80 \text{ ft/sec})(3.0 \text{ sec}) + \frac{1}{2}(-32 \text{ ft/sec}^2)(3.0 \text{ sec})^2$$

$$= 240 \text{ ft} - 144 \text{ ft} = 96 \text{ ft.}$$

As a check, s_2 can also be found by using

$$s_2 = \bar{v}t = \left(\frac{v_2 + v_0}{2}\right)t = \frac{-16 \text{ ft/sec} + 80 \text{ ft/sec}}{2} \times 3.0 \text{ sec}$$

$$= 96 \text{ ft}$$

where $\bar{v}$ is the average velocity.

Note that s is the magnitude of the displacement, not the total distance traveled. If the ball returns to the starting point or goes on past it, s will be zero or negative, respectively.

● **PROBLEM 3-22**

(a) With what speed must a ball be thrown directly upward so that it remains in the air for 10 seconds? (b) What will be its speed when it hits the ground? (c) How high does the ball rise?

Solution: Near the surface of the earth, all objects fall towards its center with a constant acceleration $g = 32 \text{ ft/sec}^2$. Therefore, when the ball is thrown, its speed must decrease by 32 ft/sec each second until it reaches its maximum height. Then it starts to fall, gaining speed at the rate of 32 ft/sec, and retraces its path, hitting the ground with the same speed at which it started the trip upward. This is so because the acceleration is constant and the distance traveled is the same during the rising and falling portions of the motion of the ball. Thus, the average velocity must have the same magnitude in each case and the time required to reach the maximum height must equal the time required to fall back to the ground.

(a) Let the upward direction be positive. Then v_0 is positive and the acceleration a is negative. After 10 seconds, v must equal $-v_0$. From the kinematics equation

$$v = v_0 + at$$

we have for the instant before it hits the ground,

$$-v_0 = v_0 - gt$$
$$-2v_0 = -gt$$

and

$$v_0 = \frac{gt}{2} = \frac{(32 \text{ ft/sec}^2)(10 \text{ sec})}{2} = 160 \text{ ft/sec}$$

(b) The speed of the ball when it hits the ground is $-v_0$ or -160 ft/sec.

(c) The height reached by the ball can be obtained by realizing that the rise of the ball must take half the total time the ball is in the air, or 5 seconds. The average velocity for this part of the motion must be

$$\bar{v} = \frac{v_i + v_f}{2} = \frac{(160 \text{ ft/sec} + 0 \text{ ft/sec})}{2} = 80 \text{ ft/sec.}$$

The height the ball rises is then

$$d = \bar{v}t = (80 \text{ ft/sec})(5 \text{ sec}) = 400 \text{ ft.}$$

This result can also be obtained using the kinematics equation

$$d = v_0 t + \tfrac{1}{2} at^2$$

Substituting values,

$$d = (160 \text{ ft/sec})(5 \text{ sec}) + \tfrac{1}{2}(-32 \text{ ft/sec}^2)(5 \text{ sec})^2$$

$$= 800 \text{ ft} - 400 \text{ ft} = 400 \text{ ft.}$$

● **PROBLEM** 3-23

A racing car passes one end of the grandstand at a speed of 50 ft/sec. It slows down at a constant acceleration $\vec{a}$, such that its speed as it passes the other end of the grandstand is 10 ft/sec. (a) If this process takes 20 seconds, calculate the acceleration $\vec{a}$ and (b) the length of the grandstand .

Solution: (a) For constant acceleration, we have

$$a = \frac{\text{change in velocity}}{\text{time elapsed}} = \frac{\Delta v}{\Delta t}$$

Therefore

$$a = \frac{v_f - v_i}{\Delta t} = \frac{10 \text{ ft/sec} - 50 \text{ ft/sec}}{20 \text{ seconds}} = -2 \text{ ft/sec}^2$$

where v_f and v_i are the final and initial velocities, respectively.

(b) The length of the grandstand is equal to the distance d the car travels during the 20 seconds. This distance is equal to its final position x_f minus its initial position x_i and can be found from the kinematics equation

$$x_f = x_i + v_i t + \tfrac{1}{2}at^2 .$$

Hence,

$$d = x_f - x_i = v_i t + \tfrac{1}{2}at^2$$

$$= (50 \text{ ft/sec})(20 \text{ sec}) + \tfrac{1}{2}(-2 \text{ ft/sec}^2)(20 \text{ sec})^2$$

$$= 1000 \text{ ft} - 400 \text{ ft} = 600 \text{ ft}$$

The length d can also be found using $d = \bar{v}t$ where $\bar{v}$ is the average velocity. For constant acceleration, $\bar{v}$ is given by

$$\bar{v} = \frac{v_i + v_f}{2} = \frac{50 \text{ ft/sec} + 10 \text{ ft/sec}}{2} = 30 \text{ ft/sec}.$$

Then,

$$d = \bar{v}t = (30 \text{ ft/sec})(20 \text{ sec}) = 600 \text{ ft}.$$

which agrees with the first answer.

VECTOR COMPONENTS OF VELOCITY AND ACCELERATION

● **PROBLEM** 3-24

The pilot of an airplane flying on a straight course knows from his instruments that his airspeed is 300 mph. He also knows that a 60-mph gale is blowing at an angle of 60° to his course. How can he calculate his velocity relative to the ground?

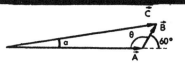

Solution: Relative to an observer on the ground, the airplane has two velocities, one of 300 mph relative to the air and the other of 60 mph at an angle of 60° to the course, due to the fact that it is carried along by the moving air mass.

To obtain the resultant velocity, it is therefore necessary to add the two components by vector addition. In the diagram, $\vec{A}$ represents the velocity of the aircraft relative to the air, and $\vec{B}$ the velocity of the air relative to the ground. When they are added in the normal manner of vector addition, $\vec{C}$ is their resultant. The magnitude of $\vec{C}$ is given by the trigonometric formula known as the law of cosines (see figure).

$$C^2 = A^2 + B^2 - 2AB \cos \theta.$$
But A = 300 mph, B = 60 mph, and θ = (180° - 60°) = 120°. Therefore
$$C^2 = (300 \text{ mph})^2 + (60 \text{ mph})^2 - 2 \times 300 \text{ mph}$$

$$\times 60 \text{ mph } (-\tfrac{1}{2}) = 111{,}600 \text{ (mph)}^2;$$

$$\therefore \qquad C = 334 \text{ mph}.$$

Also, from the addition formula for vectors, we have

$$\sin \alpha = \frac{B}{C} \sin \theta = \frac{60 \text{ mph}}{334 \text{ mph}} \times \frac{\sqrt{3}}{2} = 0.156.$$

$$\therefore \qquad \alpha = 9°.$$

● **PROBLEM** 3-25

A motor boat can move with a maximum speed of 10 m/sec, relative to the water. A river 400 m wide flowing at 5 m/sec must be crossed in the shortest possible time to reach a point on the other bank directly opposite the starting point. In which direction must the boat be pointed and how long will it take to cross?

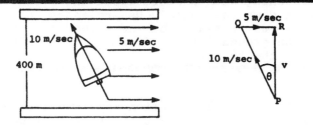

Solution: If the boat were pointed directly at the opposite bank, then during the crossing it would drift downstream and it would not reach the other bank at a point directly opposite the starting point. It must therefore be pointed in a direction tilted in the up-stream direction as shown in the figure. As illustrated in the vector diagram PQR, the result of adding the velocity of the boat relative to the water to the velocity of the water must be a resultant velocity $\vec{v}$ pointing directly toward the opposite bank. We cannot draw this triangle of vectors immediately be-cause we do not know the angle θ between the direction of motion and the direction straight across the stream. However, inspecting the triangle PQR and remembering that in trigonometry the sine of the angle θ is defined as
$$\sin \theta = \frac{QR}{PQ}$$

$$= \frac{5}{10} = 0.5$$

we refer to table of sines and find that the angle whose sine is 0.5 is 30°. The boat must therefore be pointed upstream at an angle of 30° from the direction perpendicular to the bank.

Applying Pythagoras' theorem to the triangle PQR

$$PQ^2 = QR^2 + PR^2$$

or $PR^2 = PQ^2 - QR^2$

52

that is; $v^2 = 10^2 - 5^2 = 75$

$$v = \sqrt{75} = 8.66 \text{ m/sec}$$

The boat therefore crosses the river at a speed of 8.66 m/sec. Since the distance across the river is 400 m, the time taken is, since v = constant,

$$t = \frac{d}{v} = \frac{400 \text{ m}}{8.66 \text{ m/sec}}$$

$t = 46.2$ sec.

● **PROBLEM 3-26**

A boy leaning over a railway bridge 49 ft high sees a train approaching with uniform speed and attempts to drop a stone down the funnel. He releases the stone when the engine is 80 ft away from the bridge and sees the stone hit the ground 3 ft in front of the engine. What is the speed of the train?

Solution: Applying the equation applicable to uniform acceleration, $x - x_0 = v_0 t + \frac{1}{2}at^2$, to the dropping of the stone 49 ft from rest under the action of gravity, we can find the time t the stone is in motion. The initial velocity of the stone v_0 is zero. The distance the stone travels, $x - x_0 = 49$ ft. Therefore,

$$49 \text{ ft} = 0 + (\tfrac{1}{2})(32 \text{ ft/sec}^2)(t^2)$$

$$\therefore t = \sqrt{\frac{2 \times 49 \text{ ft}}{32 \text{ ft/s}^2}} = \frac{7}{4} \text{ s.}$$

In the time of 7/4 s it takes the stone to drop, the engine has moved with uniform speed u a distance of (80 − 3) ft.

$$\therefore \quad u = \frac{d}{t} = \frac{77 \text{ ft}}{7/4 \text{ sec}} = 44 \text{ ft/sec} = 30 \text{ mph.}$$

● **PROBLEM 3-27**

An airplane lands on a carrier deck at 150 mi/hr and is brought to a stop uniformly, by an arresting device, in 500 ft. Find the acceleration and the time required to stop.

Solution. Converting units to ft-sec,

$$v_0 = (150 \text{ mi/hr}) \times \left(\frac{5280 \text{ ft/mi}}{3600 \text{ sec/hr}} \right) = 220 \text{ ft/sec}.$$

Since there is a constant deceleration,

$$2as = v_1^2 - v_0^2$$

$$2a(500 \text{ ft}) = 0 - (220 \text{ ft/sec})^2$$

$$a = \frac{-(220 \text{ ft/sec})^2}{2(500 \text{ ft})} = -48.4 \text{ ft/sec}^2.$$

Solving for t in the following formula,

$$v_1 = v_0 + at$$

$$t = \frac{v_1 - v_0}{a} = \frac{0 - 220 \text{ ft/sec}}{-48.4 \text{ ft/sec}^2} = 4.55 \text{ sec}.$$

● PROBLEM 3-28

A ball is projected horizontally with a velocity v_0 of 8 ft/sec. Find its position and velocity after $\frac{1}{4}$ sec (see the figure).

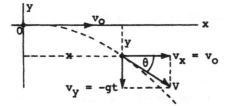

Solution: Since the acceleration of gravity, g, is constant, we may use the equations for constant acceleration to find the velocity $\left(v_y \right)$ and position (y) of a particle undergoing free fall motion

$$v_y = v_{0_y} - gt$$

$$y = y_0 + v_{0_y} - \tfrac{1}{2}gt^2$$

Here, y_0 and v_{0_y} are the initial y position and velocity of the particle. In this case, the departure angle is zero. The initial vertical velocity component is therefore zero. The horizontal velocity component equals the initial velocity and is constant. Since no horizontal force acts on the flying object, it is not accelerated in the horizontal direction. Therefore,

$$v_y = -gt \qquad\qquad y = \tfrac{1}{2}gt^2$$

$$v_x = v_{0_x} \qquad\qquad x = v_{0_x} t$$

and, at $t = \frac{1}{4}$ sec,

$v_y = (-32 \text{ ft/sec}^2)(\frac{1}{4} \text{ sec})$

$\quad = -8 \text{ ft/sec}$

$v_x = 8 \text{ ft/sec}$

$y = (-\frac{1}{2})(32 \text{ ft/sec}^2)(\frac{1}{16} \text{ sec}^2) = -1 \text{ ft.}$

$x = (8 \text{ ft/sec})(\frac{1}{4} \text{ sec}) = 2 \text{ ft.}$

● **PROBLEM** 3-29

A ball is thrown with an initial velocity, v_0, of 160 ft/sec,
directed at an angle, θ_0, of 53° with the ground.
(a) Find the x- and y-components of v_0.

(b) Find the position of the ball and the magnitude and direction of
its velocity when $t = 2$ sec.
(c) At the highest point of the ball's path, what is the ball's alti-
tude (h) and how much time has elapsed?
(d) What is the ball's range d? (See figure).

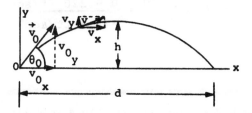

Solution: (a) Using the figure

$$v_{0_x} = v_0 \cos \theta_0; \quad v_{0_y} = v_0 \sin \theta_0$$

Hence,

$$v_{0_x} = 160 \text{ ft/sec} \cdot \cos 53° = 160 \text{ ft/sec } (3/5) = 96 \text{ ft/sec}$$

$$v_{0_y} = 160 \text{ ft/sec} \cdot \sin 53° = 160 \text{ ft/sec } (4/5)$$

$$= 128 \text{ ft/sec}$$

(b) The acceleration due to gravity is constant. Furthermore, there
is no force acting on the projectile in the x-direction, and its acceleration in the x-direction is therefore zero. Hence

$$a_x(t) = 0 \qquad\qquad a_y(t) = -g$$

$$v_x(t) = v_{0_x} \qquad\qquad v_y(t) = v_{0_y} - gt$$

$$x(t) = x_0 + v_{0_x} t \qquad\qquad y(t) = y_0 t \, v_{0_y} t - \frac{1}{2}gt^2$$

Here, x_0, y_0 are the initial coordinates of the projectile, and v_{0_x},
v_{0_y} are the initial x and y components of the ball's velocity.

Taking the origin (0) as shown in the figure, we have, at $t = 2$ sec

$$v_x = 96 \text{ ft/sec}$$

$$x = (96 \text{ ft/sec})(2 \text{ sec}) = 192 \text{ ft.}$$

$$v_y = 128 \text{ ft/sec} - \left(32 \text{ ft/sec}^2\right)(2 \text{ sec}) = 64 \text{ ft/sec}$$

$$y = (128 \text{ ft/sec})(2 \text{ sec}) - \left(\tfrac{1}{2}\right)\left(32 \text{ ft/sec}^2\right)\left(4 \text{ sec}^2\right)$$

$$y = 256 \text{ ft} - 64 \text{ ft} = 192 \text{ ft.}$$

The magnitude of the ball's velocity is

$$v = \left(v_x^2 + v_y^2\right)^{\frac{1}{2}}$$

$$v = \left((64 \text{ ft/sec})^2 + (96 \text{ ft/sec})^2\right)^{\frac{1}{2}}$$

$$v = 115.4 \text{ ft/sec.}$$

The direction of the velocity relative to the x-axis is

$$\tan \theta = \frac{v_y}{v_x} = \frac{64}{96} = 2/3$$

$$\theta = 34°$$

(c) At the highest point of the path, the ball has no vertical velocity. Then, by our kinematics equations,

$$v_y = 0 = v_0 - gt$$

$$t = \frac{v_{0_y} - 0}{g} = \frac{128 \text{ ft/sec}}{32 \text{ ft/sec}^2} = 4 \text{ sec .}$$

It takes 4 sec. for the ball to reach its maximum height. It has traveled a vertical distance,

$$y_{max} = v_{0_y} t - \tfrac{1}{2} gt^2$$

$$= (128 \text{ ft/sec})(4 \text{ sec}) - \tfrac{1}{2}\left(32 \text{ ft/sec}^2\right)(4 \text{ sec})^2$$

$$= 512 \text{ ft} - 256 \text{ ft} = 256 \text{ ft.}$$

(d) It takes the ball as much time to fall as it does to rise. Hence, the entire trajectory requires 8 sec. By the kinematics equations, we find its horizontal position at the end of its trajectory,

$$x(t) = v_{0_x} t = 96 \text{ ft/sec} \cdot 8 \text{ sec} = 768 \text{ ft.}$$

This is the range of the ball.

● PROBLEM 3-30

A workman sitting on top of the roof of a house drops his hammer. The roof is smooth and slopes at an angle of 30° to the horizontal. It is 32 ft long and its lowest point is 32 ft from the ground. How far from the house wall is the hammer when it hits the ground?

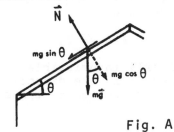

Fig. A

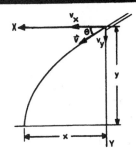

Fig. B

56

Solution: Figure A illustrates the first part of the motion. Two forces are acting on the hammer as it slides down the roof; the weight $\vec{mg}$ acting downward, one component of which, mg cos θ, balances the second force, the normal force exerted by the roof. At the same time, the component parallel to the roof, mg sin θ, is unbalanced and produces the acceleration on the hammer.

Apply Newton's second law to the unbalanced force to obtain mg sin θ = ma. Thus the hammer accelerates down the roof with acceleration a = g sin θ. In this case sin θ = sin 30° = ½. The kinematic relation for constant acceleration which does not involve time is used to find the velocity with which the hammer leaves the roof. It is $v^2 = v_0^2 + 2as$, where v_0, the initial velocity, is 0 and s is the distance the hammer moves on the roof (= 25 ft). Hence, v is obtained from

$$v^2 = 2 \times \frac{32}{2} \text{ ft/sec}^2 \times 32 \text{ ft; that is,}$$

v = 32 ft/sec.

In the second stage of the fall, the hammer undergoes projectile motion. It drops 32 ft in time t while traveling a distance x horizontally. Let the positive direction of y be taken as downward, and resolve v into its vertical and its horizontal components: v sin θ and v cos θ, respectively (see fig. B). θ is the same as the angle of the slope of the roof. Since there is no horizontal component of force acting on the hammer when it leaves the roof, there is then no horizontal acceleration. The kinematic equation for constant velocity is then x = (v cos θ)t. The vertical acceleration is the constant acceleration of gravity g. Therefore $y = (v \sin θ)t + \frac{1}{2} gt^2$ where t = x/v cos θ.

$$y = v \sin θ \frac{x}{v \cos θ} + \frac{g}{2} \times \frac{x^2}{v^2 \cos^2 θ} \; .$$

$$\frac{x^2 \times 32 \text{ ft/sec}^2}{2 \times (32 \text{ ft/sec})^2 \times \frac{3}{4}} + \frac{x}{\sqrt{3}} - 32 \text{ ft} = 0$$

or $x^2 + 16 \sqrt{3} \, x \text{ ft} - 1536 \text{ ft}^2 = 0$

$(x + 32 \sqrt{3} \text{ ft})(x - 16 \sqrt{3} \text{ ft}) = 0$

x = - 32 $\sqrt{3}$ ft   or   +16 $\sqrt{3}$ ft.

The negative answer is clearly inadmissible. It is the answer that would result if the direction of projection were reversed. Hence the correct answer is

x = 16 $\sqrt{3}$ ft = 27.7 ft from the house.

The moon revolves about the earth in a circle (very nearly) of radius R = 239,000 mi or 12.6×10^8 ft, and requires 27.3 days or 23.4×10^5 sec to make a complete revolution. (a) What is the acceleration of the moon toward the earth?

(b) If the gravitational force exerted on a body by the earth is inversely proportional to the square of the distance from the earth's center, the acceleration produced by this force should vary in the same way. Therefore, if the acceleration of the moon is caused by the gravitational attraction of the earth, the ratio of the moon's acceleration to that of a falling body at the earth's surface should equal the ratio of the square of the earth's radius (3950 mi or 2.09×10^6 ft) to the square of the radius of the moon's orbit. Is this true?

EARTH

Solution: (a) The velocity of the moon is

$$v = \frac{\text{distance}}{\text{time}} = \frac{\text{circumference}}{\text{time for one orbit}} = \frac{2\pi R}{T} = \frac{2\pi \times 12.6 \times 10^8 \text{ ft}}{23.4 \times 10^5 \text{ sec}}$$

$$= 3360 \frac{\text{ft}}{\text{sec}} .$$

Its radial acceleration is therefore

$$a = \frac{v^2}{R} = \frac{(3360 \text{ ft/sec})^2}{12.6 \times 10^8 \text{ ft}} = 0.00896 \frac{\text{ft}}{\text{sec}^2} = 8.96 \times 10^{-3} \frac{\text{ft}}{\text{sec}^2}$$

(b) The ratio of the moon's acceleration to the acceleration of a falling body at the earth's surface is:

$$\frac{a}{g} = \frac{8.96 \times 10^{-3} \text{ ft/sec}^2}{32.2 \text{ ft/sec}^2} = 2.78 \times 10^{-4}$$

The ratio of the square of the earth's radius to the square of the moon's orbit is:

$$\frac{(2.09 \times 10^6 \text{ ft})^2}{(12.6 \times 10^8 \text{ ft})^2} = 2.75 \times 10^{-4}$$

The agreement is very close, although not exact because we have used average values.

CHAPTER 4

DYNAMICS

Basic Attacks and Strategies for Solving Problems in this Chapter

---

Dynamics is the study of motion using mathematics and the concepts of space and time, with especial regard to the forces involved. According to Newton's second law, the sum of the forces acting on an object is equal to the time rate of change of the object's momentum

$$\Sigma \vec{F} = \Delta \vec{p} / \Delta t$$

where $\vec{p} = m\vec{v}$ is the momentum. Note that this is both a definition of force and a law of nature. Both force and momentum are vector quantities. Since the mass is constant in Newtonian mechanics, this law is often written as $\Sigma \vec{F} = m\vec{a}$ or simply $F = ma$.

Newton's second law can be used to find the force if the mass and acceleration are known, to find the mass if the force and acceleration are known, or to find the acceleration if the force and mass are known. Once the acceleration is found, one may use the methods of translational or rotational kinematics to find, e.g., the distance traversed during a given time interval (see KINEMATICS). The gravitational force $W = mg$ is a special case of $F = ma$. If the acceleration is zero (constant velocity motion), then we can solve the problem using the methods of translational or rotational equilibrium (see STATICS).

Problems in dynamics involve the forces of tension, gravitation or weight, and friction. One must always decide what the relevant forces are.

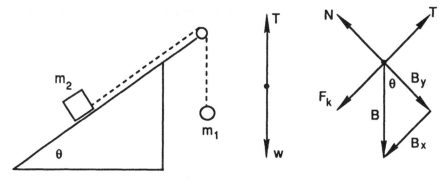

Figure 1

Consider the problem of Figure 1a, where the mass m_1 accelerates downward. Just as with statics, we need an accurate picture of the problem and the appropriate free body diagrams. The first mass has weight $W = m_1 g$ and the second mass has weight $B = m_2 g$. The first free body diagram (Figure 1b) gives $\Sigma F = W - T = m_1 a$. In the second free body diagram (Figure 1c), taking the x–direction along the incline, we get

$$\Sigma F_x = T - F_k - B_x = m_2 a \text{ and } \Sigma F_y = N - B_y = 0.$$

The weight B has components $B_x = B \sin \theta$ and $B_y = B \cos \theta$. If the tension and acceleration are unknown, one may solve for them algebraically.

One force which we have not considered up to now is the resistive force F_R (see Figure 2) which an object feels when falling in a viscous medium. This is the force which allows the parachutist to arrive safely at the ground. Newton's law gives

$$W - F_R = ma.$$

Physical intuition can, however, be used to see that after a certain time, the resistive force grows to cancel out the gravitational force. The object then moves at terminal velocity $v_T = mg / b$.

Another force important in our everyday lives and also in astrophysics is the universal force of gravitation. Newton's law of gravitation states that between every two masses in the universe, there exists an attractive force of gravitation (see Figure 3) given by

$$F = G\, m_1 m_2 / r^2.$$

Since near the surface of the Earth the gravitational force is the weight $F = m_1 g$ and $m_2 = m_E$, we can use this law to find the mass of the Earth $m_E = gr^2_E / G$ if we know its radius. The same holds true for the moon and other planets, so long as one plugs in the correct gravitational acceleration on the surface of the object.

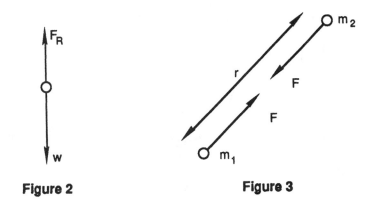

Figure 2   Figure 3

The escape speed of a rocket is given by $v_e = \sqrt{2\,gr}$ where $g = GM / r^2$ is the gravitational acceleration at a distance r from the center of the planet. The properties of the orbits of planets and satellites can be derived from Newton's law of universal gravitation. For example, using the concept of centripetal force $F_c = mv^2/r$ where $v = r\omega$, one may derive Kepler's third law, which says that the square of the orbital period is proportional to the cube of the semi-major axis or orbital radius $T^2 = k\,r^3$. Note that the period is reciprocally related to the linear frequency of the motion: $T = 2\pi r/v = 1/\upsilon$. The constant k depends only on the central massive body.

As another application of centripetal force, consider Figure 4b showing a pilot flying a loop-the-loop. At the bottom of the loop (Figure 4a), Newton's second law gives $\Sigma F = N - W = F_c$, or we find that the pilot has an apparent weight $N = mg + mv^2/r$. At the top of the loop (Figure 4c), Newton's law gives $\Sigma F = W - N = F_c$, or the pilot has an apparent weight given by $N = mg - mv^2/r$. If the pilot flies fast enough, s/he feels weightless at the top of the loop. In the same way, when we stand in an elevator and accelerate up or down, our weight can appear to increase or decrease.

In solving problems in curvilinear dynamics, we use techniques similar to those used above in translational dynamics. However, now Newton's second law is written as

$$\Sigma \vec{\tau} = \Delta \vec{L} / \Delta t$$

where $\vec{L} = \vec{r} \times \vec{p}$ is the angular momentum of a rotating object. Often, the angular momentum is written as $I\vec{\omega}$ where I is the moment of inertia of an object. By substitution, one obtains $\tau = I\,\alpha$ for Newton's second law for rotation, which is similar to $F = ma$. In rotation, torque, moment of inertia, and angular acceleration are analogous to force, mass, and acceleration. Hence, given any two of τ, I, and α in a problem, one may calculate the third. One may also have to use the methods of rotational

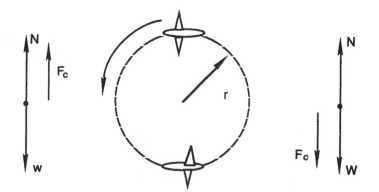

Figure 4

kinematics to find the angular acceleration from given values of angle and time.

In the absence of external torques, the angular momentum of a system must be constant: $\Sigma L_0 = \Sigma L$. Consider in Figure 5 that one platter, not initially rotating, falls onto and sticks to a second platter rotating at angular velocity ω_0. The total initial angular momentum is $I_1 \cdot 0 + I_2 \omega_0$ and the total final angular momentum is $I_1 \omega + I_2 \omega$. Equating the initial and final angular momentum gives the final angular velocity $\omega = I_2 \omega_0 / (I_1 + I_2)$.

In solving rotational dynamics problems, one must usually deal first with the translational dynamics. However, along with finding the relevant forces, one must also identify the torques. Shown in Figure 6a is a sphere about to begin rolling without slipping down an incline. In the free body diagram (Figure 6b), the weight of the sphere is broken up into components along the incline $W_x = W \sin \theta$ and perpendicular to it $W_y = W \cos \theta$ (just as with the translational dynamics problem of Figure 1). Newton's second law for translation then gives

$$\Sigma F_x = W_x - F_k = ma \text{ and } \Sigma F_y = N - W_y = 0.$$

Newton's second law for rotation gives $\Sigma \tau = rF_k = I\alpha$. Using the connecting equation $a = r\alpha$ and the fact that the moment of inertia of a sphere is $I = 2/5 \ mr^2$ would enable us to find the acceleration and any other desired observable.

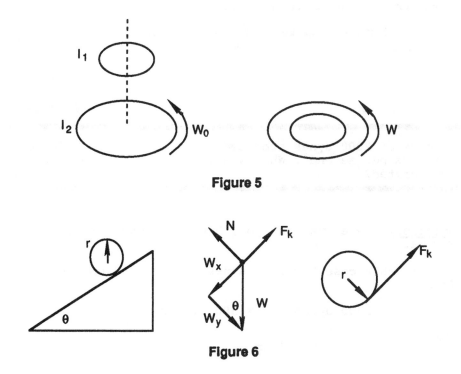

Figure 5

Figure 6

CHAPTER 4

DYNAMICS

RECTILINEAR DYNAMICS

What is the resultant force on a body of mass 48 kg when its acceleration is 6 m/sec^2?

Solution: The relationship between a body's acceleration and the net force on it is given by Newton's Second Law. The mass of the body is given, hence the net force on the body is

$$\Sigma F = ma = 48 \text{ kg} \times 6 \frac{m}{\sec^2} = 288 \text{ newtons.}$$

A force of 2000 dynes produced an acceleration of 500 centimeters per second^2. What was the mass of the object accelerated?

Solution: Here, we can apply Newton's Second Law, F = ma.

In this case F = 2000 dynes and a = 500 cm/sec^2. Then

$$2000 \text{ dynes} = M \times 500 \text{ cm/sec}^2$$

whence

$$M = 4 \text{ gm}$$

A force of 0.20 newton acts on a mass of 100 grams. What is the acceleration?

Solution: From Newton's Second Law we have

$$F = ma$$

$$a = \frac{F}{m}$$

Also, 100 grams = 0.10 kg. Therefore

$$a = \frac{0.20 \text{ nt}}{0.10 \text{ kg}} = \frac{0.20 \text{ kg-m/g}^2}{0.10 \text{ kg}}$$

$$= 2.0 \text{ m/sec}^2.$$

What is the resultant force on a body weighing 48 lb when its acceleration is 6 ft/sec^2?

Solution: We find the resultant force by using Newton's Second Law, $F = ma$. Here, F is the net force on a body of mass m having a net acceleration a. In order to use this law, we must first find the mass of the body. Since the weight of a body is defined as the gravitational force of attraction on it, we have

$$w = mg$$

where g is the acceleration due to gravity. Hence

$$m = \frac{w}{g}$$

and

$$F = \frac{w}{g} a = \frac{(48 \text{ lb})(6 \text{ ft/s}^2)}{(32 \text{ ft/s}^2)}$$

$$F = 9 \text{ lb}.$$

A 65-lb horizontal force is sufficient to draw a 1200-lb sled on level, well-packed snow at uniform speed. What is the value of the coefficient of friction?

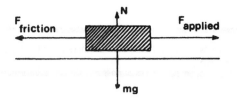

Solution: If the sled moves at constant velocity, it
experiences no net force. Therefore, the applied force
must be equal to the frictional force.

$$F_{applied} = 65 \text{ lb} = F_{friction}$$

Since the frictional force is proportional to the normal
force

$$F_{friction} = \mu_k N$$

Applying Newton's Second Law, F = ma, to the vertical
forces acting on the block, we find

$$N - mg = ma_y$$

where a_y is the vertical acceleration. In this problem,

a_y = 0 because the sled doesn't rise off the surface upon
which it slides. Hence

$$N = mg$$

and $F_{friction} = \mu_k N = \mu_k mg$

But $F_{friction} = 65 \text{ lb}$

Therefore $(65 \text{ lb}) = \mu_k (mg)$

$$\mu_k = \frac{65 \text{ lb}}{1200 \text{ lb}} = .054$$

● **PROBLEM** 4-6

What is the gravitational force on a person whose mass is
70 kg when he is sitting in an automobile that accelerates
at 4 m/s^2?

Solution: The mass, m = 70 kg, and the acceleration,
g = 9.8 m/s^2, are the known observables. The gravitational
force on the person is given by Newton's Second Law,

$$F = mg$$

61

where g is the acceleration due to gravity.

$$F = mg = (70 \text{ kg})\left(9.8 \text{ m/s}^2\right) = 6.86 \times 10^2 \text{N}.$$

Although the person will experience the force causing the acceleration, 4 m/s^2, his weight is unaffected by the car's motion. This occurs since the acceleration of the automobile is perpendicular to that caused by gravity and has no effect upon the person in the downward direction.

● PROBLEM 4-7

An object of mass 100 g is at rest. A net force of 2000 dynes is applied for 10 sec. What is the final velocity? How far will the object have moved in the 10-sec interval?

Solution. Since the force is constant, the acceleration is also. To find a, apply Newton's second law of motion.

$$a = \frac{F}{m}$$

$$= \frac{2000 \text{ dynes}}{100 \text{ g}} = 20 \text{ cm/sec}^2.$$

The kinematics equations for constant acceleration can be used to find the final velocity. The initial velocity is zero in this problem, since the object is initially at rest.

$$v = v_0 + at$$

$$v = at$$

$$= (20 \text{ cm/sec}^2) \times (10 \text{ sec})$$

$$= 200 \text{ cm/sec}.$$

To find the distance traveled in 10 seconds, use $s = v_0 t + \frac{1}{2}at^2$, and since $v_0 = 0$

$$s = \frac{1}{2} at^2$$

$$= \frac{1}{2}(20 \text{ cm/sec}^2) \times (10 \text{ sec})^2$$

$$= 1000 \text{ cm} = 10 \text{ m}.$$

In what distance can a 3000-lb automobile be stopped from a speed of 30 mi/hr (44 ft/sec) if the coefficient of friction between tires and roadway is 0.70?

Solution: The retarding force furnished by the roadway can be no greater than

$$F_s = \mu N = (0.70)(3000 \text{ lb}) = 2100 \text{ lb}.$$

Since the work done by this force is equal to the kinetic energy of the car, the stopping distance can be found from

$$W = Fs = 1/2 mv^2.$$

We must divide the weight by the acceleration due to gravity, g, to obtain the mass

$$m = \frac{W}{g} = \frac{3000 \text{ lb}}{32 \text{ ft/sec}^2} = 94 \text{ slugs}$$

$$s = \frac{1/2 mv^2}{F} = \frac{94 \text{ slugs } (44 \text{ ft/sec})^2}{2 \times 2100 \text{ lb}} = 43 \text{ ft}.$$

A drag racer achieves an acceleration of 32 (mi/hr)/sec. Compare this value with g.

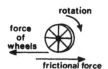

force of wheels ← → frictional force, rotation

Solution: To remain consistent with the units in which g is given, we convert to m/sec^2.

$$a = 32 \frac{mi}{hr\text{-}sec}$$

$$= 32 \frac{mi}{hr} \times \frac{1}{sec} \times \frac{5280 \text{ ft}}{1 \text{ mi}} \times \frac{1 \text{ hr}}{3600 \text{ sec}}$$

$$= 32 \times \frac{5280}{3600} \frac{ft}{sec^2}$$

$$= 1.46 \times 32 \text{ ft/sec}^2$$

$$= 1.46 \text{ g}$$

This acceleration is about the maximum that can be achieved by a vehicle that travels on wheels and depends on the friction between the wheels and the road for its thrust. A vehicle moves according to Newton's third law of motion: Every action has an equal but opposite reaction. The wheels of a car exert a force on the road in the backward direction. The reaction force is the force which acts in the direction opposite to the friction on the wheels, pushing the car forward. There is a maximum reaction force that the road can exert on the wheels, limited by the coefficient of friction which depends on the smoothness of the road, and by the weight of the car. This maximum thrust which the frictional force can exert on the car, limits its maximum acceleration. Attempts to surpass this maximum value by using a more powerful engine will result merely in spinning tires. (Rocket-powered cars and sleds can, of course, achieve much greater accelerations.)

● PROBLEM 4-10

A 1000-gram mass slides down an inclined plane 81 centimeters long in 0.60 seconds, starting from rest. What is the force acting on the 1000 grams?

Solution: Given the mass of an object, we must know its acceleration in order to calculate the force acting upon it. For an object starting at rest

$$\tfrac{1}{2}at^2 = d$$

where d is the distance travelled. In our case:

$$\tfrac{1}{2}a(0.60s)^2 = 81 \text{ cm}$$

$$a = 450 \text{ cm/s}^2$$

Therefore

$$F = ma$$

$$1000 \text{ gm} \times 450 \text{ cm/s}^2 = 450,000 \text{ dynes.}$$

● PROBLEM 4-11

A baseball pitcher throws a ball weighing 1/3 pound with an acceleration of 480 feet per second^2. How much force does he apply to the ball?

Solution: Newton's Second Law tells us that F = ma. However, we do not have the mass of the ball, but its weight which has the units of force. Since

$$W = mg$$

$$m = \frac{W}{g}$$

where W is weight, m is mass, and g is the acceleration due to gravity. Therefore,

$$m = \frac{\frac{1}{3} \text{ lb}}{32 \text{ ft/sec}^2} = \frac{32}{3} \text{ slugs}$$

Since the pitcher accelerates an object of mass $\frac{32}{3}$ slugs with an acceleration of 480 ft/s^2, the force is

$$F = \frac{32}{3} \frac{\text{lb} - \text{s}^2}{32 \text{ ft}} \times 480 \frac{\text{ft}}{\text{s}^2} = 5 \text{ lbs. of force.}$$

● **PROBLEM** 4-12

A 3200-lb car is slowed down uniformly from 60 mph to 15 mph along a level road by a force of 1100 lb. How far does it travel while being slowed down?

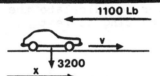

Solution: A diagram should first be drawn so that our sign conventions are consistent (see diagram).

We are given the change in velocity of the car in the positive x direction, the force acting against it in the negative x direction, and the weight of the car. We can calculate the deceleration of the car, and from this we can calculate the time the car is decelerated by its change in velocity.

First, we must find the mass of the car, given its weight. W = mg

$$3200 \text{ lb} = m \ 32 \text{ ft/s}^2$$

$$m = 100 \text{ lb-s}^2/\text{ft[slugs]}$$

From this we can calculate the deceleration of the car. Remember that the force acts in the negative x direction. F = ma

$$- 1100 \text{ lb} = 100 \text{ lb-s}^2/\text{ft a}$$

65

$$a = -11 \text{ ft/s}^2$$

Assuming constant deceleration:

$$a = \frac{\Delta v}{\Delta t}$$

where Δv = 15 mph - 60 mph = - 45 mph.

A useful conversion factor to remember is 60 mph = 88 ft/s, so that - 45 mph = - 66 ft/s. Hence,

$$-11 \text{ ft/s}^2 = -\frac{66 \text{ ft/s}}{\Delta t}$$

$$\Delta t = 6s$$

Distance is given by the formula

$$\tfrac{1}{2} at^2 + v_i t + d_i = d$$

where v_i is initial velocity, and d_i is the initial position (which we will here set equal to 0). Therefore

$$d = \tfrac{1}{2} \left(-11 \text{ ft/s}^2\right)(6s)^2 + 88 \text{ ft/s}^2 (6s) + 0$$

$$d = 330 \text{ ft.}$$

● **PROBLEM 4-13**

In a car which is accelerating, a plumb line hanging from the roof maintains a constant angle of 30 with the vertical. What is the acceleration value?

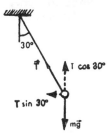

Solution: Since the plumb line maintains a constant angle, the acceleration of the car must be constant.

There are only two forces acting on the bob of the plumb line, the weight $\vec{W}$ = mg acting downward, and the tension $\vec{T}$ in the string. Splitting $\vec{T}$ into its vertical and horizontal components (see figure) one obtains for the vertical direction

$$T \cos 30° = mg, \tag{1}$$

This results because the bob does not move in the vertical direction, hence the vertical forces must balance.

By Newton's second law,

$$T \sin 30° = ma, \tag{2}$$

since the horizontal force must produce acceleration a to match the motion of the car. Dividing equation (2) by equation (1)

$$\frac{T \sin 30°}{T \cos 30°} = \tan 30° = \frac{a}{g}$$

Thus $a = g \tan 30° = g\left(\frac{1}{\sqrt{3}}\right) = \frac{32 \text{ ft/sec}^2}{1.732}$

$$= 18.47 \text{ ft/sec}^2.$$

● **PROBLEM** 4-14

An elevator is accelerated upward at 2 ft/sec^2. If the elevator weighs 500 lb, what is the tension in the supporting cable?

Solution: The net force acting on the elevator is

$$\Sigma F = T - mg$$

where T is the cable tension, and mg is the elevator's weight. (Note that the positive direction is taken as upward). By Newton's Second Law, this must equal the product of the elevator's mass and acceleration, whence

$$T - mg = ma$$

Solving for T

$$T = m(g + a) \tag{1}$$

We don't know the mass, m, of the elevator, but we do know its weight W. Since

$$W = mg$$

(1) becomes

$$T = \frac{W}{g} (g + a)$$

Using the data provided

$$T = \left(\frac{500 \text{ lb}}{32 \text{ ft/s}^2}\right) (32 \text{ ft/s}^2 + 2 \text{ ft/s}^2)$$

$$T = \left(\frac{34}{32}\right) 500 \text{ lb}$$

$$T = 531.2 \text{ lb.}$$

● **PROBLEM** 4-15

A 60.0-lb block rests on a smooth plane inclined at an angle of 20° with the horizontal. The block is pulled up the plane with a force of 30.0 lb parallel to the plane. What is its acceleration?

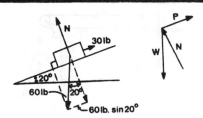

Solution. Here three forces are acting on the block. Its weight W is 60 lb downward. The force of the plane on the block is a thrust N normal to the plane. There is a pull P parallel to the plane. The force acting on the block can be resolved into forces acting normal and parallel to the plane.

The weight of the block may be resolved into components of 60.0 lb × cos 20° normal to the plane and 60.0 lb × sin 20° parallel to the plane.

Since there is no motion in the direction perpendicular to the plane, forces in that direction cancel each other. Therefore, the normal component of the weight is balanced by the force N. Parallel to the plane, taking the direction of P as positive, the sum of the forces is

$$F = 30.0 \text{ lb} - 60.0 \text{ lb} \times \sin 20°$$

$$= 30.0 \text{ lb} - (60.0 \times 0.342) \text{lb} = 9.5 \text{ lb}$$

$$m = \frac{W}{g} = \frac{60.0 \text{ lb}}{32 \text{ ft/sec}^2} = 1.87 \text{ slugs}$$

From F = ma,

$$a = \frac{F}{m} = \frac{9.5 \text{ lb}}{1.87 \text{ slugs}} = 5.1 \text{ ft/sec}^2.$$

Note that if the angle were 30°, the component of the weight
down the plane would be equal to the force up the plane and
there would be no unbalanced force acting on the block. Hence
it would not be accelerated. If the angle were greater than
30°, the block would be accelerated down the plane.

● PROBLEM 4-16

As shown in the figure, a block of mass .5 slugs moves on
a level frictionless surface, connected by a light flexible
cord passing over a small frictionless pulley to a second
hanging block of mass .25 slugs. What is the acceleration
of the system, and what is the tension in the cord connecting the two blocks?

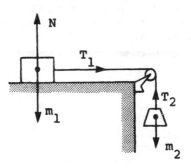

Solution: In order to find the system's acceleration, we
must relate the net force on the system to the acceleration
via Newton's Second Law. First we isolate the rope, and
calculate its acceleration. By the second law,

$$T_1 - T_2 = m_{rope}a$$

where T_1 and T_2 are in opposite directions. In this
problem, we sume m_{rope} = 0, and

$$T_1 = T_2$$

Hence, the rope acts only to transmit the force of tension
to the block.

Applying Newton's Second Law to the horizontal (x) and
vertical (y) directions of motion of the block on the table,
we obtain

$$T = m_1 a_{x_1}$$

$$N - w_1 = a_{y_1}$$

where m_1 is the mass of the block on the table, and a_{x_1} is
its horizontal acceleration. Noting that a_{y_1} = 0, since
the block doesn't accelerate vertically, we find

$$T = m_1 a_{x_1} \qquad (1)$$

$$N = w_1 \qquad (2)$$

We next apply the third law to the hanging block of mass m_2, and

$$m_2 g - T = m_2 a_{y_2} \qquad (3)$$

where a_{y_2} is the vertical acceleration of block 2. Now, since the 2-block system moves as a unit, $a_{x_1} = a_{y_2} = a$, and, using (1), (2) and (3)

$$T = m_1 a \qquad (4)$$

$$N = w_1 \qquad (5)$$

$$m_2 g - T = m_2 a \qquad (6)$$

Substituting (4) in (6), and solving for a

$$m_2 g - m_1 a = m_2 a$$

$$a = \frac{m_2 g}{m_1 + m_2}$$

From (4),

$$T = \frac{m_1 m_2 g}{m_1 + m_2}$$

Substituting the given data in these equations

$$a = \frac{(.25 \text{ sl})(32 \text{ f/s}^2)}{(.75 \text{ sl})} = 10.7 \text{ f/s}^2$$

$$T = \frac{m_1 m_2 g}{m_1 + m_2} = m_1 a = (.50 \text{ sl})(10.7 \text{ f/s}^2)$$

$$T = 5.4 \text{ lb}$$

● **PROBLEM 4-17**

(a) Calculate the acceleration experienced by the two weights, shown in the figure, if the coefficient of friction between the 32 lb. weight and the plane is 0.2. (b) Calculate also the tension in the cable, whose weight we assume to be negligible.

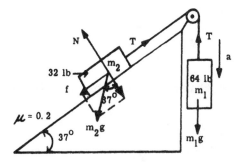

Solution: Consider the two weights as a system. This implies that the cable does not stretch and no internal forces have to be considered, since they consist of action-reaction forces and therefore cancel. The external forces acting on the system are the frictional force on the 32 lb block and the gravitational force on both weights. Since the frictional force F_f is proportional to the normal force, we first find N. The 32 lb block has no movement perpendicular to the plane. Setting the sum of the forces in this direction equal to zero, we get from the diagram,

$$N - mg \cos 37° = 0$$

Therefore

$$N = 32 \cos 37°$$

and

$$F_f = \mu N = (0.2)(32 \cos 37°)$$

with direction down the plane, since it opposes the motion. All the cable does is change the direction of forces which are applied to each weight and which are in line with the cable. In the same direction as the 64 lb. force on m_1 (the cable makes it so), the 32 lb. weight experiences the frictional force and the component of the gravitational force parallel to the cable or 32 sin 37°. Applying Newton's second law to the system, we have

$$\Sigma F = (m_1 + m_2)a$$

since both weights experience the same acceleration. Then

$$64 - 32 \sin 37° - (0.2)(32 \cos 37°) = (\frac{64}{32} + \frac{32}{32})a$$

$$64 - 19.2 - 5.1 = 3a$$

$$39.7 = 3a$$

$$a = 13.2 \text{ ft/sec}^2 \tag{a}$$

The tension is obtained by isolating the 64 lb weight and noting that the only two forces acting on it are T and the force of gravity. Calling the downward direction positive, we obtain from Newton's second law,

$$64 - T = m_1 a = (\frac{64}{32})(13.2) = 26.4$$

$$T = 64 - 26.4 + 37.6 \text{ lbs.}$$

What is the acceleration of a block on a frictionless plane inclined at an angle θ with the horizontal?

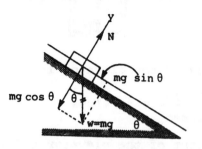

Solution: In order to find the acceleration, a, of the block, we must
calculate the net force, F, on the block, and relate this to its acceleration via Newton's Second Law, F = ma. (Here m is the mass of the
block).
     The only forces acting on the block are its weight mg and the
normal force N exerted by the plane (see figure). Take axes parallel
and perpendicular to the surface of the plane and resolve the weight
into x- and y-components. Then

$$\Sigma F_y = N - mg \cos \theta \ ,$$

$$\Sigma F_x = mg \sin \theta \ .$$

But we know that the acceleration in the y direction, a_y = 0, since
the block doesn't accelerate off the surface of the inclined plane.
From the equation $\Sigma F_y = ma_y$ we find that N = mg cos θ. From the
equation $\Sigma F_x = ma_x$, where a_x is the acceleration of the block in the
x direction, we have

$$mg \sin \theta = ma_x \ ,$$

$$a_x = g \sin \theta.$$

     The mass does not appear in the final result, which means that any
block, regardless of its mass, will slide on a frictionless inclined
plane with an acceleration down the plane of g sin θ. (Note that the
velocity is not necessarily down the plane).

An elevator and its load weigh a total of 1600 lb. Find the
tension T in the supporting cable when the elevator, originally moving downward at 20 ft/sec, is brought to rest with
constant acceleration in a distance of 50 ft. (See fig.)

Solution: The mass of the elevator is

$$m = \frac{w}{g} = \frac{1600 \text{ lb}}{32 \text{ ft/sec}^2} = 50 \text{ slugs}$$

where w is the weight of the elevator and its load. From the equations of motion with constant acceleration,

$$v^2 = v_0^2 + 2ay, \quad a = \frac{v^2 - v_0^2}{2y}.$$

Let the upward direction be positive and the origin (y = 0) be at the point where the deceleration begins. Then the initial velocity v_0 is -20 ft/sec, the final velocity v is zero, and its displacement during this interval is y = -50 ft. Therefore

$$a = \frac{0 - (-20 \text{ ft/sec})^2}{-2 \times 50 \text{ ft}} = 4 \frac{\text{ft}}{\text{sec}^2}.$$

The acceleration is therefore positive (upward). From the free-body diagram (Fig.) the resultant force is

$$\sum F = T - w = T - 1600 \text{ lb}.$$

Hence, from Newton's second law,

$$\sum F = ma,$$

$$T - 1600 \text{ lb} = 50 \text{ slugs} \times 4 \frac{\text{ft}}{\text{sec}^2} = 200 \text{ lb},$$

$$T = 1800 \text{ lb}.$$

● PROBLEM 4-20

With what force will the feet of a passenger press downward on the elevator floor when the elevator has an acceleration of 4 ft/sec^2 upward if the passenger weighs 160 lb?

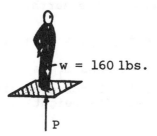

w = 160 lbs.

P

Solution: This example illustrates a problem that is frequently encountered, in which it is necessary to find a desired force by first computing the force that is the reaction to the one desired, and then using Newton's third law. That is, we first calculate the force with which the elevator floor pushes upward on the passenger P; the force desired is the reaction to this. The figure shows the forces acting on the passenger. We may use Newton's Second Law, F = ma, to relate the net force on the man to his acceleration. The resultant force is P - w. The mass m of the passenger is his weight, mg, divided by

$32 \ f/s^2$, or 5 slugs, and his acceleration is the same as that of the elevator,

$$\Sigma F = ma$$

$$P - 160 \ lb = 5 \ slugs \times 4 \ \frac{ft}{sec^2} = 20 \ lb,$$

$$.P = 180 \ lb.$$

The passenger exerts an equal and opposite force downward on the elevator floor.

GRAVITATIONAL FORCES

● **PROBLEM** 4-21

Calculate the value of the universal gravitational constant, G, assuming that the earth's radius is 6.4×10^6 m the earth has an average density of 5.5×10^3 kg/m^3. The volume V of a sphere is $V = \frac{4}{3}\pi r^3$, where r is the radius of the sphere.

Solution: Begin by computing the volume of the earth:

$$V = \frac{4}{3}\pi r^3 = \left(\frac{4}{3}\pi\right)\left(6.4 \times 10^6 \ m\right)^3 = 1.1 \times 10^{21} \ m^3.$$

Since Density = $\frac{Mass}{Volume}$, we have

$$Mass = Density \times Volume$$

74

or, the total mass of the earth,

$$m_2 = \left(1.1 \times 10^{21}\ m^3\right)\left(5.5 \times 10^3\ kg/m^3\right) = 6.0 \times 10^{24}\ kg.$$

If an object of mass m_1 is placed on the Earth's surface, the gravitational force of attraction (W) between it and the Earth (i.e., its weight) is found by use of Newton's second law.

$$W = m_1 g$$

where g is the acceleration of the object due to the gravitational force (i.e., acceleration of gravity). According to the Universal Law of Gravitation, however, the gravitattional force of attraction between m_1 and m_2 is

$$W = \frac{Gm_1m_2}{d^2}$$

where d is the radius of the Earth. Then

$$\frac{Gm_1m_2}{d^2} = m_1 g$$

After rearranging,

$$G = \frac{gd^2}{m_2} = \frac{\left(9.8\ m/s^2\right)\left(6.4 \times 10^6\ m\right)^2}{6.0 \times 10^{24}\ kg} = 6.7 \times 10^{-11}\ N\ m^2/kg^2$$

Since the value of the earth's radius is more accurately known today, Newton's estimate of G differed from this calculated value.

● PROBLEM 4-22

With what force does the Earth attract the moon?

Solution: By the Universal Law of Gravitation, we have

$$F_G = G\frac{m_m m_E}{r_m^2}$$

where r_m is the distance between the earth and moon, and m_m and m_e are the masses of the moon and the earth respectively.

$$G = 6.67 \times 10^{-8}\ \frac{dyne - cm^2}{g^2}$$

$$r_m = 3.84 \times 10^{10}\ cm$$

$$m_m = 7.35 \times 10^{25} \text{ g}$$

$$m_e = 5.98 \times 10^{27} \text{ g}$$

$$F_G = \left(6.67 \times 10^{-8} \text{ dyne-cm}^2/\text{g}^2\right) \times \frac{\left(7.35 \times 10^{25} \text{ g}\right) \times \left(5.98 \times 10^{27} \text{ g}\right)}{\left(3.84 \times 10^{10} \text{ cm}\right)^2}$$

$$= 2.0 \times 10^{25} \text{ dynes .}$$

● **PROBLEM** 4-23

Compute the force of gravitational attraction between the large and small spheres of a Cavendish balance, if m = 1 gm, m' = 500 gm, r = 5 cm.

Solution: Two uniform spheres attract each other as if the mass of each were concentrated at its center. By Newton's Law of Universal Gravitation, the force of attraction between 2 masses m and m' separated by a distance r is

$$F = \frac{Gmm'}{r^2} = \frac{\left(6.67 \times 10^{-8} \text{ dyne} \cdot \text{cm}^2/\text{gm}^2\right) \times (1 \text{ gm}) \times (500 \text{ gm})}{(5 \text{ cm})^2}$$

$$= 1.33 \times 10^{-6} \text{ dyne,}$$

or about one-millionth of a dyne.

● **PROBLEM** 4-24

(1) Two lead balls whose masses are 5.20 kg and .250 kg are placed with their centers 50.0 cm apart. With what force do they attract each other?

(2) At the surface of the earth g = 9.806 m/s². Assuming the earth to be a sphere of radius 6.371×10^6 m, compute the mass of the earth.

Solution: (1). The force of gravitational attraction between two bodies with masses m_1 and m_2 separated by a distance s is

$$F = \frac{G\, m_1 m_2}{s^2}$$

$$= \left(6.67 \times 10^{-11} \frac{\text{nt} - \text{m}^2}{\text{kg}^2}\right) \left(\frac{5.20 \text{ kg} \times .250 \text{ kg}}{(.500 \text{ m})^2}\right)$$

$$= 3.46 \times 10^{-10} \text{ nt}$$

(2). The only force acting on a body of mass m near

the surface of the earth is the gravitational force.
Hence, using Newton's Second Law

$$F = ma = \frac{G\,m\,m_e}{r^2}$$

where r is the distance of m from the earth's center.
At the surface of the earth, a = g and $r = R_e$

$$mg = \frac{Gmm_e}{R_e^2}$$

whence

$$m_e = \frac{gR_e^2}{G}$$

$$= \frac{(9.806 \text{ m/s}^2)\,(6.371 \times 10^6 \text{ m})^2}{6.670 \times 10^{-11} \text{ nt} \cdot \text{m}^2/\text{kg}^2}$$

$$= 5.967 \times 10^{24} \text{ kg}$$

● **PROBLEM** 4-25

At what point between moon and earth do the gravitational
fields of these two bodies cancel? The earth's mass is
5.98×10^{24} kg, and the moon's is 7.35×10^{22} kg. The
distance between the centers of the earth and the moon
is 3.85×10^7 m.

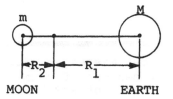

MOON   EARTH

Solution: Let the point where the gravitational fields
cancel be at a distance R_1 from the earth's center, R_2
from the moon's center. The attraction of the earth at
this point will equal that of the moon's:

$$G = \frac{M\mu}{R_1^2} = G\,\frac{m\mu}{R_2^2}$$

where G is the gravitational constant, M the mass of the
earth, and m that of the moon, or

$$G = \frac{M}{R_1^2} = G\,\frac{m}{R_2^2}\;.$$

The term on the left side of the equation is called
the earth's gravitational field, the term on the right
is the moon's. The gravitational field at a point in space
is the gravitational force experienced by a unit mass at
that point. (It is similar to the electric field, which
is the electrostatic force per unit charge experienced
due to a particular charged body). Gravitational fields

77

are vector fields and the resultant gravitational field due to two or more masses is calculated by adding the field vectors from all sources at every point in space.

The only point in space where the gravitational fields of the earth and the moon cancel, must be collinear to the centers of both bodies since no two vectors cancel if they are not oppositely directed. From the equation above, we get

$$\left(\frac{R_1}{R_2}\right)^2 = \frac{M}{m}$$

$$\frac{R_1}{R_2} = \left(\frac{M}{m}\right)^{\frac{1}{2}} = \left(\frac{5.98 \times 10^{24} \text{ kg}}{7.35 \times 10^{22} \text{ kg}}\right)^{\frac{1}{2}} = 9.$$

Since the point in question is collinear to both the earth and moon's centers, the distance between the centers must equal $R_1 + R_2$ (see diagram), thus:

$$R_1 + R_2 = 3.85 \times 10^8 \text{ m}$$
$$R_1 = 3.85 \times 10^8 \text{ m} - R_2$$
$$\frac{R_1}{R_2} = \frac{3.85 \times 10^8 \text{ m} - R_2}{R_2} = \frac{3.85 \times 10^8 \text{ m}}{R_2} - 1 = 9$$
$$R_2 = 3.85 \times 10^7 \text{ m}$$
$$R_1 = 9R_2 = 9(3.85 \times 10^7 \text{ m}) = 34.7 \times 10^7 \text{ m}.$$

● PROBLEM 4-26

A parachutist, after bailing out, falls 50 meters without friction. When the parachute opens, he decelerates downward 2.0 meters/sec^2. He reaches the ground with a speed of 3.0 meters/sec. (a) How long is the parachutist in the air? (b) At what height did he bail out?

Solution: (a) The parachutist, starting at rest, falls 50 m at an acceleration equal to g, the acceleration of gravity. Since this is constant

$$s = v_0 t + \tfrac{1}{2}at^2, \text{ where } v_0 \text{ is the initial velocity.}$$

Here $v_0 = 0$ and

$$50 = \tfrac{1}{2} gt^2, \quad t = \sqrt{100/g} = 10/g^{\frac{1}{2}} = 10(3.13) = 3.2 \text{ sec}$$

He then decelerates at 2.0 m/sec^2 until he reaches a final velocity, v_f of 3 m/sec^2. When he begins his deceleration he has reached a speed:

$$v_f = v_0 + at, \qquad v_0 = 0$$

$$= gt = 9.8(3.2)$$

$$= 31.3 \text{ m/sec}$$

Thus: $v_f' = v_0' + a't'$

$$3 = 31.3 - 2t'; \quad 2t' = 31.3 - 3; \quad t' = 14.2$$

total time of flight $= t + t' = 3.2$ sec $+ 14.2$ sec

$$= 17.4 \text{ sec.}$$

(b) We know that the parachutist falls 50 meters before the parachute opens. Thus, the problem reduces to one in which we must find the distance s the parachutist travels until he is decelerated to a speed of 3.0 m/sec, having started at velocity $v = 31.3$ m/sec.
We know that:

$$s = vt' + \tfrac{1}{2} at'^2$$

$$s = (31.3 \text{ m/sec})(14.2 \text{ sec}) + \tfrac{1}{2}(-2.0 \text{ m/sec}^2)(14.2 \text{ sec})^2$$

$$= 444.5 - 201.6 = 242.9 \text{ meters.}$$

Hence the parachutist bailed out from a height of 50 + 242.9 = 292.9 meters.

● **PROBLEM 4-27**

A 2.0-ton elevator is supported by a cable that can safely support 6400 lb. What is the shortest distance in which the elevator can be brought to a stop when it is descending with a speed of 4.0 ft/sec?

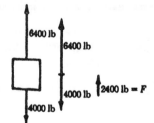

Solution. The maximum force that can be used to stop the elevator without breaking the cable is 6400 lb - 4000 lb = 2400 lb upward (4000 lb. is the weight of the elevator).
This maximum force gives the shortest distance in which the elevator can be stopped since it provides a maximum deceleration $a_{max} = \dfrac{F_{max}}{m}$.

$$m = \frac{W}{g} = \frac{4000 \text{ lb}}{32 \text{ ft/sec}^2} = 125 \text{ slugs}$$

$$a = \frac{F}{m} = \frac{2400 \text{ lb}}{125 \text{ slugs}} = 19.2 \text{ ft/sec}^2 .$$

With $v_{final} = 0$ and taking up as positive, the minimum stopping distance can be found using the kinematics equation

$$v_f^2 = 2as + v^2$$

$$s = \frac{-v^2}{2a} = \frac{-(-4.0 \text{ ft/sec})^2}{2 \times 19.2 \text{ ft/sec}^2} = -0.42 \text{ ft.}$$

● PROBLEM 4-28

At what distance from the center of the earth does the acceleration due to gravity have one half of the value that it has on the surface of the earth?

Solution: Newton's Second Law implies that $W = mg$. W is the weight of an object of mass m (that is, the grav- itational force of attraction between the earth and the object), and g is the acceleration due to gravity. Then, by Newton's Law of universal gravitation,

$$W = \frac{GM_e m}{R^2} = mg$$

where R is the distance of the object of mass m from the center of the earth, and M_e is the mass of the earth. Therefore.

$$g(R) = \frac{GM_e}{R^2}$$

At the surface of the earth,

$$g(R_e) = \frac{GM_e}{R_e^2}$$

But we want $g(R) = \tfrac{1}{2}g(R_e)$. Therefore,

$$\frac{GM_e}{R^2} = \frac{1}{2} \frac{GM_e}{R_e^2}$$

$$R^2 = 2R_e^2$$

$$R = \sqrt{2} \, R_e$$

$$= 1,414 \times 6.38 \times 10^6 \text{ m} = 9.02 \times 10^6 \text{ m}$$

The acceleration due to gravity is reduced to one half of its usual value at a distance of 9.02×10^6 meters from the center of the earth. This is equivalent to a height of 2.64×10^6 meters or 1640 miles above the surface of the earth.

CURVILINEAR DYNAMICS

What is the acceleration of a point on the rim of a flywheel 0.90 m in diameter, turning at the rate of 1200 rev/min?

<u>Solution:</u> For uniform circular motion, the acceleration of a particle at distance r from the axis of rotation is given by

$$a = \frac{v^2}{r} \tag{1}$$

and is directed towards the center of the circle. Linear velocity, v, is related to angular velocity, ω, by the relationship

$$v = \omega r \tag{2}$$

Substitution of (2) into the equation for linear acceleration gives

$$a = \frac{(\omega r)^2}{r} = \omega^2 r$$

where ω is expressed in radians/second. For the point on the rim of the flywheel

$$\omega = 1200 \text{ rev/min} = 20 \text{ rev/sec}$$

$$= 20 \times 2\pi \text{ rad/sec}$$

$$r = 0.45 \text{ m}$$

$$a = \omega^2 r = (20 \times 2\pi \text{ rad/sec})^2 (0.45 \text{ m})$$

$$= 7100 \text{ m/sec}^2$$

Ignoring the motion of the earth around the sun and the motion of the sun through space, calculate (a) the angular velocity, (b) the velocity, and (c) the acceleration of a body resting on the ground at the equator.

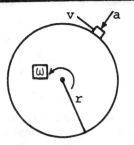

View from the North Pole.

Solution: Because of the rotation of the earth the body at the equator moves in a circle whose radius is equal to the radius of the earth (see figure).

$$r = \text{radius of earth}$$
$$= 6.37 \times 10^6 \text{ meters}$$

We are going to use the MKS System of units. One revolution, which is 2π radians, takes 1 day or

$$\frac{24 \text{ hr}}{1 \text{ day}} \times \frac{60 \text{ min}}{1 \text{ hr}} \times \frac{60 \text{ sec}}{1 \text{ min}} = 24 \times 60 \times 60 \frac{\text{secs}}{\text{day}}$$

(a) Since the frequency of revolution is $f = \frac{1}{T}$, where T is the period (the time for one revolution), then

$$2\pi f = \omega = \frac{2\pi}{T} \quad .$$

This equals the number of radians traveled per unit time, or the angular velocity ω.

$$\omega = \frac{2\pi}{24 \times 60 \times 60}$$
$$= 7.27 \times 10^{-5} \text{ radians per second}$$

(b) The linear velocity is, by definition

$$v = \omega r$$
$$= \left(7.27 \times 10^{-5}\right) \times \left(6.37 \times 10^6\right) \frac{\text{rad}}{\text{s}} \cdot \text{m}$$
$$= 4.64 \times 10^2 \text{ m/sec} \quad .$$

Since 1 mph = 0.447 m/sec

$$v = \left(4.64 \times 10^2 \ \frac{\text{m}}{\text{sec}}\right)\left(\frac{1}{.447} \ \frac{\text{sec}}{\text{m}}\right)$$
$$= 1040 \text{ mph}$$

(c) The acceleration toward the center of the earth is, since the motion is circular,

$$a = \frac{v^2}{r}$$
$$= \frac{\left(4.64 \times 10^2 \text{ m/sec}\right)^2}{\left(6.38 \times 10^6 \text{ m}\right)} = 3.37 \times 10^{-2} \text{ m/sec}^2$$

A stone of mass 100 grams is whirled in a horizontal circle at the end of a cord 100 cm long. If the tension in the cord is 2.5 newtons, what is the speed of the stone?

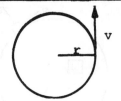

Solution: First, we shall calculate the acceleration of the object, and from that we may calculate its velocity. Firstly,

$$F = mg$$

$$2.5 \text{ newtons} = 100 \text{ gm} \times a$$

Newtons have the units $\frac{kg - m}{s^2}$, and 100 gm = 0.100 kg,

so that

$$2.5 \; \frac{kg-m}{s^2} = 0.100 \text{ kg} \times a$$

$$a = 25 \text{ m/s}^2$$

Also $a = \frac{v^2}{r}$ for uniform circular motion, where a is the linear acceleration and v is the linear velocity of the object. Therefore,

$$25 \; \frac{m}{s^2} = \frac{v^2}{1 \text{ m}}$$

$$v = 5 \; \frac{m}{s} \; .$$

What is the centripetal force required to cause a 3200-pound car to go around a curve of 880-ft radius at a speed of 60 mph?

Solution: When a body travels in uniform circular motion, it experiences an acceleration towards the center of the circle. Since the object has a mass, a force towards the center of the circle is produced.

In circular motion, the acceleration of the body is given by

$$a = \frac{v^2}{r}$$

where v is the linear velocity of the object and r is the radius of the circle. In our case (using 60 mph = 88 ft/sec):

$$a = \frac{(88 \text{ ft/sec})^2}{880 \text{ ft}} = 8.8 \text{ ft/sec}^2$$

The mass of the car is

$$m = \frac{Wt}{a} = \frac{3200 \text{ lb}}{32 \text{ ft/sec}^2} = 100 \frac{\text{lb} - \text{sec}^2}{\text{ft}} \quad [\text{slugs}]$$

And $F = ma$

$$F = 100 \frac{\text{lb} - \text{sec}^2}{\text{ft}} \times 8.8 \frac{\text{ft}}{\text{sec}^2}$$

$$= 880 \text{ lb.}$$

● PROBLEM 4-33

A racing car traveling in a circular path maintains a constant speed of 120 miles per hour. If the radius of the circular track is 1000 ft, what if any acceleration does the center of gravity of the car exhibit?

Solution: Since the car is traveling a circular path at constant speed, v, its acceleration is radial, and given by

$$a = \frac{v^2}{R}$$

Here, R is the radius of the circular path. Using the given data

$$a = \frac{(120 \text{ miles/hr})^2}{(1000 \text{ ft})} = \frac{14400 \text{ miles}^2}{1000 \text{ ft} \cdot \text{hr}^2}$$

$$a = 14.4 \text{ miles}^2/\text{ft} \cdot \text{hr}^2$$

In order to keep units consistent, note that

    1 hr = 3600 s

and 1 mile = 5280 ft

Then $a = \dfrac{14.4(5280 \text{ ft})^2}{(1 \text{ ft})(3600 \text{ s})^2}$

$a = 30.98 \text{ ft/s}^2$

A 3200-lb car traveling with a speed of 60 mi/hr rounds a curve whose radius is 484 ft. Find the necessary centripetal force.

<u>Solution:</u> A centripetal force is a force which results when a particle executes circular motion with constant speed. It is called centripetal because it points to the center of the circle. Note that although the speed of the particle is constant, its velocity is not, because the latter is continually changing in direction. As a result, the centripetal force is responsible for changing the velocity of the particle.

Using Newton's Second Law, we may write

$$F = ma \qquad\qquad (1)$$

where F is the net force acting on the mass, m.

Because this is uniform circular motion, $a = \dfrac{v^2}{R}$, where v is the speed of the particle in a circular orbit of radius R. Inserting this result in (1),

$$F = \dfrac{mv^2}{R} \qquad\qquad (2)$$

Equation (2) gives the centripetal force needed to accelerate m. In order to use this formula, we must transform the weight, mg, given in the question as 3200 lb., into a mass by dividing by 32 ft/sec.^{2} . Then, using (2)

$$F = \left[\dfrac{3200}{32} \text{ sl} \right] \dfrac{(88 \text{ f/s})^2}{(484 \text{ ft})} = 1600 \text{ lb.}$$

A train whose speed is 60 mi/hr rounds a curve whose radius of curvature is 484 ft. What is its acceleration?

Solution: For uniform circular motion, we have an acceleration directed towards the center of curvature of magnitude

$$a = \frac{v^2}{R}$$

where v is the speed of the object, and R is the radius of the circle. To keep the units consistent, we have to convert the speed from mi/hr to ft/sec, since R is in feet.

$$v = \left(60 \ \frac{mi}{hr}\right)\left(\frac{5280 \ ft/mi}{3600 \ sec/hr}\right) = 88 \ ft/sec.$$

Substituting the appropriate values, we find the acceleration to be

$$a = \frac{v^2}{R} = \frac{(88 \ ft/sec)^2}{484 \ ft} = 16 \ ft/sec^2.$$

● **PROBLEM** 4-36

The angular velocity of a body is 4 rad/sec at time $t = 0$, and its angular acceleration is constant and equal to 2 rad/sec^2. A line OP in the body is horizontal $\left(\theta_0 = 0\right)$ at time $t = 0$. (a) What angle does this line make with the horizontal at time $t = 3$ sec? (b) What is the angular velocity at this time?

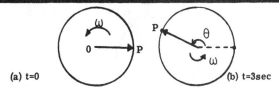

(a) t=0   (b) t=3sec

Solution: The angular kinematics equations for constant angular acceleration are identical in form to the linear kinematic equations with α corresponding to a, ω to v, and θ to x.
  (a) Comparable to $x = x_0 + \omega_0 t + \frac{1}{2}\alpha t^2$, we have

$\theta = \theta_0 + \omega_0 t + \frac{1}{2}\alpha t^2$ where θ_0, ω_0 are the initial position and velocity of the body.
  Since $\theta_0 = 0$, we have

$$\theta = \omega_0 t + \frac{1}{2}\alpha t^2$$

$$= 4 \ \frac{rad}{sec} \times 3 \ sec + \frac{1}{2} \times 2 \ \frac{rad}{sec^2} \times (3 \ sec)^2$$

$$= 21 \text{ radians}$$

$$= 21 \text{ radians} \quad \frac{1 \text{ revolution}}{2\pi \text{ radians}}$$

$$= 3.34 \text{ revolutions.}$$

The angle θ is then

$$\theta = 0.34 \times \text{one revolution} = 0.34 \times 360° \approx 122°.$$

(b) $\omega = \omega_0 + \alpha t$

$$= 4 \frac{\text{rad}}{\text{sec}} + 2 \frac{\text{rad}}{\text{sec}^2} \times 3 \text{ sec} = 10 \frac{\text{rad}}{\text{sec}}.$$

Alternatively,

$$\omega^2 = \omega_0^2 + 2\alpha\theta$$

$$= 4\left(\frac{\text{rad}}{\text{sec}}\right)^2 + 2 \times 2 \frac{\text{rad}}{\text{sec}^2} \times 21 \text{ rad}$$

$$= 100 \frac{\text{rad}^2}{\text{sec}^2}, \qquad \omega = 10 \frac{\text{rad}}{\text{sec}}.$$

● PROBLEM 4-37

Suppose that a satellite is placed in a circular orbit 100 miles above the earth's surface. Determine the orbital speed v and the time t required for one complete revolution of the satellite.

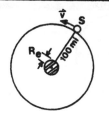

Solution: The radius R of the circular path is determined as follows (see the figure).

$R = R_e + 100$ miles where R_e, the earth's radius, is 6.378×10^6 m; a distance of 1 mile is equal to 1,609m; therefore, 100 miles $= 1.61 \times 10^5$ m

$R = 6.378 \times 10^6$ m $+ 1.61 \times 10^5$ m $= 6.539 \times 10^6$ m .

For our purposes, it is sufficient to retain only the first two digits:

$$R = 6.5 \times 10^6 \text{m}$$

The gravitational pull on the satellite is

$$F_g = mg .$$

This pull provides the centripetal force for the circular motion, therefore

$$F_{centr} = \frac{mv^2}{R} = mg$$

or

$$v^2 = gR = \left(9.8 \text{m/s}^2\right)\left(6.5 \times 10^6 \text{m}\right)$$
$$= 63.7 \times 10^6 \text{m}^2/\text{s}^2 \approx 64 \times 10^6 \text{m}^2/\text{s}^2$$
$$v = 8 \times 10^3 \text{m/s}$$

This orbital speed is only approximately correct because it has been assumed that the effect of gravity 100 miles above the earth is the same as at the earth's surface. The gravitational "pull" weakens as one recedes from the earth's surface, but at 100 miles above the earth it is only slightly different from the value g, so the calculation above is reasonably accurate. To determine the time interval required for one revolution of the satellite, the distance the satellite travels in one revolution must be calculated. This is just the circumference C of a circle of radius R:

$$C = 2\pi R = (2)(3.14)\left(6.5 \times 10^6 \text{m}\right) = 4.1 \times 10^7 \text{m}$$

The period of the motion is

$$t = \frac{C}{v} = \frac{4.1 \times 10^7 \cancel{m}}{8 \times 10^3 \cancel{m}/\text{s}} = 5.1 \times 10^3 \text{s}$$

$$t = \frac{5.1 \times 10^3 \cancel{s}}{60 \cancel{s}/\text{min}} = 85 \text{ min}$$

The time required for one complete revolution of the satellite is about 85 min.

ROTATION OF RIGID BODIES ABOUT FIXED AXES

● PROBLEM 4-38

A force F = 10 newtons in the +y-direction is applied to a wrench which extends in the +x-direction and grasps a bolt. What is the resulting torque about the bolt if the point of application of the force is 30 cm = 0.3 m away from the bolt?

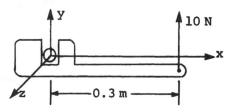

Solution: Torque is calculated from the relation:

$$\vec{\tau} = \vec{r} \times \vec{F}$$

where τ stands for torque, F stands for the force, and r

denotes the distance from the origin, about which the torque is calculated, of the point of application of the force. In this problem we use the bolt as our origin about which we calculate the torque (see the Figure above). Then,

$$\vec{\tau} = 0.3 \text{ m } \hat{i} \times 10N \hat{j} = 3 \text{ N·m } \left(\hat{i} \times \hat{j} \right) = 3 \text{ N·m } \hat{k}$$

where $\hat{i}$, $\hat{j}$, and $\hat{k}$ are the unit vectors in the +x, +y, and +z directions respectively.

● PROBLEM 4-39

The motor driving a grindstone is switched off when the latter has a rotational speed of 240 rev·min^{-1}. After 10 s the speed is 180 rev·min^{-1}. If the angular retardation remains constant, how many additional revolutions does it make before coming to rest?

Solution: The initial speed ω_0 is 240 rev·min^{-1} and the later speed ω is 180 rev·min^{-1}. Thus since the angular acceleration, α, is constant, we may write $\omega = \omega_0 + \alpha t$. Here, t is the time it takes for the grindstone's angular velocity to go from ω_0 to ω. Solving for α,

$$\alpha = \frac{\omega - \omega_0}{t} = \frac{180 \text{ rev·min}^{-1} - 240 \text{ rev·min}^{-1}}{10 \text{ s}}$$

Noting that $1 \text{ min}^{-1} = 1/60 \text{ s}^{-1}$, we find

$$\alpha = -\frac{60 \text{ rev·s}^{-1}}{60 \times 100 \text{ s}} = -.1 \text{ rev·s}^{-2}$$

Considering the subsequent slowing-down period, the final speed is zero and the grindstone traverses an angular distance θ. Hence, using the equation

$$\omega^2 = \omega_0^2 + 2\alpha\theta$$

with $\omega = 0$ and $\omega_0 = 180 \text{ rev·min}^{-1} = 3 \text{ rev·s}^{-1}$, we find

$$0 = 9 \text{ rev}^2 \cdot \text{s}^{-2} + 2 \left(-.1 \text{ rev·s}^{-2} \right) \theta$$

or $\theta = \frac{9 \text{ rev}}{.2} = 45 \text{ rev.}$

A flywheel, in the form of a uniform disk 4.0 ft in diameter, weighs 600 lb. What will be its angular acceleration if it is acted upon by a net torque of 225 lb-ft? (The rotational inertia of a wheel is $I = \frac{1}{2}mR^2$, where m is the wheel's mass and R is its radius.)

<u>Solution:</u> The flywheel is a massive wheel whose use is the "storing" of kinetic energy. The problem is one of applying the formula $\vec{\tau} = I\vec{\alpha}$ (analogous to $\vec{F} = m\vec{a}$), in which $\vec{\tau}$ is applied torque, and $\vec{\alpha}$ is the resulting angular acceleration. We are given $\vec{\tau}$, we can determine I, and solve for $\vec{\alpha}$. Since the weight (W) of any object is

$$W = mg$$

where m is its mass and g is the acceleration due to gravity, we can find m

$$m = \frac{W}{g} = \frac{600 \text{ lb}}{32 \text{ ft/sec}^2} = 18.8 \text{ slugs}$$

$$I = \tfrac{1}{2}mR^2 = \tfrac{1}{2}(18.8 \text{ slugs})(2.0 \text{ ft})^2$$

$$= 38 \text{ slug-ft}^2$$

Therefore, substituting into $\tau = I\alpha$,

$$225 \text{ lb-ft} = \left(38 \text{ slug-ft}^2\right)\alpha$$

$$\alpha = 5.9 \text{ rad/sec}^2$$

In radian measure the angle is a ratio of two lengths and hence is a pure number. The unit "radian" therefore does not always appear in the algebraic handling of units.

ROLLING BODIES

A solid cylinder 30 cm in diameter at the top of an incline 2.0 m high is released and rolls down the incline without loss of energy due to friction. Find the linear and angular speeds at the bottom.

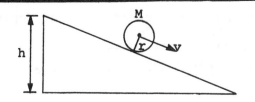

Solution: This problem can be solved using the conservation of energy principle. The cylinder initially at rest at the top of the incline has only gravitational (potential) energy. Taking the bottom of the incline as the zero level of the potential energy (see the figure above), we get

$$E_p = mgh$$

where m is the mass of the cylinder, g is the acceleration of gravity, and h = 2.0 m is its height above ground level. When the cylinder reaches the bottom of the incline, all of its energy will be kinetic:

$$E_k = \frac{1}{2} mv^2 + \frac{1}{2} I\omega^2$$

where v is the cylinder's linear velocity, I its moment of inertia about the central axis, and ω its angular momentum. $\left(I = \frac{1}{2} mR^2\right.$ for cylinders, where R is the radius.$\left.\right)$

In the process of rolling down the incline the cylinder's potential energy turns to kinetic, the total change in each being equal to:

$$\Delta E_p = \Delta E_k$$
$$mgh = \frac{1}{2} mv^2 + \frac{1}{2} I\omega^2$$
$$= \frac{1}{2} mv^2 + \frac{1}{2} \left[\frac{1}{2} mR^2\right]\left(\frac{v}{R}\right)^2$$
$$= \frac{1}{2} mv^2 + \frac{1}{4} mv^2 = \frac{3}{4} mv^2$$

using $\omega = \frac{v}{R}$

Thus, $gh = \frac{3}{4} v^2$

$$v = \frac{2\sqrt{3}}{3} (gh)^{\frac{1}{2}} = 1.15 \left[(9.8 \text{ m/sec}^2)(2.0 \text{ m})\right]^{\frac{1}{2}}$$
$$= 5.09 \text{ m/sec.}$$

Note that the linear speed does not depend upon the size or mass of the cylinder.

To find ω, we use the formula:

$$w = \frac{v}{R} = \frac{5.09 \text{ m/sec}}{0.15 \text{ m}} = 34 \text{ rad/sec.}$$

A string is wrapped around a uniform homogeneous 3 lb cylinder with a 6 in. radius. The free end is attached to the ceiling from which the cylinder is then allowed to fall (as in the Figure), starting from rest. As the string unwraps, the cylinder revolves. (a) What is the linear acceleration of the center of mass? (b) What is the linear velocity, and (c) how fast is the cylinder revolving after a drop of 6 ft? (d) What is the tension in the cord?

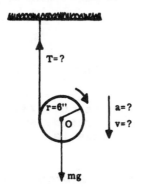

Solution: (a) Isolate the cylinder, and indicate forces acting on it.

There is no need to tabulate x- and y-components since they are all up or down forces.

Set $\Sigma F = ma$

where ΣF is the net force acting on the cylinder, a is the acceleration of the cylinder's center of mass, and m is its mass. (Note that in problems such as this one, it is convenient to take the direction of motion as positive.)

$$mg - T = ma \qquad \therefore\ a = g - \frac{T}{m} \qquad\qquad (1)$$

Now, consider rotation.

Consider torques about the center of mass 0, and set $\Sigma L = I\alpha$, where ΣL is the net torque about 0, I is the moment of inertia at the cylinder about 0, and α is its angular acceleration. Hence

$$\Sigma L = rT = I\alpha$$

$$\therefore\ T = I\ \frac{\alpha}{r}$$

(Clockwise rotation corresponds to downward motion, already assumed to have the positive direction.)

But I for a cylinder = ½ mr², where r is the cylinder radius.

In this problem $a = r\alpha$

$$T = \frac{1}{2}\frac{mr^2}{r}\frac{a}{r} = \frac{ma}{2}$$

whereupon, using (1),

$$a = \frac{-ma}{2m} + g = \frac{-a}{2} + g$$

$$\therefore \quad 3a = 2g$$

$$a = \frac{2}{3}g = 21.3 \text{ ft/sec}^2 \quad \text{(downward)}$$

(b) Now since a = constant (2/3 g), the linear motion is uniformly accelerated, such that the velocity of the center of mass is

$$v^2 = v_0^2 + 2as, \quad \text{where s becomes the drop, h,}$$

that the cylinder experiences, and v_0 is its initial velocity.

$$v^2 = 0 + (2)\left(21.3 \text{ ft/sec}^2\right)(6 \text{ ft})$$
$$v^2 = (12)\left(21.3 \text{ ft}^2/\text{sec}^2\right)$$

$$\therefore \quad v = \sqrt{256} = 16 \text{ ft/sec}$$

(c) The angular velocity $\omega = \frac{v}{r}$

$$= \frac{16 \text{ ft/sec}}{\frac{1}{2} \text{ ft}} = 32 \text{ rad/sec}$$

(d) From (1)

$$T = m(g - a) = m\left(g - \frac{2}{3}g\right)$$
$$T = \frac{1}{3}mg = \left(\frac{1}{3}\right)(3 \text{ lb}) = 1 \text{ lb}$$

● PROBLEM 4-43

A yo-yo rests on a level surface. A gentle horizontal pull (see the figure) is exerted on the cord so that the yo-yo rolls without slipping. Which way does it move and why?

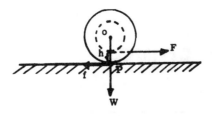

Solution: The forces acting on the yo-yo are the horizontal pull F and the frictional force f

$$f = \mu W$$

where μ is the coefficient of friction.

   Instantaneous rotation takes place about an axis
through the point of contact P (not about the center of
the yo-yo, although it might appear so) since the instantaneous velocity of the contact point is zero. Therefore,
the yo-yo rolls in the direction of the pull and its rotation is determined by the torque about P,

$$\tau = Fh.$$

It should be observed that the frictional force does not
contribute to this torque, since f is acting at P.

CHAPTER 5

ENERGY AND POWER

Conservation laws are fundamental to physics. In Newtonian mechanics, these are seen to follow from definitions and the laws of Newton. However, in more advanced treatments of mechanics and modern physics, they are considered to be laws of nature and forces often are not even mentioned.

The law of conservation of mass *states that the total quantity of matter does not change:*

$$\Sigma \, m_0 = \Sigma \, m.$$

Mass cannot be created or destroyed (in special relativity, it can be converted into energy). Work is given by the dot product of the force and displacement; if the force and displacement are in the same direction, then the work is simply the force times the distance. In general, one must calculate Fd cos θ as in Figure 1. The work can also be negative, for example, frictional work is energy dissipative and in the simplest case given by $-\mu_k N x$.

Kinetic energy is energy of motion and for a single particle given by $KE = 1/2 \, mv^2 = p^2/2m$. *Hence, given the speed and mass of the momentum and mass, one can calculate numerically the kinetic energy. Consider the kinematics of a single particle subject to acceleration:* $v^2 = v^2_0 + 2a(x - x_0)$ *(see KINEMATICS). By multiplying this equation by* 1/2 m, *we get the*

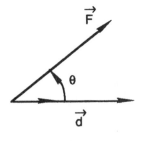

Figure 1

result

$$W = \Delta T = T - T_0$$

which is the work energy theorem. Work done on an object changes the kinetic energy of that object.

The concept of work leads immediately to the idea of potential or stored energy P.E. = Fs. For the gravitational force, in moving an object up, the force and the displacement point in opposite directions; hence the potential energy is just mgh near the surface of the Earth.

For every conservative force, we can define a potential energy. *If a spring is compressed or stretched a distance x from equilibrium, the Hooke's law potential energy is 1/2 kx². One may simply plug numbers into formulae to calculate the potential energy in solving a problem. Or one may have to use the fact that potential energy can be transformed. For example, a mass can fall and compress a spring transforming the gravitational potential energy mgh into compressional potential energy 1/2 kx².*

The law of conservation of mechanical energy *states that the total mechanical energy E = KE + PE is conserved:* $\Sigma E_0 = \Sigma E$. *For a single particle, this means that $\Delta KE = -$ PE. For the mass on a spring system of Figure 2, this means that 1/2 kA² = 1/2 mv² + 1/2 kx² for any value of the displacement x. For example, as a mass on a spring moves from x = A to x = 0 to x = $-$ A, the potential energy 1/2 kx² is transformed into kinetic energy KE = 1/2 mv² and then back again into stored energy. A good method of attack in solving energy problems is to draw two pictures, one showing the initial situation (e.g., mass on spring stretched to x = A) and the other showing the final situation (e.g., mass on spring at x = 0).*

For an object projected upward (Figure 3), one can use this principle to find the height since $1/2 mv^2_0 = mgh + 1/2 mv^2_{ox}$, or $1/2 mv^2_{oy} = mgh$; note that the energy problem-solving method gives the same answer as we get from kinematics: $h = v^2_{oy}/2g$. For distances in between y = 0 and y = h, for an object projected straight upward ($\theta = 90°$), we have 1/2 mv² + mgy = mgh.

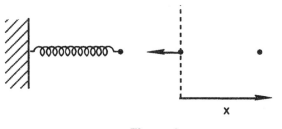

Figure 2

If friction is involved in a problem, then one must take into account that some energy is lost or goes into frictional heat. For example, in sliding down the incline of Figure 4, the law of conservation of energy must be written as $mgh = mgy + 1/2\, mv^2 + \mu_x Nx$ and the usual dynamics approach used to find N.

Energy methods are also used in rotational motion. Here, the total kinetic energy of a rigid body is $T = 1/2\, I\, \omega^2 + 1/2\, mv^2$. Work is also done by torques and calculated from

$$W = \tau\Delta\theta.$$

Power is the work done per unit time $\Delta W/\Delta t$. In the simplest case, one can find the work done by simply multiplying the power times the time. For translational motion, power is $P = \vec{F} \cdot \vec{v}$; for rotational motion, it is $\tau \cdot \omega$. In our electric bills we pay for kilowatt-hours of energy used, or 10^3 W·3600 s $= 3.6 \times 10^6$ J or 3.6 Megajoules.

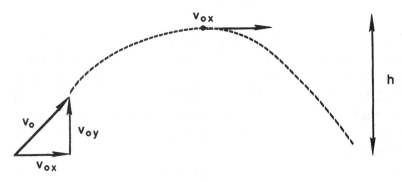

Figure 3

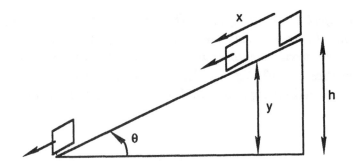

Figure 4

CHAPTER 5

ENERGY/POWER

POTENTIAL ENERGY

What is the potential energy of a 1-pound weight that has been raised 16 feet?

<u>Solution</u>: Potential energy is given by mgs, where mg is the weight of the object that has been raised. But mg is also the net force acting on this object, hence, via Newton's Second Law, we obtain

$$F = mg$$

Therefore

$$P.E. = mgs = Fs$$

Substituting the given data into this relation, we find

$$P.E. = Fs = 1 \times 16 = 16 \text{ ft-lb.}$$

A 200-kg satellite is lifted to an orbit of 2.20×10^4 mi radius. How much additional potential energy does it acquire relative to the surface of the earth?

<u>Solution</u>: As in the diagram, R is the earth's radius, M is the earth's mass, m is the satellite mass, and r is the distance between the earth's center and the satellite.

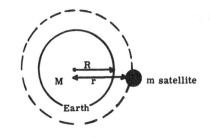

$R = 6.37 \times 10^6 \text{ m}$

$r = 2.20 \times 10^4 \text{ mi} = 3.54 \times 10^7 \text{ m}$

$M = 5.98 \times 10^{24} \text{ kg}$

$m = 200 \text{ kg}$

The additional potential energy is equal to the work done against the earth's gravitational field. At a distance R from the earth's center, that is, on the earth's surface, the satellite has a potential energy, $U_{surface}$

$$U_{surface} = -\frac{GMm}{R}$$

In orbit of radius r the potential is $U_{orbit} = -\frac{GMm}{r}$

Then the additional potential energy involved in launching the rocket to its orbit, ΔU, is given by

$$\Delta U = U_{orbit} - U_{surface} = -\frac{GMm}{r} - \left(-\frac{GMm}{R}\right) = GMm\left(\frac{1}{R} - \frac{1}{r}\right)$$

$$= (6.67 \times 10^{-11} \text{ nt} - \text{m}^2/\text{kg}^2)(5.98 \times 10^{24} \text{ kg})(200 \text{kg})$$

$$\times \left(\frac{1}{6.37 \times 10^6 \text{ m}} - \frac{1}{3.54 \times 10^7 \text{ m}}\right)$$

$$= 1.03 \times 10^{10} \text{ joules}$$

This is about equal to the work needed to lift an object weighing 3800 tons to a height of 1000 ft above the earth.
Note that the change in potential energy of the satellite cannot be found by using U = mgh. This formula applies only to objects near the earth's surface, where g is approximately constant.

KINETIC ENERGY

● PROBLEM 5-3

The mass of a bullet is 2 grams and its velocity is 30,000 centimeters per second (approximately true for a .22 caliber bullet). What is its kinetic energy?

Solution: $K.E. = \frac{1}{2} Mv^2$

$$= \frac{2 \text{ gm} \times (30,000 \text{ cm/sec})^2}{2}$$

$$= (30,000)^2 \text{ergs.}$$

Air consists of a mixture of gas molecules which are constantly moving. Compute the kinetic energy K of a molecule that is moving with a speed of 500 m/s. Assume that the mass of this particle is 4.6×10^{-26} kg.

Solution: The mass of the gas molecule, m = 4.6×10^{-26} kg, and its speed v = 5×10^2 m/s, are the known observables. Using the equation:

$K = \frac{1}{2} mv^2$

$K = (\frac{1}{2})(4.6 \times 10^{-26} \text{ kg})(5.0 \times 10^2 \text{ m/s})^2$

$= 5.75 \times 10^{-21}$ J.

A pitcher can throw a baseball weighing 5 ounces so that it will have a velocity of 96 feet per second. What is its kinetic energy?

Solution: $5 \text{ oz} = \frac{5}{16}$ lb

Therefore, since

$K.\ E.\ = \frac{1}{2} mv^2 = \frac{1}{2} \left(\frac{W}{g}\right) v^2$

where W is the weight of the ball. This is equal to

$$\frac{5 \text{ lb} \times (96 \text{ ft/sec})^2}{2 \times 16 \times (32 \text{ ft/sec}^2)} = 45 \text{ ft-lb.}$$

If we project a body upward with speed 1000 cm/s, how high will it rise?

Solution: We use the principle of energy conservation to find the height h. Assume that the level of projection is the position of zero potential energy. Then at the point of projection the total energy is purely kinetic

$$E = 0 + \tfrac{1}{2}Mv^2 = \tfrac{1}{2}M \times (10^6 \text{ cm}^2/\text{s}^2)$$

At maximum height v = 0, and the total energy is now purely potential, hence E = Mgh

By equating the two expressions for E, we have

$$Mgh = \tfrac{1}{2}M \times (10^6 \text{ cm}^2/\text{s}^2)$$

$$h = \frac{\tfrac{1}{2} \times 10^6 \text{ cm}^2/\text{s}^2}{g} = \frac{10^6 \text{ cm}^2/\text{s}^2}{2(980 \text{ cm/s}^2)}$$

$$h = .51 \times 10^3 \text{ cm}$$

$$h = 510 \text{ cm.}$$

● **PROBLEM** 5-7

A free particle, which has a mass of 20 grams is initially at rest. If a force of 100 dynes is applied for a period of 10 sec, what kinetic energy is acquired by the particle?

Solution: In order to calculate the kinetic energy we must compute the final velocity acquired by the particle: $v = at + v_o$ where v_o is the initial velocity. Since we are told that initially the particle is at rest, the expression for velocity becomes v = at. Now, from Newton's Laws we know that $a = \frac{F}{m}$. Substituting this for a yields

$$v = \left(\frac{F}{m}\right) t$$

$$= \left(\frac{100 \text{ dynes}}{20 \text{ g}}\right) \times (10 \text{ sec}) = 50 \text{ cm/sec}$$

Then,

$$KE = \tfrac{1}{2} mv^2$$

$$= \tfrac{1}{2} \times (20 \text{ g}) \times (50 \text{ cm/sec})^2 = 25,000 \text{ ergs}$$

How much work was done by the applied force? The distance moved is

$$s = \tfrac{1}{2} at^2 = \tfrac{1}{2}\left(\frac{F}{m}\right)t^2$$

$$= \frac{1}{2} \times \left(\frac{100 \text{ dynes}}{20 \text{ g}} \right) \times (10 \text{ sec})^2 = 250 \text{ cm}$$

so that the work done is W = Fs since the force and displacement are in the same direction.

$$W = (100 \text{ dynes}) \times (250 \text{ cm}) = 25{,}000 \text{ ergs}$$

Thus, the work done is transformed entirely into the kinetic energy of the particle.

● **PROBLEM** 5-8

A 1-kg block slides down a rough inclined plane whose height is 1 m. At the bottom, the block has a velocity of 4 m/sec. Is energy conserved?

Solution: Energy will be conserved if the kinetic energy gained by the block is equal to the potential energy lost.
At top: PE = mgh

$$= (1 \text{ kg}) \times \left(9.8 \text{ m/sec}^2 \right) \times (1 \text{ m})$$

$$= 9.8 \text{ J.}$$

At bottom: $KE = \frac{1}{2} mv^2$

$$= \frac{1}{2} \times (1 \text{ kg}) \times (4 \text{ m/sec})^2$$

$$= 8 \text{ J.}$$

Apparently, energy is not conserved. But we know that friction is present between the block and the rough plane. A certain amount of energy (1.8 J) has evidently been expended in overcoming this friction. This amount of energy appears as thermal energy and could be detected by measuring the temperature rise in the block and the plane after the slide is completed.

WORK AND ENERGY CONVERSION

● **PROBLEM** 5-9

What is the kinetic energy of a 1-pound weight that has fallen 16 feet?

Solution: Kinetic energy is the energy of an object due to its motion, and it is given by $\frac{1}{2} mv^2$. The mass of a 1 lb object is

$$F = mg$$

$$m = \frac{F}{g}$$

$$m = \frac{1 \text{ lb}}{32 \text{ ft/s}^2} = \frac{1}{32} \text{ slug}$$

We now calculate the velocity of the object after falling 16 feet:

$$\tfrac{1}{2} gt^2 = d \quad \text{and } gt = v \quad \text{so } v = \sqrt{2gd},$$

Substituting in this equation we have:

$$v = \sqrt{2(32 \text{ ft/s}^2)(16 \text{ ft})} = 32 \text{ ft/s}$$

The kinetic energy is

$$K.E. = \tfrac{1}{2} mv^2$$

$$K.E. = \frac{1}{2} \frac{1}{32} \text{ slug } (32 \text{ ft/s})^2 = 16 \text{ ft-lb.}$$

● **PROBLEM 5-10**

A car coasts down a long hill and then up a smaller one onto a level surface, where it has a speed of 32 ft/sec. If the car started 200 ft above the lowest point on the track, how far above this lowest point is the level surface? Ignore friction.

Solution: The initial velocity of the car is zero. Since there is no friction, the change in potential energy of the car equals its increase in kinetic energy. On the smaller hill of height h, the change in potential energy with respect to the starting point is

$$PE = mg(200 - h)$$

Its kinetic energy is given as

$$kE = \tfrac{1}{2}mv^2 = \tfrac{1}{2}m(32)^2$$

Equating the two,

$$mg(200 - h) = \tfrac{1}{2}m(32)^2$$

$$g(200 - h) = 32(200 - h) = \tfrac{1}{2}(32)^2$$

$$200 - h = \tfrac{1}{2}(32)$$

$$h = 200 - 16 = 184 \text{ ft.}$$

Therefore in order for the car to have speed 32 ft/sec, the lower hill must be at a height of 184 ft above the lowest point on the track.

A simple pendulum consists of a small object (a so-called bob) hanging from a relatively long cord whose weight is negligible with respect to the bob. The to-and-fro motion of this bob in a vertical plane is called pendulum motion. If the cord is 3 ft long and the suspended bob is drawn back so as to allow the cord to make an angle of 10° with the vertical before being released, calculate the speed of the bob as it passes through its lowest position.

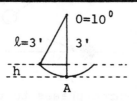

Solution: This problem can be solved by force analysis, but it lends itself most readily to a solution by the energy method.

By the principle of conservation of energy, the energy of the bob at the top of its swing must equal its energy at the bottom of its swing. At the top of its swing, the bob is momentarily at rest and it has only potential energy. Taking point A as the reference level for potential energy (see figure), and letting h be the height of the bob at the top of its swing, we may write

$$E_{top} = mgh$$

At the bottom of its swing (that is, point A), the bob has only kinetic energy. Hence

$$E_{bottom} = \tfrac{1}{2} mv^2 .$$

where v is the bob's speed at A. But

$$E_{top} = E_{bottom}$$

or $mgh = \tfrac{1}{2} mv^2$

whence $v = \sqrt{2gh}$

To determine h, use the figure and note that is is $\ell - \ell \cos \theta$

$$= 3 - 3 \cos 10° = 3 - 3(.985)$$

$$= 3 - 2.96 = .04 \text{ ft.}$$

whence $v = \sqrt{2(32 \text{ ft/s}^2)(.04 \text{ ft})}$

$$v = \sqrt{2.56 \text{ ft}^2/s^2}$$

$$v = 1.6 \text{ ft/s}$$

A pendulum with a bob of mass M is raised to height H and released. At the bottom of its swing, it picks up a piece of putty whose mass is m. To what height h will the combination (M + m) rise?

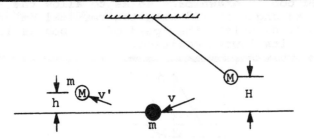

Solution: There are three phases to the problem—the fall of M, the collision of M and m, and the rise of M + m. The first and last phases involve energy conservation and the second phase involves momentum conservation.

(1) Fall: $(PE)_{initial} = (KE)_{final}$

$$MgH = \frac{1}{2} Mv^2$$

from which $v = \sqrt{2gH}$

(2) Collision: $P_{initial} = P_{final}$

$$Mv = (M + m)v'$$

(3) Rise: $(KE)_{initial} = (PE)_{final}$

$$\frac{1}{2}(M + m)v'^2 = (M + m)gh$$

from which

$$v' = \sqrt{2gh}$$

Substituting Eqs. 1 and 3 into Eq. 2 gives

$$M\sqrt{2gH} = (M + m)\sqrt{2gh}$$

Canceling $\sqrt{2g}$ and squaring, we have

$$M^2H = (m + M)^2h$$

so that the final height is

$$h = \left(\frac{M}{m + M}\right)^2 H$$

A block starting from rest slides a distance of 5 meters down an inclined plane which makes an angle of 37° with the horizontal. The coefficient of friction between block and plane is 0.2. (a) What is the velocity of the block after sliding 5 meters? (b) What would the velocity be if the coefficient of friction were negligible?

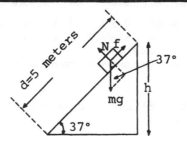

Solution: The change in potential energy of the block is
$$\Delta PE = mgh$$
where h is the height of the block and equals 5 sin 37°. Some of this energy goes into doing work against the frictional force f. The frictional force is proportional to the normal force N. The block is in equilibrium in the direction perpendicular to the inclined plane. Therefore, the sum of the forces in that direction must equal zero.

$$N - mg \cos 37° = 0$$
thus
$$N = mg \cos 37°$$

Then the frictional force is
$$F_f = \mu N = 0.2 \; mg \cos 37°$$
where μ is the coefficient of friction. The energy expended in combating this force equals the work done against it. The work equals the product of the frictional force and the distance over which it acts.

$$W = F_f d = (0.2 \; mg \cos 37°)(5) = mg \cos 37°$$

From the conservation of energy principle, the change in potential energy of an object equals its change in kinetic energy plus the work it does.

$$\Delta PE = W + \Delta KE = W + \tfrac{1}{2}m(v^2 - v_0^2)$$

Since the initial velocity v_0 of the block is zero, and its height h is d sin 37° = 5 sin 37°,

$$\Delta PE = mgh = mg \cos 37° + \tfrac{1}{2}mv^2$$
$$\tfrac{1}{2}v^2 = g(h - \cos 37°) = g(5 \sin 37° - \cos 37°)$$

$$v = \sqrt{2g(5 \sin 37° - \cos 37°)}$$
$$= \sqrt{2(9.8)[(5)(0.602) - (0.799)]}$$
$$= \sqrt{43.3} \approx 6.57 \; m/sec$$

where v is the final velocity of the block.

(b) If friction can be neglected, then we have
$$\Delta PE = \Delta KE$$
or
$$mgh = \tfrac{1}{2}mv^2$$

$$g(5 \sin 37^\circ) = \tfrac{1}{2}v^2$$
$$v = \sqrt{(2)(g)(5 \sin 37^\circ)}$$
$$= \sqrt{(2)(9.8)(5)(0.602)}$$
$$= \sqrt{59} \approx 7.68 \text{ m/sec}$$

● PROBLEM 5-14

A flywheel has a mass of 30 kg and a radius of gyration of 2 m. If it turns at a rate of 2.4 rev/sec, what is its rotational kinetic energy?

Solution: The rotational kinetic energy of a body about a given axis is

$$T = \tfrac{1}{2} I \omega^2 \qquad\qquad (1)$$

where I and ω are the rotational inertia and angular velocity of the body about the given axis. By definition of the radius of gyration, ρ, we may write

$$m\rho^2 = I \qquad\qquad (2)$$

where m is the body's mass. Using (2) in (1)

$$T = \tfrac{1}{2} m \rho^2 \omega^2$$

Using the given data

$$T = (\tfrac{1}{2})(30 \text{ kg})\left(4 \text{ m}^2\right)(2.4 \text{ rev/s})^2$$

$$T = 345.6 \text{ kg·m}^2\text{·rev}^2/\text{s}^2$$

To put this answer in conventional energy units, note that

$$1 \text{ rev/s} = 2\pi \text{ rad/s}$$

whence $T = 1382.4\pi^2$ Joules

$$T = 13643.74 \text{ Joules}$$

● PROBLEM 5-15

How much work is done in joules when a mass of 5 kilograms is raised a height of 2 meters?

Solution: Mechanical work is given by the product of the force applied to a body, and the distance for which it is applied (W = Fs when force is constant and force and line of travel are in the same direction). The force of gravity on the 5 kilogram weight is equal to the force exerted against gravity (by Newton's Third Law) and is given by:

$$F = mg$$

$$F = 5 \text{ kg } \left(9.80 \text{ m/sec}^2\right) = 49.0 \text{ } \frac{\text{k-m}}{\text{sec}^2} \text{ (newtons)}$$

and the work is given by

$$W = 49.0 \text{ newtons} (2m) = 98 \text{ joules.}$$

● **PROBLEM** 5-16

How much work is required to raise a 100-g block to a height of 200 cm and simultaneously give it a velocity of 300 cm/sec?

<u>Solution</u>: The work done is the sum of the potential energy, PE = mgh, and the kinetic energy, $KE = \frac{1}{2} mv^2$:

$$PE = mgh$$
$$= (100 \text{ g}) \times (980 \text{ cm/sec}^2) \times (200 \text{ cm})$$
$$= 1.96 \times 10^7 \text{ g-cm}^2/\text{sec}^2$$
$$= 1.96 \times 10^7 \text{ ergs}$$

$$KE = \frac{1}{2} mv^2$$
$$= \frac{1}{2} \times (100 \text{ g}) \times (300 \text{ cm/sec})^2$$
$$= 4.5 \times 10^6 \text{ g-cm}^2/\text{sec}^2$$

$$W = PE + KE$$
$$= 1.96 \times 10^7 \text{ ergs} + 0.45 \times 10^7 \text{ ergs}$$
$$= 2.41 \times 10^7 \text{ ergs}$$
$$= 2.41 \text{ J}$$

● **PROBLEM** 5-17

If a 50 g bullet traveling at 40,000 cm/sec is stopped by a steel plate, how much heat is generated, on the assumption that the energy is completely converted into heat?

<u>Solution</u>: We are told that all of the bullet's energy is converted into heat, Q. Since the bullet has only

kinetic energy

$$Q = \tfrac{1}{2} mv^2$$

where m is the bullet's mass, and v is its speed.
Hence, the amount of heat energy produced is

$$Q = (\tfrac{1}{2})(50 \text{ g})\left(4 \times 10^4 \text{ cm/s}\right)^2$$

$$Q = 25 \times 16 \times 10^8 \text{ ergs}$$

$$Q = 4 \times 10^{10} \text{ ergs}$$

● PROBLEM 5-18

A suitcase is dragged 30 m along a floor by a force F =
10 newtons inclined at an angle 30° to the floor. How
much work is done on the suitcase?

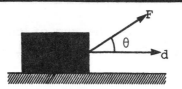

Solution: Work is defined as the scalar product of the
force acting on an object, and the distance through
which the object moves while the force is being applied.

$$\vec{W} = \vec{F} \cdot \vec{d}$$

where $\vec{F}$ is the force and $\vec{d}$ is the distance. (See the
figure above.) Note that the force and distance are
vectors while work is a scalar, hence the "scalar
product" nomenclature for the dot.

$$W = \vec{F} \cdot \vec{d} = Fd \cos \theta = Fd \cos 30°$$

$$= (10N)(30 \text{ m}) \left[\frac{\sqrt{3}}{2}\right] = 150 \sqrt{3} \text{ N·m}$$

● PROBLEM 5-19

A horizontal force of 5 N is required to maintain a velocity
of 2 m/sec for a box of mass 10 kg sliding over a certain
rough surface. How much work is done by the force in 1 min?

Solution: First, we must calculate the distance traveled:

$$s = vt$$
$$= (2 \text{ m/sec}) \times (60 \text{ sec})$$
$$= 120 \text{ m.}$$

Then, $W = Fs \cos \theta$, where θ is the angle between the force and the distance. In this case $\theta = 0°$ so we can write,

$$W = Fs$$
$$= (5 \text{ N}) \times (120 \text{ m})$$
$$= 600 \text{ N-m} = 600 \text{ J}$$

● PROBLEM 5-20

How much work in joules is done when a mass of 150 kilograms is dragged a distance of 10 meters if the coefficient of sliding friction is 0.30?

Solution: Work is given by $F \cdot s$ when the force is constant and is applied in the direction of travel (F being force and s being distance). To calculate the force needed to move the object at constant velocity against the force of friction, we use

$$F = \mu_{kinetic} \cdot N$$

where N is the normal force which in this case is the weight of the object:

$$N = mg$$
$$N = 150 \text{ kg } 9 \cdot 80 \text{ m/s}^2 = 1470 \text{ nt}$$

and the force of friction is:

$$F = 0.30 \cdot (1470 \text{ nt}) = 441 \text{ nt}$$

The work done

$$= W = Fs = 441 \text{ nt} \times 10 \text{ m} = 4410 \text{ joules.}$$

● PROBLEM 5-21

A 40-lb stone is carried up a ramp, along a path making a 30° angle to the horizontal, to the top of a building 100 ft high. How much work is done? (Neglect friction.)

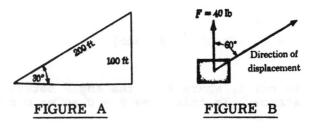

FIGURE A   FIGURE B

Solution: Work is defined as the component of the force in the direction of the displacement multiplied by the displacement, for constant forces. In mathematical terms,

$$W = \vec{F} \cdot \vec{S} = FS \cos \theta$$

where θ is the angle between the force and the displacement. We may compute the length of the ramp because from the figure (part a),

$$\sin 30° = \frac{1}{2} = \frac{100}{\text{length of ramp}}$$

Therefore, length of ramp = 200 ft. Since the stone is being carried up the ramp the force is upwards and we see that the angle θ is $60°$ (see figure (b)). Hence the work is

$$W = (40 \text{ lb})(200 \text{ ft})\cos 60° = (40)(200)\left(\frac{1}{2}\right)\text{ft-lbs}$$

$$= 4000 \text{ ft-lbs.}$$

As a check we can use the fact that this work done must equal the change in the potential energy of the stone.

$$\Delta PE = (\text{weight})(\Delta \text{ height}) = (40 \text{ lb})(100 \text{ ft}) = 4000 \text{ ft-lbs.}$$

● **PROBLEM** 5-22

A 5 -kg block slides down a frictionless plane inclined at an angle of 30° with the horizontal as shown in figure (a). Calculate the amount of work W done by the force of gravity for a displacement of 8 m along the plane.

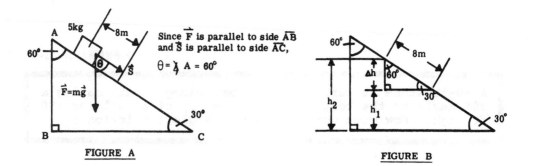

FIGURE A   FIGURE B

Solution: We will solve this problem first by the dynamics method and then by the energy method.

The formula for calculating work is:

$$W = \vec{F} \cdot \vec{s}$$

$$= F s \cos \theta$$

where θ is the angle between the force $\vec{F}$ and the displacement $\vec{s}$ of the mass in question. We see from figure (a) that the angle between $\vec{F}$ and $\vec{s}$ is $60°$:

$$W = Fs \cos 60° = \tfrac{1}{2} mgs$$

$$= \tfrac{1}{2}(5 \text{ kg}) \left(9.8 \text{ m/sec}^2\right) (8 \text{ m}) = 196 \text{ kg-m}^2/\text{sec}^2$$

$$= 196 \text{ Joules}$$

Another way to solve this problem is to calculate the difference in gravitational potential energy that the block goes through as it slides 8 m down the incline.

We know that this equals the amount of work that gravity does on the block.

As the block slides 8 m down the incline it falls through a vertical height Δh (see figure (b)) :

$$\Delta h = 8(\sin 30°)m = 4m$$

The gravitational potential energy difference that the block experiences is:

$$W = \Delta E_p = mgh_2 - mgh_1 = mg\left(h_2 - h_1\right) = mg\Delta h$$

$$= (5 \text{ kg}) \left(9.8 \text{ m/sec}^2\right) (4 \text{ m}) = 196 \text{ Joules}$$

● PROBLEM 5-23

A stone of mass 5 kg drops through a distance of 15 m under the influence of gravity. Draw graphs of the work done by the stone and the power of the stone as a function of time.

Solution. This is a case of constant acceleration with $a = g = 9.8 \text{ m/sec}^2$. The equation $d = v_0 t + \tfrac{1}{2}at^2$ can be used to find the total time the stone is in motion.

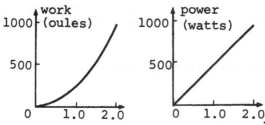

The initial velocity is zero, thus $d = \frac{1}{2}gt^2$ where

d = 15 m. The time required for the stone to fall through
15 m is

$$t^2 = \frac{2 \times 15}{9.8} = 3.06$$

$$t = 1.75 \text{ sec.}$$

The force acting on the stone is constant at

$$F = mg = 5 \text{ kg} \times 9.8 \text{ m/sec}^2 = 49 \text{ newtons.}$$

The work done by the stone is equal to W = Fd.

To find the power of the stone, note that P = Fv. The
velocity can be found from $v = v_0 + at = gt$. Below are the

calculated values of d, v, W, and P for intervals of 0.25
seconds and the graphs requested.

t	$v = gt$	$d = \frac{1}{2}gt^2$	W = Fd	P = Fv
0	0 m/sec	0 m	0 J	0 W
0.25	2.45	0.31	15.2	120
0.5	4.9	1.23	60	240
0.75	7.35	2.76	135	360
1.0	9.8	4.90	240	480
1.25	12.3	7.66	376	600
1.50	14.7	11.0	540	720
1.75	17.2	15.0	735	840

POWER

● PROBLEM 5-24

A constant horizontal force of 10 N is required to drag an
object across a rough surface at a constant speed of 5 m/sec.
What power is being expended? How much work would be done in
30 min?

Solution: Power is the rate of doing work,

$$P = \frac{\Delta W}{\Delta t} = \frac{F \Delta s}{\Delta t} .$$

(Note that in this problem the work reduces to the force multiplied by the distance the object is moved.) But $\frac{\Delta s}{\Delta t}$ is just the velocity. Therefore,

$$P = Fv$$
$$= (10 \text{ N}) \times (5 \text{ m/sec})$$
$$= 50 \text{ J/sec}$$
$$= 50 \text{ W}$$

$$W = Pt$$
$$= (50 \text{ W}) \times \left(\frac{1}{2} \text{ hr}\right)$$
$$= 25 \text{ W-hr.}$$

The work, of course, is done against the force of sliding friction.

● **PROBLEM 5-25**

The engine of a jet aircraft develops a thrust of 3000 lb. What horsepower does it develop at a velocity of 600 mi/hr = 880 ft/sec?

Solution: Power $= \dfrac{\text{Work}}{\text{Time}} = \dfrac{Fs}{T}$ (1)

where F is the force acting on a body and s is the displacement of the object in the direction of F in time t. By definition of velocity

$$v = \frac{s}{t}$$ (2)

Therefore, combining equations (1) and (2)

$$P = Fv$$

In this example,

$$P = Fv = 3000 \text{ lb} \times 880 \frac{\text{ft}}{\text{sec}} = 2,640,000 \frac{\text{ft·lb}}{\text{sec}}$$

Since 1 hp $= 550 \dfrac{\text{ft·lb}}{\text{sec}}$

$$= \frac{2.64 \times 10^6 \text{ft·lb/sec}}{550 (\text{ft·lb/sec})/\text{hp}} = 4800 \text{ hp.}$$

● **PROBLEM 5-26**

A string of freight cars weighs 200 tons. The coefficient of rolling friction is 0.005. How fast can a freight engine of 400 hp pull the string of cars along?

Solution: Power is defined as Work divided by time.

$$P = \frac{W}{t}$$

and W = Fs (where F and s are in the same direction and are force and distance respectively). Then,

$$P = \frac{Fs}{t} \quad \text{and since} \quad \frac{s}{t} = v$$

$$p = Fv$$

The force of friction can be calculated from $F = \mu N$, where μ is the coefficient of rolling friction and N is the normal force:

F = 0.005 ×(200 ton × 2000 lb/ton) = 2000 lb

Using P = Fv from above and the conversion factor

$\left(\dfrac{550 \text{ ft-lb/sec}}{1 \text{ hp}} \right)$ to convert 400 hp to power in units

$\dfrac{\text{ft-lb}}{\text{sec}}$:

400 hp (550 ft-lb/sec/hp) = 2000 lb × v

v = 110 ft/sec = 75 mi/hr.

● **PROBLEM 5-27**

A mass of 100 kilograms is pushed along the floor at a constant rate of 2 m/sec. If the coefficient of sliding friction is 0.25, at what rate is work being done in watts, in horsepower?

Solution: The weight of the mass is

$$100 \text{ kg} \times 9.8 \text{ m/sec}^2 = 980 \text{ nt} = N$$

The force of friction = F = μ × N=0.25 × 980 nt= 245 nt

Power = Fv = 245 nt × 2 m/sec = 490 watts

$$= \frac{490 \text{ watts}}{746 \text{ watts/hp}} = 0.66$$

112

EFFICIENCY

An inclined plane 5 meters long has its upper end 1 meter above the ground. A load of 100 newtons is pushed up the plane against a force of friction of 5 newtons. What is the effort, the work input, the work output, the AMA, the IMA, and the efficiency?

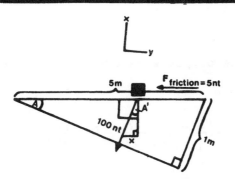

Solution: We first construct a diagram (see diagram). A vector is drawn vertically downward representing the force of gravity. Orienting our axes so that the y-axis coincides with the inclined plane, we resolve the gravitational force into its x and y components. This gives us a right triangle in which angle A' is equal to angle A, which the inclined plane forms with the ground, since they both are complements of the same angle. Therefore, since both large and small right triangles have equal angles, they are similar, so that we can write a proportion:

$$\frac{1 \text{ m}}{5 \text{ m}} = \frac{x}{100 \text{ nt}}$$

$$x = 20 \text{ nt}$$

Therefore, the force that the load exerts parallel to the inclined plane is 20 nt. This, plus the frictional force, is the effort. Hence,

Effort = Gravitational force along plane
        + frictional force

$$E = 20 \text{ nt} + 5 \text{ nt} = 25 \text{ nt}$$

Work is force × distance when the force is in the direction of the distance. Therefore, the work input (W_i) is:

$$W_i = 25 \text{ nt} \times 5 \text{ m} = 125 \text{ joules}$$

AMA (actual mechanical advantage) is:

$$AMA = \frac{R}{E}$$

where R is resistance (load), and E is effort. Then,

$$AMA = \frac{100 \text{ nt}}{25 \text{ nt}} = 4$$

The IMA (imaginary mechanical advantage) is the ratio of the length of the plane to its height:

$$IMA = \frac{5 \text{ m}}{1 \text{ m}} = 5$$

Efficiency is output work over input work.

$$\text{Efficiency} = \frac{W_o}{W_i} = \frac{100 \text{ joules}}{125 \text{ joules}} = \frac{AMA}{IMA} = \frac{4}{5}$$

$$= 0.80 = 80\%$$

● **PROBLEM 5-29**

A box weighing 100 pounds is pushed up an inclined plane 10 feet long with its upper end 4 feet above the ground. If the plane is 80% efficient, what is the force of friction?

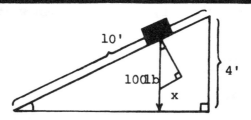

Solution: In approaching this problem, a careful plan of attack must be laid out. We are asked to find the force of friction in an inclined plane, given the dimensions and efficiency of the plane. Reasoning backwards, we begin by noticing that the effort consists of the force gravity exerts down the plane, plus the friction. The force exerted down the plane by gravity is calculable from the dimensions of the inclined plane and the weight of the box by constructing a proportion between the force triangle and the inclined plane (see diagram).

$$\frac{4'}{10'} = \frac{x}{100 \text{ lb}}$$

$$x = 40 \text{ lb}$$

114

Efficiency is calculated from AMA over IMA. IMA is calculated from the dimensions of the inclined plane (length over height, in this case 10 ft/4 ft = 2.5). The AMA is resistance over effort. The resistance is simply the weight of the box. We are only left with one unknown - the frictional force, which we now solve for

$$\text{efficiency} = \frac{AMA}{IMA} = \frac{\text{resistance/effort}}{2.5}$$

$$= \frac{\text{resistance/}\left[x + F_{friction}\right]}{2.5}$$

$$= \frac{100 \text{ lb/}\left[40 \text{ lb} + F_{friction}\right]}{2.5} = 80\%$$

$$= .80$$

Hence, $F_{friction} = 10 \text{ lb.}$

● PROBLEM 5-30

A pulley system consisting of two fixed and two movable pulleys (making four supporting strands) is used to lift a weight. If the system has an efficiency of 60%, how much weight can be lifted by an applied effort of 50 pounds?

Solution: With four supporting strands the IMA = 4.

IMA = imaginary mechanical advantage

AMA = actual mechanical advantage

E = effort

R = resistance (weight of load)

Since efficiency = $\frac{AMA}{IMA}$, $0.60 = \frac{AMA}{4}$,

whence AMA = 2.4.

Since AMA = $\frac{R}{E}$, $2.4 = \frac{R}{50 \text{ lb}}$,

whence   R = 120 lb.

● PROBLEM 5-31

A hoist raises a load of 330 pounds a distance of 15 feet in 5 seconds. At what rate in horsepower is the hoist working?

Solution: Power is equivalent to work per unit of time. In 5 seconds, the hoist does

$$W = Fs = 330 \text{ lbs} \times 15 \text{ ft} = 4950 \text{ ft-lbs}$$

of work. The rate at which work is done (the power) is:

$$\frac{4950 \text{ ft-lb}}{5 \text{ sec}} = 990 \frac{\text{ft-lbs}}{\text{sec}}$$

Since there are 550 ft-lb/sec per horsepower,

$$\frac{990 \dfrac{\text{ft-lbs}}{\text{sec}}}{550 \dfrac{\text{ft-lbs}}{\text{sec-hp}}} = 1.8 \text{ hp}$$

● **PROBLEM 5-32**

An engine used to pump water out of a mine shaft raises the water 150 ft and discharges it on the surface with a speed of 20 mph. It removes 2 slugs per second from the mine. One-fifth of the work it does is used in overcoming frictional forces. What is the horsepower of the engine?

Solution: During the process of removal from the mine, the water gains both potential and kinetic energy. The potential energy acquired per second is the weight of water ejected per second times the height raised. Thus

$$E_p = mgh = 2 \text{ slugs/s} \times 32 \text{ ft/s}^2 \times 150 \text{ ft} = 9600 \text{ ft·lb/s}$$

The water also acquires kinetic energy, the final speed of ejection being 20 mph = 88/3 ft/s . The kinetic energy acquired per second is thus

$$E_k = \tfrac{1}{2} mv^2 = \tfrac{1}{2} \times 2 \text{ slugs/s} \times \left(\frac{88}{3}\right)^2 \text{ ft}^2/\text{s}^2$$

$$= 860 \tfrac{4}{9} \text{ ft} \cdot \text{lb/s} .$$

The total energy acquired by the water is thus

$$E = E_p + E_k = 10{,}460 \tfrac{4}{9} \text{ ft} \cdot \text{lb/s}.$$

The work done by the engine, including the quantity used in overcoming friction is, if the given conditions are to be maintained,

$$W = \tfrac{5}{4} E = \tfrac{5}{4} \times 10{,}460 \tfrac{4}{9} \text{ ft} \cdot \text{lb/s}$$

and its rate of working is

$$P = \frac{\frac{5}{4} \times 10,460 \, \frac{4}{9} \, \text{ft} \cdot \text{lb/s}}{550 \, \text{ft} \cdot \text{lb/s} \cdot (\text{hp})^{-1}} = 23.8 \, \text{hp}.$$

Here, we have used the fact that

$$1 \, \text{hp} = 550 \, \text{ft} \cdot \text{lb/s}.$$

CHAPTER 6

IMPULSE/MOMENTUM

> **Basic Attacks and Strategies for Solving Problems in this Chapter**

Recall that the momentum of an object is given by $\vec{p} = m\vec{v}$. Since the momentum is a vector, one must keep track of the components when calculating it. The law of conservation of momentum states that the total momentum of a system of particles is conserved in the absence of external forces:

$$\Sigma \vec{p_0} = \Sigma \vec{p}$$

Consider the problem of Figure 1. One object of mass m_1 and speed v_1 is about to collide with another of mass m_2 at rest. This is the initial situation. Then the two objects collide or interact via internal forces. The final situation is given by Figure 2: the first mass moves off with velocity (v'_1, θ) and the second mass with velocity $(v'_2, -\phi)$. From Figure 1, conservation of momentum in the x–direction gives

$$m_1 v_1 = m_1 v'_1 \cos \theta + m_2 v'_2 \cos \theta.$$

Similarly, in the y–direction we have

$$0 = m_1 v'_1 \sin \theta - m_2 v'_2 \sin \phi.$$

If the collision is elastic, then the kinetic energy also is conserved: $\Sigma K_0 E = \Sigma KE$. This means that

$$\tfrac{1}{2} m_1 v_1^2 = \tfrac{1}{2} m_1 v'^2_1 + \tfrac{1}{2} m_2 v'^2_2$$

and so given v_1 one can solve for v'_2 (for example) in terms of v'_1. The

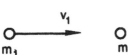

Figure 1

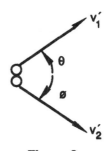

Figure 2

momentum conservation equations then become two equations in two unknowns.

If the collision is inelastic, then the loss of kinetic energy is given by

$$\Delta KE = KE - K_0E = 1/2\, m_1 v_1'^2 + 1/2\, m_2 v_2'^2 - 1/2\, m_1 v_1^2 - 1/2\, m_2 v_2^2.$$

Some problems can have both elastic and inelastic parts, as in the ballistic pendulum problem of Figure 3. The first initial situation is given by Figure 3a and the first final situation by Figure 3b. Here, the bullet becomes embedded in the block in an inelastic fashion; however, momentum is conserved (see Problem 326). The second initial situation is given by Figure 3b and the final situation by Figure 3c; now conservation of mechanical energy may be applied.

Some special cases of the scattering problem of Figures 1 and 2 are solved more simply. If $\theta = \phi = 0$, then $m_1 v_1 = m_1 v'_1 + m_2 v'_2$; given the masses and two of the speeds, one can calculate the third speed to solve a problem. If $\theta = 180°$ and $\phi = 0°$, then $m_1 v_1 = m_1 v'_1 + m_2 v'_2$. For the case of particles of equal mass ($m_1 = m_2 = m$) scattering in Figure 1, using conservation of kinetic energy one may prove that $\theta + \phi = 90°$. Hence, given θ, one can easily find ϕ. Given one of v_1, v'_1, v'_2 we then need only solve a system of two equations in two unknowns by algebra.

In an explosion where one mass fragments into several, the law of conservation of momentum is applicable and one may use it to find the velocities of the fragments. The momentum principle problem-solving approach is also useful when one mass (e.g., a car or lump of clay) collides with and sticks to another.

The impulse-momentum theorem follows from Newton's second law: $\vec{F} = \Delta\vec{p}\,/\,\Delta t$. Therefore, the impulse is

$$\vec{I} = \Delta\vec{p} = Ft.$$

In Figure 4a, this is just the area under the force versus time curve. The

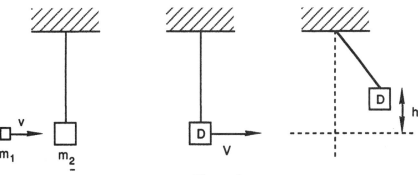

Figure 3

average force is found from

$$\langle \vec{F} \rangle = \vec{F} \, \Delta t / t$$

Impulse may also be found in rotational dynamics

$$\vec{I} = \Delta \vec{L} = \vec{\tau} \, t$$

and the graphical interpretation is the same (Figure 4b).

For rotational motion, the law of conservation of angular momentum (see DYNAMICS) must be used to solve a collision problem where one rotating mass interacts with another. If the interaction is inelastic then the amount of lost rotational kinetic energy is found from

$$\Delta KE = KE - K_0 E = 1/2 \; I_1 \omega_1'^2 + 1/2 \; I_2 \omega_2'^2 - 1/2 \; I_1 \omega_1^2 - 1/2 \; I_2 \omega_2^2 .$$

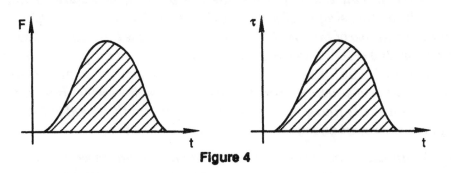

Figure 4

IMPULSE/MOMENTUM

● **PROBLEM** 6-1

A cue ball traveling at a speed of 3 m/s collides with
a stationary billiard ball and imparts a speed of
1.8 m/s to the billiard ball. If the billiard ball moves
in the same direction as the oncoming cue ball, what
is the velocity of the cue ball after the collision?
Assume that both balls have the same mass.

$V_1 = 3m/s$ $V_2 = 0$

m   m

before collision

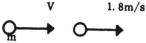

V   1. 8m/s

m

after collision

Solution: Linear momentum must be conserved in this
isolated, two particle system. Thus, the initial momentum
of the system must equal the system's final momentum.
Since the collision is 1-dimensional, we may drop the
vector nature of momentum and write

$$P_f = P_i$$

$$mv + m(1.8 \text{ m/sec}) = m \ (3 \text{ m/sec}) + m(0 \text{ m/sec})$$

$$m(v + 1.8 \text{ m/sec}) = m(3 \text{ m/sec})$$

$$v + 1.8 \text{ m/sec} = 3 \text{ m/sec}$$

$$v = 1.2 \text{ m/sec.}$$

A 100-gram marble strikes a 25-gram marble lying on a
smooth horizontal surface squarely. In the impact, the
speed of the larger marble is reduced from 100 cm/sec to
60 cm/sec. What is the speed of the smaller marble immediately after impact?

Solution: The law of conservation of momentum is applicable here, as it is in all collision problems. Therefore,
Momentum after impact = Momentum before impact.

$$\text{Momentum before impact} = M_{B1} \times V_{B1}$$

$$= 100 \text{ gm} \times 100 \text{ cm/sec}$$

$$= 10,000 \text{ gm-cm/sec}$$

$$\text{Momentum after impact} = M_{A1} \times V_{A1} + M_{A2} \times V_{A2}$$

$$= 100 \text{ gm} \times 60 \text{ cm/sec}$$

$$+ 25 \text{ gm} \times V_{A2} \text{ cm/sec}$$

Then

$$10,000 \text{ gm-cm/sec} = 6000 \text{ gm-cm/sec} + 25 \text{ g} \times V_{A2}$$

whence $V_{A2} = 160 \text{ cm/sec}$.

A 4.0-gm bullet is fired from a 5.0-kg gun with a
speed of 600 m/sec. What is the speed of recoil of
the gun?

Solution: Originally, the momentum of the system
consisting of the gun and the bullet is zero. Even
if external forces act on the system, the principle
of momentum conservation can be applied if the time
interval of "collision" is small enough. Therefore we
can say that after the bullet has been fired from
the gun, the total momentum of the system remains
zero. Letting m_1 be the mass of the gun and m_2 the
mass of the bullet, with v_1 and v_2 their respective
final velocities, we have

$$m_1 v_1 + m_2 v_2 = 0$$

$$v_1 = - \frac{m_2}{m_1} v_2$$

$$v_1 = - \frac{0.0040 \text{ kg}}{5.0 \text{ kg}} (600 \text{ m/s})$$

$$= - 0.48 \text{ m/sec}$$

where the minus sign indicates that the gun moves in a direction opposite to that of the bullet.

● PROBLEM 6-4

A cart of mass 5 kg moves horizontally across a frictionless table with a speed of 1 m/sec. When a brick of mass 5 kg is dropped on the cart, what is the change in velocity of the cart?

Solution: Assume that the brick has no horizontal velocity when it is dropped on the cart. Its initial horizontal momentum is therefore zero. Since no external horizontal forces act on the system of cart and brick, horizontal momentum must be conserved. We can say, for the horizontal direction,

$$m_c v_{ci} + m_b v_{bi} = m_c v_{cf} + m_b v_{bf}$$

Since the final velocities of the brick and cart are the same,

$$m_c v_{ci} = \left(m_c + m_b \right) v_f$$

Substituting values,

$$v_f = \frac{m_c v_{ci}}{m_c + m_b} = \frac{(5 \text{ kg})(1 \text{ m/sec})}{(5 \text{ kg} + 5 \text{ kg})} = .5 \text{ m/sec}$$

The change in velocity of the cart is

$$v_f - v_{ci} = (0.5 - 1.0) \text{m/sec} = - 0.5 \text{ m/sec}.$$

● PROBLEM 6-5

Suppose a 15-g bullet is fired into a 10-kg wooden block that is mounted on wheels and the time required for the block to travel a distance of 45cm is measured. This can easily be accomplished with a pair of photocells and an electronic clock. If the measured time is 1 sec, what is the muzzle velocity of the bullet?

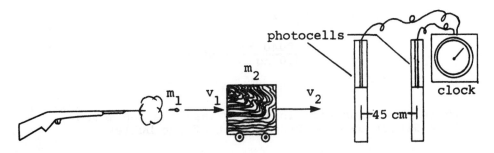

Solution: In this example, the bullet comes to rest in the block and imparts its momentum to the block. Since the block travels 45 cm in one second, the recoil velocity of the block is 45 cm/sec, and from momentum conservation we have

$$m_1 v_1 = m_2 v_2$$

(Here, we do not have a negative sign because both velocities are in the same direction. Also, we take m_2 to be 10 kg, that is, we neglect the mass of the bullet embedded in the block.) Then,

$$v_1 = \frac{m_2 v_2}{m_1}$$

$$= \frac{\left(10^4 g\right) \times (45 \text{ cm/sec})}{15 \text{ g}}$$

$$= 3 \times 10^4 \text{ cm/sec}$$

$$= 300 \text{ m/sec}$$

$$\cong 985 \text{ ft/sec}$$

● **PROBLEM** 6-6

Two particles of equal mass and equal but opposite velocities $\pm v_i$ collide. What are the velocities after the collision?

Solution: Since no external forces act on the 2 particle system, we may use the principle of conservation of momentum. This principle will relate the velocities of the particles after the collision to their velocities before the collision. Therefore,

$$m \vec{v}_{1i} + m \vec{v}_{2i} = m \vec{v}_{1f} + m \vec{v}_{2f} \qquad (1)$$

where the subscript $\vec{v}_{1_i}$ defines the initial velocity of particle 1, and similarly for $\vec{v}_{2_i}$, $\vec{v}_{1f}$, and $\vec{v}_{2f}$. Substituting $\vec{v}_{1_i} = \vec{v}_i$ and $\vec{v}_{2_i} = -\vec{v}_i$, into (1), we obtain

$$m \vec{v}_i - m \vec{v}_i = m \vec{v}_{1f} + m \vec{v}_{2f} = 0$$

Hence $\qquad \vec{v}_{1f} = -\vec{v}_{2f}.$

If the collision is elastic, then kinetic energy is conserved in the collision, and

$$\tfrac{1}{2} m v_{1_i}^2 + \tfrac{1}{2} m v_{2_i}^2 = \tfrac{1}{2} m v_{1f}^2 + \tfrac{1}{2} m v_{2f}^2 \quad .(2)$$

But $v_{1_i} = v_{2_i} = v_i$ and $v_{1f} = v_{2f} = v_f$ because we are concerned only with magnitudes in (2). Therefore,

$$\tfrac{1}{2} m v_i^2 + \tfrac{1}{2} m v_i^2 = \tfrac{1}{2} m v_f^2 + \tfrac{1}{2} m v_f^2$$

or $\qquad\qquad v_i^2 = v_f^2$

and the conservation of energy demands that the final speed v_f equal the initial speed v_i. If one or both particles are excited internally by the collision, then $v_f < v_i$ because some of the initial energy must go into the excitation energy. Hence, the final energy < initial energy. If one or both particles initially are in excited states of internal motion and on collision they give up their excitation energy into kinetic energy, then v_f can be larger than v_i.

• **PROBLEM** 6-7

A high-powered rifle whose mass is 5 kg fires a 15-g bullet with a muzzle velocity of 3×10^4 cm/sec. What is the recoil velocity of the rifle?

$m_1 = 5$ kg $\qquad m_2 = 15$ g
$v_1 = ?$ $\qquad v_2 = 3 \times 10^4$ cm/sec

Solution: The momentum of the system after the gun has fired must equal the momentum before the gun went off. Originally, the momentum of the bullet and rifle is zero since they are at rest. Using the conservation of momentum equation:

$$(m_1 + m_2)v_0 = m_1v_1 + m_2v_2 = 0$$

$$m_1v_1 = -m_2v_2$$

$$v_1 = - \frac{m_2 v_2}{m_1}$$

$$= - \frac{(15g) \times (3 \times 10^4 \text{ cm/sec})}{5 \times 10^3 \text{ g}}$$

$$= - 90 \text{ cm/sec}.$$

This is a sizable recoil velocity and if the rifle is not held firmly against the shoulder, the shooter will receive a substantial "kick". However, if he does hold the rifle firmly against his shoulder, the shooter's body as a whole absorbs the momentum. That is, we must use for m_1 the mass of the rifle plus the mass of the shooter. If his mass is 100 kg, then the recoil velocity (now of the rifle plus shooter) is

$$v_1 = - \frac{(15g) \times (3 \times 10^4 \text{ cm/sec})}{5 \times 10^3 \text{ g} + 10^5 \text{ g}}$$

$$\overset{\sim}{=} - 4.5 \text{ cm/sec}.$$

This magnitude of recoil is quite tolerable.

● **PROBLEM** 6-8

A ball of mass m_1 = 100 g traveling with a velocity v_1 = 50 cm/sec collides "head on" with a ball of mass m_2 = 200 g which is initially at rest. Calculate the final velocities, v_1' and v_2', in the event that the collision is elastic.

Before   After

<u>Solution.</u> In any collision there is conservation of momentum and since this is an elastic collision, kinetic energy is also conserved.

First, we use momentum conservation to write

p(before) = p(after)

$$m_1 v_1 + m_2 v_2 = m_1 v_1' + m_2 v_2'.$$

In order to prevent the equations from becoming too clumsy, we suppress the units (which are CGS throughout); then we have

$$100 \times 50 + 0 = 100v_1' + 200v_2'.$$

Dividing through by 100 gives

$$50 = v_1' + 2v_2' \qquad\qquad (1)$$

From energy conservation, we have (since there is no PE involved and since the collision is elastic)

$$\text{KE(before)} = \text{KE(after)}$$

$$\tfrac{1}{2}m_1v_1^2 + \tfrac{1}{2}m_2v_2^2 = \tfrac{1}{2}m_1v_1'^2 + \tfrac{1}{2}m_2v_2'^2$$

$$\tfrac{1}{2} \times 100 \times (50)^2 + 0 = \tfrac{1}{2} \times 100\ v_1'^2 + \tfrac{1}{2} \times 200\ v_2'^2.$$

Dividing through by $100/2 = 50$ gives

$$2500 = v_1'^2 + 2v_2'^2. \qquad\qquad (2)$$

We now have two equations, (1) and (2), each of which contains both of the unknowns, v_1' and v_2'. We can obtain a solution by solving Eq. 1 for v_1',

$$v_1' = 50 - 2v_2' \qquad\qquad (3)$$

and substituting this expression into Eq. 2:

$$2500 = \left(50 - 2v_2'\right)^2 + 2v_2'^2 \qquad \text{or,}$$

$$2500 = 2500 - 200v_2' + 4v_2'^2 + 2v_2'^2.$$

From this equation we find

$$6v_2'^2 = 200v_2'$$

so that

$$v_2' = \frac{200}{6} = 33\tfrac{1}{3}\ \text{cm/sec.}$$

Substituting this value into Eq. 3 we find

$$v_1' = 50 - 2 \times 33\tfrac{1}{3}$$
$$= -16\tfrac{2}{3}\ \text{cm/sec.}$$

The negative sign means that after the collision, m_1 moves in the direction opposite to its initial direction (see figure).

A 2.0-kg ball traveling with a speed of 22 m/sec over-
takes a 4.0-kg ball traveling in the same direction as
the first, with a speed of 10 m/sec. If after the
collision the balls separate with a relative speed of
9.6 m/sec, find the speed of each ball.

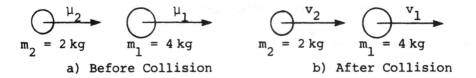

a) Before Collision   b) After Collision

<u>Solution:</u>   No external forces act on the system. Since
this is a collision problem, the principle of conservation of momentum can be used. Letting u_1 and u_2
be the initial velocities and v_1 and v_2 the final
velocities of the two masses m_1 = 4.0 kg and m_2 =
2.0 kg, we find

$$m_1u_1 + m_2u_2 = m_1v_1 + m_2v_2 \qquad (1)$$

$$(4.0 \text{ kg})(10 \text{ m/sec}) + (2.0 \text{kg})(22 \text{ m/sec}) = (4.0 \text{ kg})v_1 + (2.0 \text{ kg})v_2$$

$$(2.0 \text{ kg})v_1 + (1.0 \text{ kg})v_2 = 42 \text{ kg-m/sec}$$

or $\qquad\qquad 2.0 \ v_1 + v_2 = 42 \text{ m/sec} \qquad (2)$

The difference in speed of the two masses after
collision is given as 9.6 m/sec. Since the two masses
initially move along the same axis, they must continue
to do so after the collision, assuming their center of
mass lies along this axis of motion. Since, physically, the
2.0 kg ball cannot pass through the 4.0 kg ball, the 4.0
kg ball continues to have greater velocity in the initial
direction of motion. Taking this initial direction as
positive,

$v_1 - v_2 = 9.6 \text{ m/sec}$

Substituting $v_2 = v_1 + 9.6$ m/sec in equation (2), we
find the final velocities to be

$v_1 = 17.2 \text{ m/sec}$

$v_2 = 7.6 \text{ m/sec}$

Both balls continue to move in the initial direction but
with their speeds changed.

A proton $\left(\text{mass } 1.67 \times 10^{-27} \text{ kg}\right)$ collides with a neutron (mass almost identical to the proton) to form a deuteron. What will be the velocity of the deuteron if it is formed from a proton moving with velocity 7.0×10^6 m/sec to the left and a neutron moving with velocity 4.0×10^6 m/sec to the right? (Figure A)

4.0×10^6 m/sec -7.0×10^6 m/sec -1.5×10^6 m/sec

n   p   d

Fig. A: Before collision   Fig. B: After Collision

Solution: According to the conservation of momentum we write:

$$m_d v_d = m_p u_p + m_n v_n$$

where m_d, m_p, and m_n are the masses of the deuteron, proton, and neutron respectively. Since the masses of the proton and neutron are almost identical:

$$m_p = m_n = \tfrac{1}{2} m_d$$

Inserting this into the momentum conservation equation (we adopt the convention that velocities to the right are positive):

$$2m_p v_d = m_p v_p + m_p v_n$$

$$v_d = \frac{v_p + v_n}{2} = \frac{-7.0 \times 10^6 \text{ m/sec} + 4.0 \times 10^6 \text{ m/sec}}{2} = -1.5 \times 10^6 \text{ m/sec (figure B).}$$

Thus the neutron moves to the left with speed 1.5×10^6 m/sec. In the actual collision a photon is produced and carries off some of the momentum, therefore the velocity calculated above is somewhat too large.

● **PROBLEM** 6-11

A 100-kg man jumps into a swimming pool from a height of 5 m. It takes 0.4 sec for the water to reduce his velocity to zero. What average force did the water exert on the man?

Solution: The man's initial velocity (before jumping) is zero. Therefore, as he strikes the water, his velocity v is $v^2 = v_0^2 + 2gh$, , which reduces to $v^2 = 2gh$

$$v = \sqrt{2gh}$$

$$= \sqrt{2 \times (9.8 \text{ m/sec}^2) \times (5 \text{ m})}$$

$$= 10 \text{ m/sec}$$

Therefore, the man's momentum on striking the water was

$$p_1 = mv$$

$$= (100 \text{ kg}) \times (10 \text{ m/sc})$$

$$= 1000 \text{ kg-m/sec}$$

The final momentum was $p_2 = 0$, so that the average force was

$$\bar{F} = \frac{\Delta p}{\Delta t} = \frac{p_2 - p_1}{\Delta t}$$

$$= \frac{0 - 1000 \text{ kg-m/sec}^2}{0.4 \text{ sec}}$$

$$= - 2500 \text{ N}$$

The negative sign means that the retarding force was directed opposite to the downward velocity of the man.

● **PROBLEM** 6-12

Suppose the collision in the figure is completely in-elastic and that the masses and velocities have the values shown. What is the velocity of the 2 mass system after the collision? What is the kinetic energy before and after the collision?

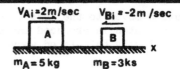

Solution: Since we wish to relate the final velocity of the system to its initial velocity, we will use conservation of momentum The total momentum before the collision is equal to the total momentum after the collision, if no forces external to the system act. Hence

$$m_A \vec{v}_{Ai} + m_B \vec{v}_{Bi} = (m_A + m_B)\vec{v}$$

where $\vec{v}_{Ai}$, $\vec{v}_{Bi}$ are the initial velocities of m_A and m_B, and $\vec{v}$ is the final velocity of the combined masses. Solving for $\vec{v}$,

$$\vec{v} = \frac{m_A \vec{v}_{Ai} + m_B \vec{v}_{Bi}}{m_A + m_B}$$

Changing the vectors to magnitudes, and noting that $\vec{v}_{Ai}$ and $\vec{v}_{Bi}$ are in the opposite directions

$$v = \frac{m_A v_{Ai} - m_B v_{Bi}}{m_A + m_B}$$

where v_{Ai} is in the positive x direction. Therefore,

$$v = \frac{(5 \text{ kg})(2 \text{ m/s}) - (3 \text{ kg})(2 \text{ m/s})}{8 \text{ kg}}$$

$$v = .5 \text{ m/s}$$

Since v_2 is positive, the system moves to the right after the collision. The kinetic energy of body A before the collision is

$$\tfrac{1}{2} m_A v_{Ai}^2 = (\tfrac{1}{2})(5 \text{ kg})(4 \text{ m}^2/\text{s}^2) = 10 \text{ joules}$$

and that of body B is

$$\tfrac{1}{2} m_B v_{Bi}^2 = (\tfrac{1}{2})(3 \text{ kg})(4 \text{ m}^2/\text{s}^2) = 6 \text{ joules}$$

The total kinetic energy before collision is therefore 16 joules.

Note that the kinetic energy of body B is positive, although its velocity v_{Bi} and its momentum mv_{Bi} are both negative.

The kinetic energy after the collision is

$$\tfrac{1}{2}(m_A + m_B)v^2 = \tfrac{1}{2}(8 \text{ kg})(.25 \text{ m}^2/\text{s}^2) = 1 \text{ joule}$$

Hence, far from remaining constant, the final kinetic energy is only 1/16 of the original, and 15/16 is "lost" in the collision. If the bodies couple together like two freight cars, most of this energy is converted to heat through the production of elastic waves which are eventually absorbed.

If there is a spring between the bodies and the bodies are locked together when their velocities become equal, the energy is trapped as potential energy in the compressed spring. If all these forms of energy are taken into account, the total energy of the system is conserved although its kinetic energy is not. However, momentum is always conserved in a collision, whether or not the collision is elastic.

● **PROBLEM 6-13**

A rifle weighing 7 pounds shoots a bullet weighing 1 ounce, giving the bullet a speed of 1120 feet per second.
(a) If the rifle is free to move, what is its recoil speed?
(b) If the rifle is held tight against the shoulder of a man weighing 133 pounds and if he were free to move, what would be the recoil speed of the rifle and man?
(c) If the bullet imbeds itself in a block of wood

weighing 3 pounds and 7 ounces and if the block were free to move, what would be the speed of the block plus bullet?

Solution: The law of conservation of momentum may be applied in an isolated system where no external forces are applied.

(a) The momentum of the gun plus bullet before firing is zero, and it is therefore also zero after firing. The momentum after firing is

$$M_{bullet} \times v_{bullet} + M_{gun} \times v_{gun} = 0 \qquad (1)$$

Since the law of conservation of momentum involves mass and not weight, we must convert weight into mass by dividing by the acceleration of gravity $\left(M = \dfrac{Wt}{g} \right)$. Therefore

$$M_{bullet} = \frac{\frac{1}{16} \text{ lb}}{32 \text{ ft/s}^2} = .001953 \text{ slugs and}$$

$$M_{gun} = \frac{7 \text{ lb}}{32 \text{ ft/s}^2} = \frac{7}{32} \text{ slugs}$$

Equation (1) then becomes

$$.001953 \text{ slugs} \times 1120 \text{ ft/sec} + 7/32 \text{ slugs} \times v_{gun} = 0$$

whence

$$v_{gun} = -10 \text{ ft/sec, or 10 ft/sec backwards}$$

(b) The momentum after firing is

$$M_{bullet} \times v_{bullet} + M_{gun + man} \times v_{gun + man} = 0 \quad \text{or}$$

$$.001953 \text{ slugs} \times 1120 \text{ ft/sec} + \left(\frac{133}{32} \text{ slugs} + \frac{7}{32} \text{ slugs} \right)$$

$$\times \ v_{gun + man} = 0$$

whence

$$v_{gun + man} = -0.5 \text{ ft/sec, or 0.5 ft/sec backwards}$$

(c) The momentum of the bullet before the collision with the block is

$$M_{bullet} \times v_{bullet} = .001953 \text{ slugs} \times 1120 \text{ ft/sec} \times 32 \text{ ft/s}^2 = 70 \text{ lb-ft/sec}$$

The momentum after collision is the same, 70 lb-ft/sec. Then

$$70 \text{ lb-ft/sec} = \left(M_{\text{bullet + block}} \right) \times \left(v_{\text{bullet + block}} \right)$$

$$= \left(\frac{3}{32} \text{ slugs} + \frac{7}{2} \text{ slugs} + 2 \text{ slugs} \right) \times \left(v_{\text{bullet+block}} \right)$$

whence

$$\left(v_{\text{bullet + block}} \right) = 20 \text{ ft/sec forwards.}$$

● PROBLEM 6-14

A satellite of mass 3×10^3 kg moves with a speed of 8×10^3 m/s in an orbit of radius 7×10^6 m. What is the angular momentum of the satellite as it revolves about the earth?

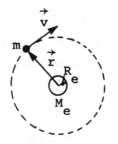

Solution: The angular momentum of an object about a point 0 is defined as

$$\vec{L} = \vec{r} \times \vec{p}$$

where $\vec{p}$ is the linear momentum of the object and $\vec{r}$ is the distance vector from 0 to the object. In this problem, $\vec{r}$ and $\vec{p}$ are perpendicular, hence the magnitude of $\vec{L}$ is

$$L = rp = r(mv) = mvr.$$

The known observables are mass, $m = 3 \times 10^3$ kg; speed $v = 8 \times 10^3$ m/s; and orbit radius, $r = 7 \times 10^6$ m; therefore,

$$L = mvr = \left(3 \times 10^3 \text{ kg} \right)\left(8 \times 10^3 \text{ m/s} \right)\left(7 \times 10^6 \text{ m} \right) =$$

$$= 1.68 \times 10^{14} \text{ Js.}$$

CHAPTER 7

HYDROSTATICS/AEROSTATICS

Fluid mechanics is an important part of physics since much of our universe consists of gases and liquids either at rest or in motion. The study of fluids at rest is called fluid statics or sometimes hydrostatics/aerostatics since water and air are two essential fluids.

The density of a fluid is its mass divided by its volume

$$\rho = m / V.$$

If one measures *the mass of a beaker with a certain volume of liquid in it,* m_{b+w}, *and without a certain volume of liquid in it,* m_b, *(Figure 1), then one can easily calculate the density of the liquid as*

$$\rho = (m_{b+w} - m_b) / V.$$

The specific gravity of an object is a dimensionless quantity defined as the ratio of its density to that of water (usually at 4°C). Since $\rho_w \cong 1$ *g/cc, the specific gravity is the same number as the density of a substance in CGS units. In solving a specific gravity problem, one must simply convert to* CGS.

For solid objects, the mass of the object is more easily measured, for example with a calibrated digital balance. Finding the volume is easy if the object has a regular shape. For example, the volume of a parallelpiped is lwh, a right circular cylinder $\pi r^2 h$, *a sphere* $4/3 \pi r^3$, *and a cone* $1/3 \pi r^2 h$.

Another common experimental way to find the volume of an object is by submerging it. For example, if a mass is placed in the fluid of Figure 1b, one can simply take the difference of the volumes before and after

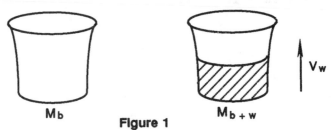

M_b Figure 1 M_{b+w}

submerging the object to get $V = V_{0+w} - V_w$. This approach works very well for irregularly shaped objects.

Archimedes' principle *states that a fluid exerts an upward or buoy-ancy force on an object equal to the weight of the fluid displaced. This can be used to understand how objects float and why objects have a different apparent weight in a fluid. Consider the situation of Figure 2. For a mass on a spring (Figure 2a), the free body diagram gives* $W - F = 0$ *or* $mg = kx$. *The stretching of the spring and knowledge of the Hooke constant may hence be used to find the weight, as with the calibrated bathroom scale. However, in Figure 2b, summing up the forces we get* $W - F - B = 0$. *The apparent weight of the object is* $F = ky = mg - B$. *If the object is a solid sphere of radius r and density* ρ, *then the buoyant force is given by* $\rho_w 4/3 \pi r^3 g$. *Clearly, for* $\rho > \rho_w$ *the solid object will sink.*

The concept of pressure is important in fluid mechanics. Pressure is the force per unit area acting on a surface. For example, if an object is beneath a column of fluid of height h and cross-sectional area A, then the pressure is $p = F/A = mg/A$. *The mass of a fluid of constant density is* $m = \rho A h$. *The pressure is thus* $p = \rho g h$. *The quantity* ρg *is sometimes called the weight density. If there is an ambient pressure then one must add that to get the absolute pressure* $p = p_a + \rho g h$.

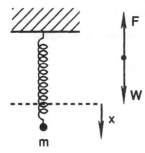
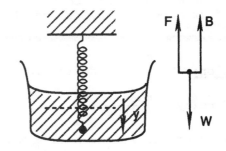

Figure 2

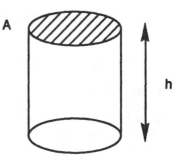

Figure 3

CHAPTER 7

HYDROSTATICS/AEROSTATICS

DENSITY, SPECIFIC GRAVITY, PRESSURE

In order to determine their density, drops of blood are placed in a mixture of xylene of density 0.867 $g \cdot cm^{-3}$, and bromobenzene of density 1.497 $g \cdot cm^{-3}$, the mixture being altered until the drops do not rise or sink. The mixture then contains 72% of xylene and 28% of bromobenzene by volume. What is the density of the blood?

Solution: Using the definition of density

$$density = \frac{mass}{volume}$$

every 72 cm^3 of xylene have a mass of 72 cm^3 × 0.867 $g \cdot cm^{-3}$ = 62.424 g, and every 28 cm^3 of bromobenzene have a mass of 28 cm^3 × 1.497 $gm \cdot cm^{-3}$ = 41.916 g. Thus, 100 cm^3 of the mixture have a mass of (62.424 + 41.916)g = 104.340 g. Thus the density of the mixture is 1.0434 $g \cdot cm^{-3}$.

But blood neither rises nor sinks in this mixture, showing that the blood has no net force acting on it. Thus the weight of any drop of blood is exactly equal to the upthrust acting on it. But, by Archimede's principle, the upthrust is the weight of an equal volume of mixture. Hence the blood and the mixture have the same densities; thus the density of blood is 1.0434 $g \cdot cm^{-3}$.

The mass of a rectangular bar of iron is 320 grams. It is $2 \times 2 \times 10$ centimeters^3. What is its specific gravity?

Solution: Specific gravity for solids is the ratio of the density of the solid to the density of water (approximately 1 gram per cubic centimeter). The specific gravity of iron is then

$$S = \frac{\rho_i}{\rho_\omega}$$

But $\rho_i = \dfrac{320 \text{ gm}}{2 \times 2 \times 10 \text{ cm}^3} = 8 \text{ gm/cm}^3$

Since $\rho_\omega = 1 \text{ gm/cm}^3$

$$S = \frac{8 \text{ gm/cm}^3}{1 \text{ gm/cm}^3} = 8$$

A water pipe in which water pressure is 80 lb/in.^{2} springs a leak, the size of which is .01 sq in. in area. How much force is required of a patch to "stop" the leak?

Solution: This problem is quickly recognized as an application of the definition of fluid pressure. Commencing with the definition of pressure as the ratio of the force f on an area a, and the area a, we find

$$p = \frac{f}{a}$$

It follows that: $f = pa$

Substituting values: $f = 80 \text{ lb/in}^2 \times .01 \text{ in}^2 = .8 \text{ lb.}$

A boy sits in a bus holding a balloon by a string. The bus accelerates forward. In which direction will the balloon move?

Solution: Our first guess is that the balloon moves backward. However, the balloon actually moves forward. This occurs due to the pressure gradient created by the motion of the bus. When the bus is at rest, the air molecules undergo random motions. On the average the molecules remain in one position. As the bus accelerates, the back of the bus "collects" the air molecules. The front of the bus leaves the air molecules behind. The net result is an increase in air density at the back of the bus, and a decrease in air density at the front. Just as a balloon rises due to the greater pressure at the lower end of the balloon than at the top of the balloon, similarly the greater pressure at the back of the balloon will cause it to move forward.

FLUID FORCES

● **PROBLEM 7-5**

Find the force acting on the bottom of an aquarium having a base 1 foot by 2 feet and containing water to a depth of one foot.

Solution: Pressure, p, is given by height times density (when density is weight per volume). The density of the water is $\dfrac{62.}{ft^3}$ lb Therefore,

$$p = hw = 1 \text{ ft} \times \frac{62.4 \text{ lb}}{ft^3} = 62.4 \frac{lb}{ft^2}$$

Force = pressure × Area of bottom, therefore,

$$F = pA = 62.4 \frac{lb}{ft^2} \times (1 \text{ ft} \times 2 \text{ ft}) = 124.8 \text{ lb.}$$

Note that the shape of the vessel is not considered in this solution. It would be the same even if the sides were sloping outward or inward.

Find the pressure due to a column of mercury 74.0 cm high.

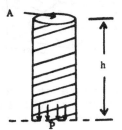

Solution: The total force F acting at the bottom of the column of mercury is due to the weight of the mercury. Or, by Newton's Second Law

$$F = W = mg.$$

Since $\text{Density}(\rho) = \dfrac{\text{mass}(m)}{\text{volume}(V)}$

and $V = Ah$ where A is the cross sectional area of the column and h is its height. We then have

$$F = \rho V g = \rho A h g$$

The pressure P at the bottom of the column is defined as

$$P = \frac{F}{A} = \frac{\rho A h g}{A} = h \rho g =$$

$$= (0.740\text{m})\left(1.36 \times 10^4 \text{ kg/m}^3\right)\left(9.80\text{m/sec}^2\right)$$

$$= 9.86 \times 10^4 \text{ nt/m}^2 .$$

In the equation derived above, the pressure is that due to the liquid alone. If there is a pressure on the surface of the liquid, this pressure must be added to that due to the liquid to find the pressure at a given level. The pressure at any level in the liquid is then

$$P = P_s + hpg$$

where P_s is the pressure at the surface of the liquid.

● PROBLEM 7-7

A rectangular tank 6.0 by 8.0 ft is filled with gasoline to a depth of 8.0 ft. The pressure at the surface of the gasoline is 14.7 lb/in². (The density of gasoline is 1.325 sl/f³). Find the pressure at the bottom of the tank and the force exerted on the bottom.

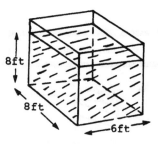

Solution: The total pressure at the tank's bottom is the sum of the air pressure at the surface of the fluid and the pressure due to the gasoline above the tank bottom:

$$P_{air} = 14.7 \quad lb/in^2$$

Since $1 \ lb/in^2 = 144 \ lb/f^2$

$$P_{air} = 14.7 \ lb/in^2 = (14.7)(144 \ lb/f^2) = 2120 \ lb/f^2 \quad (1)$$

To find the pressure on the bottom of the tank due to the gasoline, we note that the pressure is equal to the force on the bottom of the tank divided by the area of the bottom

$$P_{gas} = \frac{F}{A}$$

But $F_{gas} = \rho g V$ where ρ is the density of gasoline, g is 9.8 m/s^2, and V is the volume of the gasoline in the tank. Hence

$$P_{gas} = \frac{\rho g V}{A}$$

But $V = hA$, where h is the height of the gasoline in the tank. Therefore

$$P_{gas} = \rho g h = (1.313 \ sl/f^3)(32 \ f/s^2)(8 \ f)$$

$$P_{gas} = 336 \ lb/f^2 \quad (2)$$

Hence, using (1) and (2)

$$P_{total} = (336 + 2120) lb/f^2$$

$$P_{total} = 2456 \ lb/f^2$$

Noting that

$$P_{total} = \frac{F_{total}}{A}$$

and $\quad F_{total} = P_{total} \ A$

135

$$= (2456 \text{ lb/f}^2)(48 \text{ f}^2)$$

$$= 117888 \text{ lb}$$

● **PROBLEM** 7-8

How much pressure is needed to raise water to the top of
the Empire State Building, which is 1250 feet high?

Solution: Pressure is given by height times density
(when density is weight per volume). This is seen from the
diagram. Since pressure is force per unit area, the force
the column of water exerts is equal to its height times
the density of the material.

$$p = hw = 1250 \text{ ft} \times \frac{62.4 \text{ lb}}{\text{ft}^3} \qquad \text{or}$$

$$= \frac{78,000 \text{ lb}}{\text{ft}^2} \times \frac{1 \text{ ft}^2}{144 \text{ in.}^2} = 542 \text{ lb/in.}^2$$

● **PROBLEM** 7-9

Compute the atmospheric pressure on a day when the height of the
barometer is 76.0 cm.

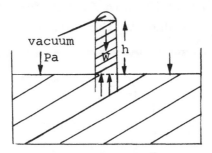

Solution: The height of the mercury column of the barometer depends
on density ρ and g as well as on the atmospheric pressure. Hence
both the density of mercury and the local acceleration of gravity must
be known. The density varies with the temperature, and g with the
latitude and elevation above sea level. All accurate barometers are
provided with a thermometer and with a table or chart from which cor-
rections for temperature and elevation can be found. Let us assume
$g = 980 \text{ cm/sec}^2$ and $p = 13.6 \text{ gm/cm}^3$. The pressure due to the atmosphere supports the weight of mercury in the column of the barometer
(see the figure). If the cross sectional area of the column is A,
then the weight of mercury in the column is

$$W = mg$$

where m is the mass of the mercury. Since

$$\text{Density}\,(\rho) \;=\; \frac{\text{mass}}{\text{volume}}$$

then

$$W = \rho(Ah)g$$

where V = Ah, h being the height of mercury in the column. Therefore

$$\frac{W}{A} = \rho gh$$

is the pressure due to the weight of the mercury acting downward. It must equal P_a for equilibrium to be maintained in the fluid. (see figure). Hence

$$P_a = \rho gh = 13.6 \frac{gm}{cm^3} \times 980 \frac{cm}{sec^2} \times 76 \text{ cm}$$

$$= 1,013,000 \frac{dynes}{cm^2}$$

(about a million dynes per square centimeter). In British engineering units,

$$76 \text{ cm} = 30 \text{ in.} = 2.5 \text{ ft,}$$

$$\rho g = 850 \frac{lb}{ft^3}$$

$$P_a = 2120 \frac{lb}{ft^2} = 14.7 \frac{lb}{in^2} \;.$$

● **PROBLEM 7-10**

The pressure in a static water pipe in the basement of an apartment house is 42 lb · in^{-2}, but four floors up it is only 20 lb · in^{-2}. What is the height between the basement and the fourth floor?

P_2=20lb-in^2

pressure due to weight of water

P_1=42lb·in^2

Solution: If A is the cross sectional area of the pipe, then the pressure $\left(P_1 = \frac{F1}{A} \text{ where } F_1 \text{ is the force exerted} \right)$ in the pipe at the basement must balance both the pressure $P_2 \left(= \frac{F_2}{A} \right)$ in the pipe at the fourth floor and the weight of the water in the column of height h (see the figure). If ρ is the density of water, then by definition

$$\rho = \frac{m}{v}$$

where m is the mass of the water in the column of volume
v = Ah. Then m = ρAh and the weight of the water is
W = mg = ρghA. Thus the pressure due to the weight of the
water is $\frac{W}{A}$ = ρgh. Hence

$$P_1 = P_2 + \rho gh$$

$$\left(P_1 - P_2\right) = (42 - 20) \text{ lb} \cdot \text{in}^{-2} = 22\frac{lb}{in^2} \times \frac{144 \text{ in}^2}{1 \text{ ft}^2}$$

$$= \rho gh = 1.94 \text{ slug} \cdot \text{ft}^{-3} \times 32 \text{ ft} \cdot \text{s}^{-2} \times h$$

$$\therefore \quad h = \frac{(22 \times 144) \text{ lb} \cdot \text{ft}^{-2}}{1.94 \text{ slug} \cdot \text{ft}^{-3} \times 32 \text{ lb} \cdot \text{ft}^{-3}} = \frac{99}{1.94} \text{ ft}$$

$$= 51.03 \text{ ft.}$$

● **PROBLEM 7-11**

In a hydraulic press the small cylinder has a diameter
of 1.0 in., while the large piston has a diameter of
8.0 in. If a force of 120 lb is applied to the small
piston, what is the force on the large piston, neglecting friction?

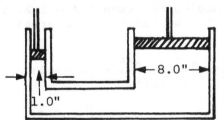

Hydraulic Press

Solution: Pascal's law states that pressure applied to
an enclosed fluid is transmitted throughout the fluid in
all directions without loss. In the hydraulic press
shown, this means that the pressure applied to the
smaller piston is transmitted unchanged to the larger
piston. Since it has a larger area, it experiences a
greater force since F = PA. Hence, we have

$$P_2 = P_1 \qquad\qquad \frac{F_2}{A_2} = \frac{F_1}{A_1}$$

$$F_2 = \frac{A_2}{A_1} F_1 = \frac{\pi (4.0 \text{ in.})^2}{\pi (0.50 \text{ in.})^2} 120 \text{ lb} = 7.7 \times 10^3 \text{ lb}$$

● **PROBLEM 7-12**

What is the diameter of the small piston of a hydraulic
press when a force of 20 pounds on it produces a force of
4 tons on the large piston whose diameter is 20 inches,

138

assuming that friction can be neglected? What is the
mechanical advantage?

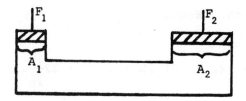

Solution: The force exerted on each piston is proportional to its area. This means:

$$\frac{F_1}{F_2} = \frac{A_1}{A_2}$$

where F_1 is the force on the small cylinder, F_2 the
force on the large cylinder, and A_1 and A_2 their respective areas. Therefore,

$$\frac{20 \text{ lbs}}{4 \text{ tons} \times 2000 \frac{\text{lbs}}{\text{ton}}} = \frac{\pi \ r^2}{\pi (10 \text{ in})^2}$$

$$r_1 = \frac{1}{2} \text{ in}^2$$

If friction is neglected, then AMA = IMA. The IMA
of a hydraulic press is the ratio of the areas of its
pistons.

$$IMA = AMA = \frac{A_2}{A_1} = \frac{\pi \ (10 \text{ in})^2}{\pi (\frac{1}{2} \text{ in})^2} = \frac{F_2}{F_1} = 400.$$

CHAPTER 8

TEMPERATURE

The amount of random motion of the particles (usually atoms and molecules) of a substance is related to the temperature *of that substance. For example, the ideal gas has a total energy <E> = 3/2 NkT where N is the number of particles and k is the Boltzmann constant. The total thermal energy of a substance hence depends on both the amount of substance (N) and the temperature (T). Defined this way, clearly it makes a difference what the units of temperature are.*

A temperature scale is usually defined by two fixed points and an assumed linear change of some property of a substance (e.g., the length of a thermometer column or the resistance of a resistance thermometer) with the temperature. For the Fahrenheit scale, the normal freezing point of water is 32°F and the normal boiling point is 212°F (at atmospheric pressure). For the Celsius scale, these same two points are 0°C and 100°C. In the Kelvin or absolute temperature scale, they are 273.15 K and 373.15 K. Most scientific formulae use the Kelvin scale where T = 0 K is the lowest possible temperature, absolute zero. Any two such temperature scales can be related using the equation

$$(y - y_1)/(x - x_1) = (y_2 - y_1)/(x_2 - x_1)$$

or y = mx + b. (See Problems 439 and 440 and refer to Figure 1.)

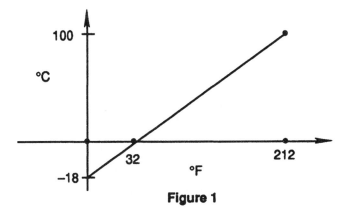

Figure 1

The ideal thermometric substance has a coefficient of linear expansion $\alpha = 1/L_0 \, \Delta L/\Delta T$ which is constant. L_0 is the length at some standard or reference temperature where α is known. This coefficient α gives the linear dependence of the length of a substance on temperature (see Figure 2). If α = constant, then one can solve a problem to find the change in length of a substance $\Delta L = \alpha L_0 \, \Delta T$. This concept is easily generalized to get the coefficient of area expansion $\delta = 1/A_0 \, \Delta A/\Delta T$ and the coefficient of volume expansion $\beta = 1/V_0 \, \Delta V/\Delta T$, If these coefficients of expansion are likewise constant, then one can solve a problem to find the change in area or volume.

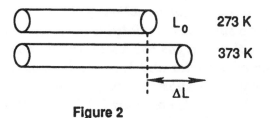

Figure 2

TEMPERATURE, THERMOMETRY, THERMAL EXPANSION

A Celsius thermometer indicates a temperature of 36.6°C. What would a Fahrenheit thermometer read at that temperature?

Solution: The relationship between the Celsius and Fahrenheit scales can be derived from a knowledge of their corresponding values at the freezing and boiling points of water. These are 0°C and 32°F for freezing and 100°C and 212°F for boiling. The temperature change between the two points is equivalent for the two scales and a temperature difference of 100 Celsius degrees equals 180 Fahrenheit degrees. Therefore one Celsius degree is $\frac{9}{5}$ as large as one Fahrenheit degree. We can then say

$$°F = \frac{9}{5}°C + B$$

where B is a constant. To find it, substitute the values known for the freezing point of water:

$$32° = \frac{9}{5} \times 0° + B = B.$$

We therefore have

$$°F = \frac{9}{5}°C + 32°.$$

For a Celsius temperature of 36.6°, the Fahrenheit temperature is

$$F = \frac{9}{5} \times 36.6° + 32° = 65.9° + 32° = 97.9°.$$

What Fahrenheit temperature corresponds to -40° Centigrade?

Solution: -40°C is 40 Centigrade degrees below the freezing point of
water. Now 40°C = 9/5(40) = 72°F since 1 Centigrade degree is 9/5
of 1 Fahrenheit degree. But 72°F below the freezing point, which is
32°F, is 40°F below 0°F (72 - 32 = 40). Thus -40°C = -40°F. This
could have been obtained directly as follows.

The formula for converting temperature in degrees Centigrade to
degrees Fahrenheit is
$$F = \frac{9}{5}°C + 32$$

If °C = -40° then

$$°C = \frac{9}{5}(-40) + 32$$

$$= -40°$$

The extremes of temperature in New York, over a period of
50 years, differ by 116 Fahrenheit degrees. Express this
range in Celsius degrees.

Solution: Fahrenheit and Celsius temperature scales are
related by

$$C° = \frac{5}{9} (F° - 32).$$

Since in this example, only a change in temperature is
being converted from one linear scale to the other, we
have

$$\Delta C° = \frac{5}{9} \Delta F°$$

Substituting, we get

$$C° = \frac{5}{9} \times 116 °F = 64.5 \ C°$$

Express 20°C and - 5°C on the Kelvin scale.

Solution: The relationship between the Celsius and Kelvin scale is

$$K° = 273° + C°$$

Therefore 20°C is

$$T = 273° + 20° = 293°K$$

and - 5°C is

$$T = 273° + (- 5°) = 268°K$$

● **PROBLEM 8-5**

A certain platinum-resistance thermometer has a resistance of 9.20 ohms when immersed in a triple-point cell. When the thermometer is placed in surroundings where its resistance becomes 12.40 ohms, what temperature will it show?

Solution: The triple-point of water occurs when water can co-exist in its three forms: liquid, gas, and solid. This can happen at a temperature of 273.16° K and a water vapor pressure of 4.58 mm-Hg. Since the resistance of a thermometer is directly proportional to the temperature, we can write

$$\frac{T_1}{R_1} = \frac{T_2}{R_2}$$

or

$$T_2 = T_1 \ (R_2/R_1)$$

$$T_2 = 273.16° \ K \left(\frac{12.40}{9.20}\right) = 368.1° \ K$$

● **PROBLEM 8-6**

A copper bar is 8.0 ft long at 68°F and has a linear expansivity of $9.4 \times 10^{-6}/F°$, What is the increase in length of the bar when it is heated to 110°F?

Solution: Change in this object's dimensions is proportional to the change in temperature and the original length. Therefore the change in length of the bar is

$$\Delta L = L_0 \alpha \ \Delta t = (8.0 \ ft)(9.4 \times 10^{-6}/F°)(110°F - 68°F)$$

$$= 0.0032 \ ft.$$

An iron steam pipe is 200 ft long at $0°C$. What will its increase in length when heated to $100°C$?

($\alpha = 10 \times 10^{-6}$ per celsius degree).

Solution: The change in length, ΔL, of a substance due to a temperature change is proportional to the change, ΔT, and to the original length, L_0, of the object:

$$\Delta L = \alpha \, L_0 \, \Delta T$$

where α is the proportionality constant and is called the coefficient of linear expension.

$L_0 = 200$ ft, $\alpha = 10 \times 10^{-6}$ per $C°$,

$T = 100°C$, $T_0 = 0°C$.

Increase in length $= \Delta L = \alpha \, L_0 \Delta T$

$$= (10 \times 10^{-6})(200)(100)$$
$$= 0.20 \text{ ft.}$$

A certain weight of alcohol has a volume of 100 cm^3 at $0°C$. What is its volume at $50°C$?

Solution: The coefficient of volume expansion of alcohol is $0.00112/°C$. Thus, the increase of 100 cubic centimeter for a $50°C$ rise is
$$\frac{0.00112}{°C} \times 100 \text{ cm}^3 \times 50°C = 5.60 \text{ cm}^3$$

The new volume is therefore 105.60 cubic centimeters.

A brass plug has a diameter of 10.000 cm at $150°C$. At what temperature will the diameter be 9.950 cm?

Solution: It is observed experimentally that when a sample is exposed to a temperature change ΔT, the sample experiences a change in length ΔL, proportional to ΔT and

L, the original length of the sample. This (approximate) result may be written as:

$$\Delta L = \alpha L \ \Delta T \qquad\qquad (1)$$

where α is the coefficient of linear thermal expansion. Solving (1) for ΔT, we find that

$$\Delta T = \frac{\Delta L}{\alpha L} \qquad\qquad (2)$$

is the change in temperature required to implement a change in length ΔL. Substituting the given data into (2), we obtain:

$$\Delta T = \frac{(9.950 - 10.00)\ \text{cm.}}{(19 \times 10^{-6}/°C)(10.000\ \text{cm})}$$

$$T = -260°\ C$$

But we want the final value of T, not ΔT. Since

$$\Delta T = T_f - T_o$$

$$T_f = \Delta T + T_o$$

$$T_f = 150°\ C - 260°\ C = -110°\ C.$$

This is the value to which the temperature must be lowered in order to shrink the diameter of the plug to 9.950 cm.

CHAPTER 9

HEAT/CALORIMETRY

| Basic Attacks and Strategies for Solving Problems in this Chapter |

One interesting fact about temperature is the concept of thermal equilibrium. This is summarized as the zeroth law of thermodynamics: if two bodies (A and B) are in thermal equilibrium with a third (C), then they are in thermal equilibrium with each other. In fact, the temperatures are then the same

$$T_A = T_B = T_C.$$

Heat is a form of energy called thermal energy. Heat always flows from a hot body to a colder one. According to the first law of thermodynamics, the change in the internal energy of a substance is equal to the amount of heat absorbed by the substance minus the amount of work done by the substance:

$$\Delta U = \Delta Q - \Delta W.$$

This is really just the conservation of energy. Heat is commonly measured in calories, where 1 cal = 4.186 J, 1 Btu = 252 cal, and 1 J = .738 ft-lb are some common conversion factors. One can solve a number of simple problems by converting calories to joules or calories to British thermal units, for example.

In many situations, the amount of work done by a system on its surroundings is zero, or can be neglected. Then, according to the first law, the change in internal energy of the system or substance of mass m is just equal to the amount of heat absorbed

$$U = Q = mc\Delta T$$

where c is the specific heat of the substance $c = 1/m \, \Delta Q/\Delta T$. If there are phase transitions, then one also has to take account of the amount of heat needed to change the phase.

For example, consider water and its three possible phases: solid, liquid, and gas as in Figure 1. The specific heat of ice (solid water) or steam (gaseous water) is $c_s = c_g = 0.5$ cal/g–K, the specific heat of liquid water is $c_1 = 1$ cal/g–K, *the* latent heat of fusion *is* $L_f = 80$ cal/g *and the* latent heat of vaporization *is* Lv = 540 cal/g. *What is the amount of heat needed to change from* m = 100 g *of ice at* $T_0 = 223$ K *to* 100 g *of steam at* T = 423 K?

To solve any problem of this type, we first find the amount of heat needed to change the temperature of the substance to the fusion or melting temperature $(T_f = 273$ K *for water)* $Q_1 = mc_s(T_f - T_0)$. *Then, one calculates the amount of heat needed to change the phase from solid to liquid* $Q_2 = mL_f$. *Next, there is an amount of heat needed to raise the temperature from the freezing temperature to the vaporization temperature* $(T_v = 373$ K *for water)* $Q_3 = mc_1(T_v - T_f)$. *Also, we must add heat to vaporize the substance* $Q_4 = mL_v$. *Finally, there is an amount of heat needed to raise the temperature from the boiling temperature to the final temperature* $Q_5 = mc_g(T - T_v)$. *The total heat is found by adding up all of the components. Clearly, one can also solve many problems which involve fewer steps and don't go through both phase transitions.*

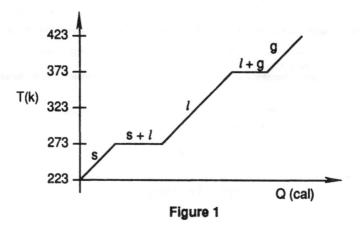

Figure 1

CHAPTER 9

HEAT/CALORIMETRY

THERMAL ENERGY

How many Btu are required to raise the temperature of 2 pounds of water from 32°F to 212°F?

Solution: The temperature rise is 180 degrees Fahrenheit. The number of Btu necessary is

$$2 \times 180° = 360 \text{ Btu},$$

since one Btu is required to raise the temperature of one pound of water one degree Fahrenheit.

A gallon of gasoline will deliver about 110,000 Btu when burned. To how many foot-pounds is this equivalent?

Solution:

$$1 \text{ Btu} = 778 \text{ foot-pounds}$$

$$110,000 \text{ Btu} = 778 \, \frac{\text{ft-lb}}{\text{Btu}} \times 110,000 \text{ Btu}$$

$$= 85,580,000 \text{ foot-pounds}.$$

How many calories of heat are required to raise 1,000 grams of water from 10°C to 100°C?

Solution: The temperature rise is 90 degrees centigrade. The number of calories needed is

$$1000 \times 90° = 90,000 \text{ calories,}$$

since one calorie is required to raise the temperature of one gram of water one degree centigrade.

● **PROBLEM** 9-4

How many calories are developed in 1.0 min in an electric heater which draws 5.0 amp when connected to a 110-volt line?

Solution: A resistance (the electric heater) which draws 5.0 amp when connected to a 110 volt line develops power (or energy per unit time) given by

$$P = \frac{\text{energy}}{\text{time}} = I^2R$$

But, by Ohm's Law, $V = IR$, hence

$$P = I(IR) = IV$$

The energy developed in 1.0 min is then

$$E = IVt = 5 \text{ amp} \times 110 \text{ volts} \times 1 \text{ min} \times \frac{60 \text{ sec}}{\text{min}}$$

$$= 33,000 \text{ Joules}$$

(The unit of time was converted to seconds to make it compatible with the MKS system being used.)

Since 1 calorie = 4.19 Joules

$$E = 33,000 \text{ Joules} \times \frac{1 \text{ cal}}{4.19 \text{ Joules}} = 7.9 \times 10^3 \text{ cal.}$$

● **PROBLEM** 9-5

A 1000-gram metal block fell through a distance of 10 meters. If all the energy of the block went into heat energy, how many units of heat energy appeared?

146

Solution:

Work is given by the force acting on the block times the distance travelled by the block, when force and distance are in the same direction. Hence,

Work = (980 × 1000)dynes × 1000 cm

= 98 × 10^7 erg.

Since 1 joule = 10^7 ergs, 98 × 10^7 ergs equals 98 joules. There are 4.19 joules/cal. Therefore,

$$\text{Heat} = \frac{98 \text{ joules}}{4.19 \text{ joules/cal}}$$

= 23.5 cal approximately.

HEAT OF FUSION

● **PROBLEM 9-6**

How much heat is required to change 25 kg of ice at -10°C to steam at 100°C?

Solution. We have 4 separate situations which we must consider in this problem. First, the ice is heated to its melting point, which involves a change in temperature. Next, the ice changes state to form water during which there is no change of temperature. Then, as heat is added the water reaches its boiling point and any further addition of heat serves only to finally change the state of the water to steam and will not raise the temperature of the boiling water. Note that the specific heat of ice is different from that of water.

Heat to raise temperature of ice to its melting point = $m_i c_i \Delta t_i$ = 25 kg(0.51 Cal/kg C°)[0 - (-10°C)] = 128 Cal.

Heat to melt ice = $m_1 L_v$ = 25 kg(80 Cal/kg) = 2000 Cal.

Heat to warm water to its boiling point = $m_w c_w \Delta t_w$ = 25 kg(1.0 Cal/kg C°)(100°C - 0°C) = 2500 Cal

Heat to vaporize water = $m_w L_v$ = 25 kg(540 Cal/kg) = 13,500

Total heat required	128 Cal
	2,000
	2,500
	14,000
	19,000 Cal

Note that in this summation 128 is negligible and may be disregarded, since there is a doubtful figure in the thousands place in 14,000.

> 500 g of lead shot at a temperature of 100° C are poured
> into a hole in a large block of ice. If the specific
> heat of lead is .03, how much ice is melted?

Solution: As the lead is poured into the hole in the
ice, the latter will melt (gain heat energy) and the
former will cool off (lose heat energy). By the principle
of conservation of energy, we may write

heat lost by lead = heat gained by ice   (1)

Now assuming that the lead doesn't undergo a phase
change during the process, we have

heat lost by lead = $m_\ell \, c_\ell \, |\Delta T|$ (2)

where m_ℓ is the mass of the lead, c_ℓ is the specific heat,
and $|\Delta T|$ is the magnitude of the temperature change ex-
perienced by the lead. Unlike the lead, the ice changes
phase during the process. Assuming that not all of the
ice is melted, the portion that is melted will be in
equilibrium with the remaining ice. Hence,

heat gained by ice = $m_i \, L$ (3)

where m_i is the mass of ice melted, and L is the heat
of fusion of ice. Then using (3) and (2) in (1)

$$m_\ell \, c_\ell \, \Delta T_\ell = m_i \, L$$

or $$m_i = \frac{m_\ell \, c_\ell \, |\Delta T_\ell|}{L}$$

$$m_i = \frac{(500 \text{ g})(.03 \text{ cal/g°C}) \, |(0°C - 100°C)|}{80 \text{ cal/g}}$$

$$m_i = 18.75 \text{ g}$$

Note that the final temperature of the lead is 0°C.
Since not all the ice is melted, the lead comes into
equilibrium with the ice and water at 0°C.

> A 200 g ice cube is placed in 500 g of water at 20°C.
> Neglecting the effects of the container, what is the
> resultant situation?

Solution: Note that a cube of ice at 0°C will lower the temperature of the water, and that for every 80 calories of heat energy absorbed by the ice, one gram will be melted without any change in temperature. If the heat given' off by the 500 g of water cooling to 0°C exceeds the amount necessary to melt the 200 g of ice, then the water will not cool to 0°C. If, however, it is less than sufficient to melt all 200 g of ice, only a fraction of the ice will be melted, and the resultant temperature will be 0°C.

The amount of heat that must be withdrawn from the water to lower its temperature to 0°C is

$$Q = mc \ \Delta T$$

where m is the mass of water, c is its specific heat, and ΔT is the change in temperature that the water experiences.

$$Q = (500 \ g)(1 \ cal/g°C)(20°C)$$

$$Q = 10000 \ cal$$

The amount of ice that 10000 calories will melt at 0°C is

$$\frac{10000}{80} = 125 \ g$$

This is less than 200 g, the original amount of ice. Therefore a 75 g block of ice finds itself floating in water at 0°C.

CALORIMETRY

● PROBLEM 9-9

A 100-gram piece of ice at 0°C is added to 400 grams of water at 30°C. Assuming we have a perfectly insulated calorimeter for this mixture, what will be its final temperature when the ice has all been melted?

Solution: The heat gained by the ice must equal the heat lost by the water. In addition energy is lost because the ice changes from the solid state to the liquid state, which requires the addition of the heat of fusion (which is 80 cal/gm for ice).

The heat gained by the ice is H_g.

$$H_g = (mass \times heat \ of \ fusion)$$

$$+ \ (mass \times specific \ heat \ of \ ice \times change \ in \ temperature)$$

$$= mL + mc\Delta t$$

$$H_g = 100 \text{ gm} \times 80 \text{ cal/gm} + 100 \text{ gm}$$
$$\times \ (1 \text{ cal/gm} \times °C) \times (t - 0°)C$$

where t is the final temperature.

The heat lost by the warm water is H_1

$$H_1 = mc\Delta t$$

$$H_1 = 400 \text{ gm} \times (1 \text{ cal/gm} \times °C) \times (30° - t°)C$$

Since heat gained must equal heat lost,

$$100 \times 8,000 \text{ cal} + 100t° \text{ cal} = 12,000 - 400t° \text{ cal}$$

whence

$$(100 + 400)t° \text{ cal} = 12,000 \text{ cal} - 8000 \text{ cal}$$

and

$$t = 8 \text{ degrees centigrade,}$$

● **PROBLEM** 9-10

Five kg of aluminum $\left(c_v = 0.91 \text{ J/gm°K.}\right)$ at 250°K. are placed in contact with 15 kg of copper $\left(c_v = 0.39 \text{ J/gm°K.}\right)$ at 375°K. If any transfer of energy to the surroundings is prevented, what will be the final temperature of the metals?

Solution: If the final temperature is T the change in the internal energy of the aluminum will be

$$\Delta U_{Al} = mc_v \Delta T$$

where m is the mass of Al, c_v is the specific heat of Al, and ΔT is the temperature change the sample experiences. Hence

$$\Delta U_{Al} = 5 \times 0.91 \ (T - 250)$$

Similarly, for Cu

$$\Delta U_{Cu} = 15 \times 0.39 \ (T - 375)$$

According to conservation of energy

$$\Delta U_{Total} = \Delta U_{Al} + \Delta U_{Cu} = 0$$

Thus $\quad 5 \times 0.91(T - 250) + 15 \times 0.39(T - 375) = 0$

from which we can calculate $T = 321°$ K.

● PROBLEM 9-11

500 g of alcohol at 75° C are poured into 500 g of water at 30° C in a 300 g glass container (c_{glass} = .14). The mixture displays a temperature of 46° C. What is the specific heat of alcohol?

Solution: When the alcohol is poured into the glass-water system, the former loses heat energy, and its temperature drops. The latter gains heat energy and its temperature rises. Hence, by the principle of conservation of energy

heat loss by alcohol = heat gained by H_2O +

heat gained by glass $\quad\quad$ (1)

In general, if a sample of mass m, composed of a substance of specific heat c, is exposed to a temperature change ΔT, it will lose or gain heat energy

$Q = m\ c\ \Delta T$.

Using this fact, we may write

heat gained by $H_2O = m_{H_2O}\ c_{H_2O}\ \Delta T_{H_2O}$

$$= (500\text{ g})(1\text{ cal/g°C})(46°C - 30°C)$$

$$= 8000\text{ cal}$$

heat gained by glass $= m_g\ c_g\ \Delta T_g$

$$= (300\text{ g})(.14\text{ cal/g°C})(46°C - 30°C)$$

$$= 672\text{ cal}$$

heat lost by alcohol $= m_a\ c_a\ \Delta T_a$

$$= (500\text{ g})(c_a)(75°C - 46°C)$$

$$= (14500\text{ cal})\ c_a$$

151

(Note that the heat gained by the alcohol is negative. Hence, the heat lost by the alcohol is positive. This is the reason why $\Delta T_a > 0$). Using these facts in (1)

$$(14500 \text{ g } ^\circ C) c_a = 8000 \text{ cal} + 672 \text{ cal} = 8672 \text{ cal}$$

or $\quad c_a = \frac{8672}{14500} \frac{cal}{g^\circ C} = .598 \frac{cal}{g^\circ C}$

● **PROBLEM 9-12**

The temperatures of three different liquids are maintained at 15°C, 20°C, and 25°C, respectively. When equal masses of the first two liquids are mixed, the final temperature is 18°C, and when equal masses of the last two liquids are mixed, the final temperature is 24°C. What temperature will be achieved by mixing equal masses of the first and the last liquid?

Solution: Let the mass used in all cases be m, and label the specific heat capacities of the liquids c_1, c_2, and c_3, respectively. The heat Q which must be supplied to a body of mass m and specific heat c to raise its temperature through an increment Δt is given by

$$Q = m c \Delta T$$

In the first mixing, the heat lost by the second liquid must equal the heat gained by the first. Thus

$$m c_2 \times (20 - 18)^\circ C = m c_1 \times (18 - 15)^\circ C$$
or
$$2c_2 = 3c_1.$$

Similarly, for the second mixing,

$$m c_3 \times (25 - 24)^\circ C = m c_2 \times (24 - 20)^\circ C$$

or $\quad c_3 = 4c_2.$

It follows that $c_3 = 6c_1$.

If the third mixing produces a final temperature t, then one applies the same argument as before, to obtain
$$m c_3 \times (25^\circ C - t) = m c_1 \times (t - 15^\circ C).$$

$$\therefore \quad 6c_1 (25^\circ C - t) = c_1 (t - 15^\circ C)$$

$$150^\circ C - 6t = t - 15^\circ C.$$

$$\therefore \quad t = \frac{165}{7} \ {}^\circ C = 23 \tfrac{4}{7} \ {}^\circ C.$$

A 1.4447-gm sample of coal is burned in an oxygen-bomb calorimeter. The rise in temperature of the bomb $\left(\text{mass } m_c\right)$ and the water surrounding it $\left(\text{mass } m_w\right)$ is 7.795 F$^\circ$ = 4.331 C$^\circ$. The water equivalent of the calorimeter $\left[= m_w + m_c\left(c_c/c_w\right)\right]$ is 2511 gm. What is the heating value of the coal sample?

Solution: The heat flowing in or out of a body of mass m with specific heat c is given by

$$Q = mc\Delta T$$

where ΔT is the change in temperature of the body. Therefore,

Heat liberated = (2511 gm)(1 cal/gm C$^\circ$)(4.331 C$^\circ$) = 10,875 cal

$$\text{Heating value} = \frac{\text{heat liberated}}{\text{mass of heating agent}} = \frac{10,875 \text{ cal}}{1.4447 \text{gm}}$$

$$= 7525 \ \frac{\text{cal}}{\text{gm}} = 13,520 \ \frac{\text{Btu}}{\text{lb}}$$

An aluminum calorimeter of mass 50 g contains 95 g of a mixture of water and ice at 0°C. When 100 g of aluminum which has been heated in a steam jacket is dropped into the mixture, the temperature rises to 5°C. Find the mass of ice originally present if the specific heat capacity of aluminum is 0.22 cal/g·C deg.

Solution: The heat lost by the cooling aluminum must equal the heat gained by the calorimeter and contents. If a mass y of ice were originally present, the total heat gained would have to include the heat acquired by the ice in melting, the heat gained by the 95 g of water in rising in temperature, and the heat gained by the calorimeter in doing likewise. The heat Q absorbed by a mass m of specific heat c as its temperature rises an amount Δt is:

$$Q = m \ c \ \Delta T$$

Also one gram of ice absorbs 80 calories of heat in changing into water. Thus,

heat gained by the aluminum
        calorimeter   = (50 g)(0.22 cal/g·C deg)
                          (5 - 0)°C

heat gained by ice as it
melts = (y)(80 cal/g)

heat gained by water = (95 g)(1 cal/g·C deg)(5 - 0)°C

heat lost by chunk of
aluminum = (100 g)(0.22 cal/g·C deg)

(100 - 5)°C

since steam has a temperature of 100°C. Thus

100 g × 0.22 cal/g·C deg × (100 - 5)°C

= y × 80 cal/g + 95 g × 1 cal/g·C deg

× (5 - 0)°C + 50 g × 0.22 cal/g·C deg × (5 - 0)°C

∴ 80 y cal/g = $\left[0.22(9500 - 250) - 95 \times 5\right]$ cal.

∴ y = $\frac{1560}{80}$ = 19.50 g.

● PROBLEM 9-15

A 100 g block of copper (s_{cu} = .095) is heated to
95°C and is then plunged quickly into 1000 g of water
at 20° C in a copper container whose mass is 700 g.
It is stirred with a copper paddle of mass 50 g until
the temperature of the water rises to a steady final
value. What is the final temperature?

Solution: The heat lost by the hot copper block as
it cools to temperature t_f

$m_{block}s_{cu}(t_{95} - t_f)$ = (100 g)(.095 cal/g)(95°C - t_f)

where s_{cu} is the specific heat of copper.

The heat gained by the water, the container, and
the paddle is

$(m_{water}s_{H_2O} + m_{container}s_{cu} + m_{paddle}s_{cu})$ $(t_f - t_{20})$

Here s_{H_2O} is the specific heat of water. Then

154

$$\left[(1000g) \ (1 \ cal/g) + (700 \ g) \ (.095 \ cal/g) + (50g) \right.$$
$$\left. (.095 \ cal/g)\right] (t_f - 20° \ C)$$

Equating the heat lost to the heat gained:

$$(100 \ g)(.095 \ cal/g)(95° \ C - t_f) = \left[(1000 \ g)(1 \ cal/g) \right.$$

$$+ (700 \ g)(0.95 \ cal/g) + (50 \ g)$$

$$\left. (.095 \ cal/g)\right] (t_f - 20° \ C)$$

Regrouping and solving for t_f:

$$(9.5)(95° \ C - t_f) = (1000 + 66.5 + 4.75)(t_f - 20° \ C)$$

$$902.5° \ C - 9.5 \ t_f = 1071.3(t_f - 20) = 1071.3t_f - 21430°C$$

$$22330° \ C = 1081t_f$$

$$t_f = \frac{22330}{1081} °C = 20.6 \ °C.$$

● **PROBLEM** 9-16

When 2.00 lb of brass at 212°F is dropped into 5.00 lb of water at 35.0°F the resulting temperature is 41.2 F. Find the specific heat of the brass. (Neglect the effect of the container.)

<u>Solution:</u> The quantity of heat Q_w added to the water is

$$Q_w = m_w c_w \Delta T_w$$

where m_w and c_w are respectively the mass and specific heat of the water, and ΔT_w is the increase in temperature of the water. Similarly, the heat Q_B lost by the brass to the water is

$$Q_B = m_B c_B \Delta T_B \ ,$$

ΔT_B being the decrease in the temperature of the brass. The heat will flow from the brass to the water until they are at the same temperature. Since the total energy of the system is conserved, the heat leaving the brass equals the heat entering the water,

$$m_B c_B \Delta T_B = m_w c_w \Delta T_w$$

$$(2.00 \ lb)(c_B)(212°F - 41.2°F) = (5.00 \ lb)(1.00 \ Btu/lbF°)(41.2°F - 35.0°F)$$

$$c_B = 0.091 \ Btu/lbF°$$

CHAPTER 10

GASES

```
Basic Attacks and Strategies for
Solving Problems in this Chapter
```

In general, gases such as the air surrounding us in a room follow the ideal gas law

$$pV = nRT.$$

In this relation, p, V, n, T are the pressure, volume, number of moles, and absolute temperature of the gas respectively. R is called the universal gas constant for any ideal gas. A gas can be considered ideal and follow the previous relation if it meets the following criteria:

— The volume of the container is very large in comparison with the size of the gas molecules. Thus, the molecules are separated from each other by a large distance compared to their individual size.

— The motion of the gas molecules is completely random. No energy is lost from collisions of molecules with one another or the walls of the container.

— The duration of the collisions are short compared to the distance travelled by the moving molecules.

Hence, if a gas fits the previous criteria, the ideal gas law can be used to analyze some of its properties. PV = nRT, says in words that, for a constant volume, the pressure of a gas is directly proportional to the absolute temperature.

CHAPTER 10

GASES

● PROBLEM 10-1

About how many molecules are there in 1 cm³ of air and what is their average distance apart?

Solution: The number of molecules in 1 cm³ can be calculated from the ideal gas equation:

$$N = \frac{pV}{kT}$$

The pressure of the air is approximately $p = 10^6$ dyne cm⁻². The temperature of the air is approximately 300° K. If V = 1 cm³,

$$N = \frac{10^6 \text{ dyne/cm}^2 \times 1 \text{ cm}^3}{(1.38 \times 10^{-16} \text{ erg/}^\circ\text{K} \times 300^\circ \text{ K})}$$

$$N = \frac{10^6 \text{ dyne/cm}^2 \times 1 \text{ cm}^3}{1.38 \times 10^{-16} \text{ dyne-cm/}^\circ\text{K} \times 300^\circ \text{ K}}$$

$$= 2.5 \times 10^{19}$$

In 1 cm³ of air there are approximately 2.5×10^{19} molecules. Imagine the 1 cm³ to be divided up into little cubes of side a, each of which contains a molecule. Then the volume of each cube is a^3. Hence, in 1 cm³, there are 1 cm³/a^3 cubes. Since there is 1 molecule in each cube, the number of cubes must equal the number of molecules in 1 cm³.

$$\frac{1 \text{ cm}^3}{a^3} = 2.5 \times 10^{19}$$

$$a^3 = \frac{1 \text{ cm}^3}{2.5 \times 10^{19}} = 4 \times 10^{-20} \text{ cm}^3$$

$$a = 3.4 \times 10^{-7} \text{ cm}$$

This is the average distance apart of the molecules and is about 20 times the size of an oxygen or nitrogen molecule.

● PROBLEM 10-2

The best vacuum that can be produced corresponds to a pressure of about 10^{-10} dyne cm^{-2} at 300° K. How many molecules remain in 1 cm^3?

Solution: We can use the ideal gas equation to calculate N, the number of molecules in the given volume:

$$N = \frac{pV}{kT}$$

$$= \frac{10^{-10} \text{ dyne/cm}^2 \times 1 \text{ cm}^3}{1.38 \times 10^{-16} \text{ dyne-cm/°K} \times 300° \text{ K}}$$

$$\approx 2,500$$

There is still a large number of molecules left.

● PROBLEM 10-3

A volume of 50 liters is filled with helium at 15° C to a pressure of 100 standard atmospheres. Assuming that the ideal gas equation is still approximately true at this high pressure, calculate approximately the mass of helium required.

Solution: From the ideal gas equation, PV = nRT (where P, V, T are the pressure, temperature and volume of the gas, R is a constant, and n is the number of moles of gas in V.) We can find the number of moles required, and from the atomic mass we can calculate the total mass required. Thus, converting all data to cgs units, we have

$$P = 100 \text{ atmospheres} \times 1.0 \times 10^6 \frac{\text{dyne}}{\text{cm}^2 \text{ atmospheres}}$$

$$= 1.0 \times 10^8 \frac{\text{dyne}}{\text{cm}^2}$$

157

$$V = 50 \text{ liters} \times 10^3 \frac{cm^3}{liter} = 5.0 \times 10^4 \ cm^3$$

$$T = 15° + 273° = 288° \ K$$

Substituting into the ideal gas equation,

$$1.0 \times 10^8 \frac{dyne}{cm^2} \ 5.0 \times 10^4 \ cm^3$$

$$= n \ \frac{8.3 \times 10^7 \ erg}{°K \ mole} \ 288° \ K$$

$$n = \frac{5 \times 10^{12} \ dyne \cdot cm}{\left(8.3 \times 10^7 \ \frac{erg}{°K \cdot mole}\right)(288° \ K)} = 2.09 \times 10^2 \text{ moles}$$

The atomic mass of helium is approximately 4 gm/mole, and since helium is a monoatomic gas, one mole of helium contains 4 gm of matter. Therefore, 210 moles of gas contains

210 moles × 4 gm/mole = 840 gm.

The helium has a mass of 840 gm.

● **PROBLEM** 10-4

Does an ideal gas get hotter or colder when it expands according to the law $pV^2 = \text{Const}$?

Solution: The ideal-gas equation states that

$$pV = nRT$$

where V is the molar volume, R is the gas constant, T is the temperature and n is the number of moles.

Therefore, for $pV^2 = \text{Const.}$, we have

$$(pV)V = \text{Const.}$$

$$nRTV = \text{Const.}$$

or

$$V = \frac{\text{Const.}}{nRT}$$

We see that as the volume increases, temperature must decrease since V is inversely proportional to T.

A certain quantity of a gas has a volume of 1200 cm^3 at 27°C. What is its volume at 127°C if its pressure remains constant?

Solution: Charles' law states that for constant pressure the volume of a gas is directly proportional to its absolute temperature (in degrees Kelvin). Converting the temperatures into Kelvin's temperatures by adding 273 we have,

$$T_1 = 27° + 273° = 300° \text{ K}$$

$$T_2 = 127° + 273° = 400° \text{ K}$$

Using Charles' law, we obtain

$$v_1 = kT_1 \quad \text{and} \quad v_2 = kT_2$$

where k is a constant.

Taking the ratio of these 2 equations, we find

$$\frac{v_2}{v_1} = \frac{T_2}{T_1}, \quad \frac{v_2}{1200 \text{ cm}^3} = \frac{400° \text{ K}}{300° \text{ K}}$$

then

$$v_2 = \frac{1200 \text{ cm}^3 \times 400° \text{ K}}{300° \text{K}} = 1600 \text{ cm}^3$$

An ideal gas is contained within a volume of 2ft^3, when the pressure is 137 atmosphere and the temperature is 27°C. What volume would be occupied by this gas if it were allowed to expand to atmospheric pressure at a temperature of 50°C?

Solution: We may use the ideal gas law to analyze the behavior of the ideal gas.

$$PV = nRT$$

where P is the pressure of a container (of volume V) of gas at an absolute temperature T. n is the number of moles of the gas and R is the universal gas constant. Since we are dealing with a fixed mass of gas, we may write

$$\frac{PV}{T} = nR = \text{constant.}$$

Alternatively,

$$\frac{P_1 V_1}{T_1} = \frac{P_2 V_2}{T_2}$$

where $\left(V_1, P_1, T_1\right)$ and $\left(V_2, P_2, T_2\right)$ are the conditions which describe the behavior of the gas before and after it expands, respectively. Since $T_1 = 273° + 27° = 300°K$ and $T_2 = 273° + 50° = 323°K$ then

$$V_2 = V_1 \frac{P_1}{P_2} \frac{T_2}{T_1} = \left(2 \times \frac{137}{1} \times \frac{323}{300}\right) ft^3 = 295 ft^3$$

• **PROBLEM** 10-7

A 5000-cm^3 container holds 4.90 gm of a gas when the pressure is 75.0 cm Hg and the temperature is 50° C. What will be the pressure if 6.00 gm of this gas is confined in a 2000-cm^3 container at 0° C?

Solution: From the ideal gas law,

$$\frac{P_1 V_1}{m_1 T_1} = \frac{P_2 V_2}{m_2 T_2}$$

Note we can use masses instead of number of moles since they are proportional.

$$\frac{P_1 \times 2000 \text{ cm}^3}{6.00 \text{ gm} \times 273° \text{ K}} = \frac{75.0 \text{ cm Hg} \times 5000 \text{ cm}^3}{4.90 \text{ gm} \times 323° \text{ K}}$$

$$P_1 = 194 \text{ cm Hg}$$

• **PROBLEM** 10-8

The pressure of the nitrogen in a constant-volume gas thermometer is 78.0 cm at 0°C. What is the temperature of a liquid in which the bulb of the thermometer is immersed when the pressure is seen to be 87.7 cm?

Solution: In a thermometer there is one physical property (thermometric property) whose change is used to indicate a change of temperature. The thermometric property of the thermometer, in this case the pressure, is taken as being directly proportional to the Kelvin temperature. Therefore

T = cp

where c is a constant of proportionality. We can then

160

state that for two temperatures on this scale, the following relationship holds:

$$\frac{T_1}{T_2} = \frac{p_1}{p_2}$$

Let T_1 be $0°C$ or $273°K$. Substituting the known values, we get

$$T_2 = \frac{T_1 p_2}{p_1} = \frac{(273°K)(87.7 \text{ cm})}{(78.0 \text{ cm})} = 307°K$$

Reconverting to the Celsius scale,

$$T_2 = 307°K - 273°K = 34°C$$

CHAPTER 11

ELECTROSTATICS

Electrostatics is the study of discrete or continuous systems of electric charge at rest. Electric charge comes in two varieties, positive and negative, the MKS *unit being the* Coulomb $\equiv$ C. *Like charges repel one another and unlike charges attract each other. Fundamental to electricity is* Coulomb's law, *which states that between every two charges, there exists an electric force given by (see Figure 1)*

$$\vec{F} = k_e q_1 q_2 / r^2 \, \hat{r}$$

where $k_e = 9.0 \times 10^9 \, N - m^2/C^2$ *is the* MKS *Coulomb force constant. If using the* CGS *system of units,* $k_e = 1$ *exactly, and the charge is measured in* esu *or electrostatic units. If there is more than one charge in the vicinity, then one must sum up the vector force from each nearby charge to get the resultant force (see VECTORS); this is called the principle of superposition.*

The electric field *acting on a charge is defined as the electric force acting on that charge divided by the magnitude of the charge. Hence, for a single point charge the electric field is given by* $\vec{E} = k_e q/r^2 \, \hat{r}$. *The electric field at a point in space due to a system of point charges can also be found using superposition, summing up the electric fields of the individual point charge. Positive charges are sources of electric field and negative charges are sinks (see Figure 2), which means that electric field vectors point away from positive charges ($\hat{r}$ direction) and towards negative charges ($-\hat{r}$ direction). Electric field lines are found by connecting electric field*

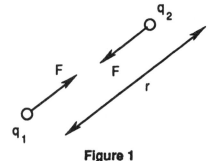

Figure 1

vectors, as shown in Figure 3.

To better understand electrostatics, one should examine how an object first obtained a charge. Most everything in nature is electrically neutral, meaning that they contain an equal amount of positive and negative charges. However, if an additional charge is added to a normally neutral object by touching the object with a charged rod, the neutral object will then have an extra positive or negative charge. This is known as charging by contact. All extra charges, now on the previously neutral object, are of the same type all positive or negative. Each charge of the same type will repel one another so they will spread out, as much as they can, throughout the object. This is why charge can be removed from an object by grounding it to the earth. The earth is very large allowing the charges to spread out far away from each other so they will leave the small charged object, making it neutral again.

In order to better study the effect of an electric charge, we can use the concept of an electrical potential. This is known to most people as voltage. Electric potential is the amount of work done when you move a single charge, let's call it a test charge, near an area with other charges. The surrounding charges will attract or repel the test charge. Therefore, work

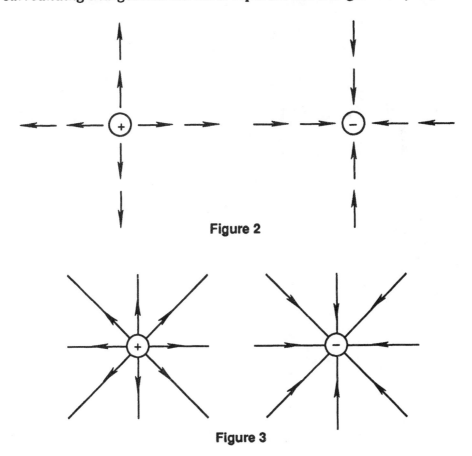

Figure 2

Figure 3

must be done to move the charge while all the other charges are acting on it. If you move the test charge from position A to position B, the amount of work done is the electrical potential or

$$V = W/Q.$$

Using the electric field, the potential difference

$$V = Va - Vb = -Ed,$$

where E is a constant electric field and d is the distance from B to A.

CHAPTER 11

FUNDAMENTAL ELECTROSTATICS

● PROBLEM 11-1

What is the electric field intensity at a point 30 centi-meters from a charge of 0.10 coulombs?

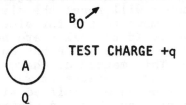

TEST CHARGE +q

Q

<u>Solution:</u> The electrostatic force on the test charge q, due to the charge Q is, by Coulomb's law, (see figure)

$$F = \frac{kQq}{r^2}$$

The electric field intensity at point B is defined as:

$$\varepsilon = \frac{F}{q} \quad \left(= \frac{kQq/r^2}{q} \right)$$

$$= \frac{kQ}{r^2}$$

In the problem we are presented with, we have

$$Q = 0.10 \text{ coulomb,}$$

$$r = 30 \text{ cm} = 3.0 \times 10^{-1} \text{ m}$$

Then

$$\epsilon = 9 \times 10^9 \frac{nt - m^2}{coulombs^2} \times \frac{0.10 \ coulombs}{(3.0 \times 10^{-1})^2 \ m^2}$$

$$= 10^{10} \ nt/coulombs$$

Show how two metallic balls that are mounted on insulating glass stands may be electrostatically charged with equal amounts but opposite sign charges.

Solution: The two metal balls are assumed to be initially uncharged and touching each other. (Any charge on them may first be removed by touching them to the earth. This will provide a path for the charge on the spheres to move to the ground). A charged piece of amber is brought near one of the balls (B) as shown in the Figure. The negative charge of the amber will repel the electrons in the metal and cause them to move to the far side of A, leaving B charged positively. If the balls are now separated, A retains a negative charge and B has an equal amount of positive charge. This method of charging is called charging by induction, because it was not necessary to touch the objects being electrified with a charged object (the amber). The charge distribution is induced by the electrical forces associated with the excess electrons present on the surface of the amber.

What is the intensity of the electric field 10 cm from a negative point charge of 500 stat-coulombs in air?

Solution: The electrostatic force on a positive test charge q' at a distance r from a charge Q is, by Coulomb's law, (in the CGS system of units)

$$\vec{F} = k \frac{Qq'}{r^2}$$

The electric field intensity E is defined as the force per unit charge, or

$$\vec{E} = \frac{\vec{F}}{q'} = \frac{kQ}{r^2}$$

$\vec{E}$ points in the direction the force on the test charge acts. In a vacuum, k = 1 (to a good approximation, k = 1 for air as well), therefore the electric field 10 cm from a point charge of 500 stat-coulomb is

$$\vec{E} = (1) \frac{500 \text{ stat-coul}}{(10 \text{ cm})^2} = 5 \text{ dyne/stat-coul} \quad \text{pointing}$$

directly toward the negative charge.

● PROBLEM 11-4

If 5 joules of work are done in moving 0.025 coulomb of positive charge from point A to point A', what is the difference in potential of the points A and A'?

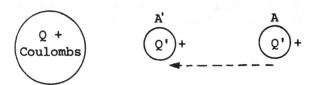

Solution: To solve this problem we use our formula for the definition of the volt, $E = \frac{W}{Q}$.

The work is 5 joules and the charge Q is 0.025 coulomb. Then the potential difference

$$E = \frac{5 \text{ joules}}{0.025 \text{ coulomb}} = 200 \text{ volts}$$

● PROBLEM 11-5

Suppose that a small, electrically charged metal ball is lowered into a metal can as illustrated in the Figure. Show how the charge is distributed when (a) the ball is inside the can but not touching and (b) after the ball touches the inside of the can.

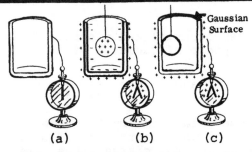

(a)   (b)   (c)

An electroscope attached to the metal can is used to detect the presence of electric charge on the outside surface of the can.

164

Solution: When the charged sphere is lowered to the position as in Figure (b), free electrons from atoms in the metal migrate to the inner surface because the positive charge of the ball exerts an attractive force. Since the net charge of the isolated can was originally zero, there is now a charge imbalance within the conductor. An excess of positive charge results. In a fraction of a second, due to transient currents within the conductor, the positive charges can be thought to mutually repel, spreading to the outside surface of the can. The outside surface then has a positive charge equal to the negative charge on the inside surface. As the ball and can touch, they form a single conductor and the electrons on the inner surface of the can move onto the metal ball and neutralize the positive charge carried by the ball. The final result is that the excess charge of the metallic sphere, placed in contact with an insulated metal can, resides entirely on its outside surface (see Figure c). This experiment provides a verification of Gauss's law. If a Gaussian surface is constructed inside the outer surface of the metal can, then there is no net charge within the surface. Then, according to Gauss's law,

$$\Phi = \frac{Q}{\varepsilon_0}$$

where Φ is the electric flux through the Gaussian surface due to the net charge Q within the surface. This then becomes $\Phi = 0$. Any excess charge must therefore reside on the outer surface of the conductor, outside the Gaussian surface.

● PROBLEM 11-6

The spherical shell of a Van de Graaff generator is to be charged to a potential of 10^6 V. Calculate the minimum radius the shell can have if the dielectric strength of air is 3×10^6 V·m^{-1}.

Solution: The potential and electric intensity at the surface of a sphere of radius R are

$$V = \frac{Q}{4\pi \varepsilon_0 R} \qquad \text{and} \qquad E = \frac{Q}{4\pi \varepsilon_0 R^2} = \frac{V}{R}$$

Note that these relations are the same as the formulae for the potential and electric field of a point charge at a distant R from the charge. Thus, the field due to a sphere of charge Q is the same as that due to a point charge of charge Q. Therefore, R = V/E. But the maximum acceptable value of E is 3×10^6 V·m^{-1} for, at any higher value of E, the air will break down, and arc discharges through the air will result. Hence, the maximum radius for the spherical shell is

$$R = \frac{10^6 \text{ V}}{3 \times 10^6 \text{ V·m}^{-1}} = \frac{1}{3} \text{ m.}$$

● **PROBLEM** 11-7

A charge of 1 C flows from a 100-V outlet through a 100-W light bulb each second. How much work is done each second by this electrical source?

Solution: The voltage, V = 100 V, and the charge, q = 1 C, are given. By definition of potential

$$V = \frac{W}{q}$$

where W is the work done in moving the charge q through a potential difference V. Then

$$W = qV = (1 \text{ C})(100 \text{ V}) = 1 \times 10^2 \text{ J}$$

Alternatively, since the power rating of the light bulb is given as 100 watt, it dissipates 100 joules of energy per second. Therefore, for each second, the source must supply 100 joules of energy (or do 100 joules of work per second) to provide the energy dissipated by the light bulb resistance.

CHAPTER 12

ELECTROSTATIC INTERACTIONS

Recall that the electric field measured at position $\vec{r}_i$ from a single point charge q_i is given by $\vec{E}_i = k_e q_i / r_i^2\, \hat{r}_i$. See Figure 1. The electric field is defined for all space around that charge. The single charge also defines a scalar potential $V_i = k_e q_i / r_i$ at position r_i. The electric potential is also defined for every point in space around that charge.

If there is another discrete charge at position $\vec{r}_j$, then that charge will experience a Columb force

$$\vec{F}_{ij} = q_j \vec{E}_i = k_e q_i q_j / r_{ij}^2\, \hat{r}_{ij}$$

where the additional subscript just makes clear the importance of the two charges. If other forces are involved such as tension, friction, weight, or resistive force, then all of these forces must be shown in a free body diagram and used with the equilibrium condition $\Sigma \vec{F} = 0$ to solve the problem. The two charges also possess an electric potential energy

$$U_{ij} = \vec{F} \cdot \vec{r} = k_e q_i q_j / r_{ij}.$$

For a set of discrete charges, one simply sums to get the total potential energy of the system $U = \Sigma U_{ij}$, where the sum only includes each pair of charges once.

Consider the situation of Figure 2, the case of $n = 2$ discrete charges producing an electric field and a scalar potential at point P in space. The electric field at point P is

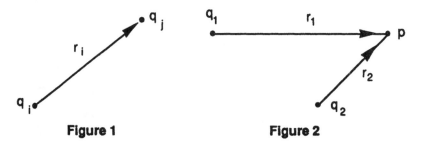

Figure 1   Figure 2

$$\vec{E} = \sum \vec{E_i} = k_e q_1 k_1^2 \hat{r}_1 + k_e q_2 k_2^2 \hat{r}_2.$$

The electric potential at point P *is* $V = \sum V_i = k_e q_1 / r_1 + k_e q_2 / r_2$. *In solving numerical problems, be sure to use the correct units and constants* $k_e = 1$ *in the CGS system and* $k_e = 9.0 \times 10^9$ *in the MKS system.*

    The exact electric field of the electric dipole configuration *(Figure 3) is given by*

$$\vec{E}(\vec{r}) = k_e q_1 k_1^2 r_1 - k_e q_2 / r_2^2 r_2.$$

If the distance between the two charges 2a *is small, then the electric field is given by* $E_r = 2 k_e p \cos \theta / r^3$ *and* $E_r = k_e p \sin \theta / r^3$, *where the dipole moment is* $p = 2qa$. *This may be calculated from the potential* $V = k_e \hat{r} \cdot \vec{p} / r^2$, *where the direction of* $\vec{p}$ *is from the negative to the positive charge.*

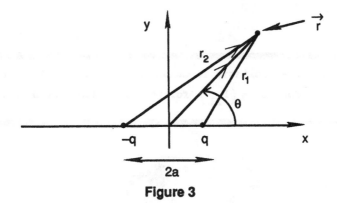

Figure 3

CHAPTER 12

ELECTROSTATIC INTERACTIONS AMONG PARTICLES AND BODIES

● **PROBLEM 12-1**

Calculate the electrostatic force on q_1 due to $q_2 (F_{12})$ and the force on q_2 due to $q_1 (F_{21})$ for the case illustrated in the figure.

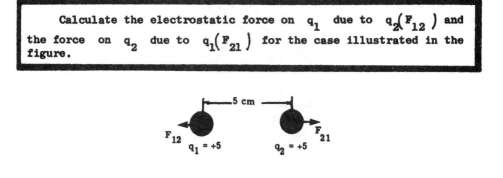

Solution: Using Coulomb's law and doing the calculation in the CGS system, of units we have

$$F_{12} = \frac{(+3 \text{ stat C})(+5 \text{ stat C})}{(5 \text{cm})^2} = +0.6 \text{ dyne (to the left)}$$

$$F_{21} = \frac{(+5 \text{ stat C})(+3 \text{ stat C})}{(5 \text{ cm})^2} = +0.6 \text{ dyne (to the right)}$$

Both forces have the same magnitude (Newton's third law for electro-statis forces) and are repulsive.

● **PROBLEM 12-2**

Calculate the resultant force, on the charge q_3 in the figure.

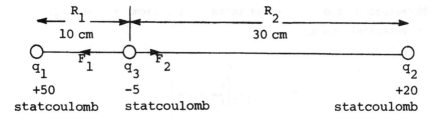

Solution: The force exerted by q_1 on q_3 is

$$F_1 = \frac{q_1 q_3}{R_1^2}$$

$$= \frac{(50)(-5)}{(10)^2} = -2.5 \text{ dyne}$$

The negative sign denotes an attractive force. The force exerted on q_3 by q_2 is

$$F_2 = \frac{q_2 q_3}{R_2^2}$$

$$= \frac{(20)(-5)}{(30)^2} = \frac{-100}{900}$$

$$= -0.111 \text{ dyne}$$

Since q_2 is positive and q_3 is negative this force is attractive and is directed to the right toward q_2.

The resultant force on q_3 is

$$F_R = F_1 - F_2 = -2.5 - (-0.111)$$

$$= -2.389 \text{ dyne}$$

and is directed to the left.

● PROBLEM 12-3

Suppose we have two charges, $q_1 = +4$ statC and $q_2 = -6$ statC, with an initial separation of $r_1 = 3$ cm. What is the change in potential energy if we increase the separation to 8 cm?

Solution: The potential energy of two point charges, q_1 and q_2, separated by a distance r_1, is given by

$$V_{12} = \frac{q_1 q_2}{r_1} \quad .$$

Therefore as the separation is increased from r_1 to r_2, the change in potential energy is

$$\Delta V_{12} = q_1 q_2 \left(\frac{1}{r_2} - \frac{1}{r_1} \right)$$

$$= (4 \text{ statC})(-6 \text{ statC}) \times \left(\frac{1}{8 \text{cm}} - \frac{1}{3 \text{cm}} \right)$$

$$= (-24 \text{ statC}^2) \left(\frac{-5 \text{cm}}{24 \text{cm}^2} \right)$$

$$= +5 \frac{\text{statC}^2}{\text{cm}}$$

$$= +5 \text{ ergs}$$

In this case, there is a net increase in the electrostatic potential energy (that is, $\Delta V_{12} > 0$) because work was done by an outside agent against the attractive electrostatic force.

● PROBLEM 12-4

What is the force between two positive charges of 100μ coulombs and 200μ coulombs, respectively, when they are separated a distance of 3 centimeters?

Solution: Using Coulomb's Law,

$$F = k \frac{Q_1 Q_2}{r^2}$$

we have

$Q_1 = 100\mu \text{ coulombs} = 10^{-4} \text{ coulombs}$

$Q_2 = 2 \times 10^{-4} \text{ coulombs}$

$k = \text{electrostatic constant} = 9 \times 10^9 \frac{(\text{nt-m}^2)}{\text{coulombs}^2}$

and $r = 3 \text{ cm} = 3 \times 10^{-2} \text{ m}$

Then $F = 9 \times 10^9 \frac{(\text{nt- m}^2)}{\text{coulombs}^2}$

$$\times \frac{10^{-4} \text{ coulombs} \times 2 \times 10^{-4} \text{ coulombs}}{(3 \times 10^{-2})^2 \text{ m}^2}$$

$$= 2 \times 10^5 \text{ nt}$$

Two equal conducting spheres of negligible size are charged with 16.0×10^{-14} C and -6.4×10^{-14} C, respectively, and are placed 20 cm apart. They are then moved to a distance of 50 cm apart. Compare the forces between them in the two positions. The spheres are connected by a thin wire. What force does each now exert on the other?

Solution: The equation giving the force between the spheres, which may be considered as point charges, is by Coulomb's law,

$$F = \frac{1}{4\pi\varepsilon_0}\frac{q_1 q_2}{r^2}$$

where q_1, q_2 are the charges on the spheres, and r is their separation. Thus

$$F_1 = \frac{1}{4\pi\varepsilon_0}\frac{q_1 q_2}{(0.2)^2 \text{ m}^2} \quad \text{and} \quad F_2 = \frac{1}{4\pi\varepsilon_0}\frac{q_1 q_2}{(0.5)^2 \text{ m}^2}$$

$$\therefore \quad \frac{F_1}{F_2} = \frac{(0.5)^2}{(0.2)^2} = 6\tfrac{1}{4}$$

If the spheres are joined by a wire, the charges, which are attracted to one another, can flow in the wire under the influence of the forces acting on them. The charges will neutralize as far as possible and $\left[16.0 \times 10^{-14} + \left(-6.4 \times 10^{-14}\right)\right] = 9.6 \times 10^{-14}$ C will be left distributed over the system. Neglecting the effect of the wire, by symmetry 4.8×10^{-14} C will reside on each sphere. The force between the two spheres is now

$$F = \frac{1}{4\pi\varepsilon_0}\frac{q^2}{r^2}$$

$$= 9 \times 10^9 \text{ N} \cdot \text{m}^2 \cdot \text{C}^{-2} \times \frac{(4.8 \times 10^{-14})^2 \text{C}^2}{(0.5)^2 \text{ m}^2}$$

$$= 8.29 \times 10^{-17} \text{ N.}$$

Compute the electric field and the electric potential at point P midway between two charges, $Q_1 = Q_2 = +5$ statC, separated by 1 m.

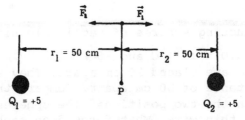

Solution: The magnitude of a test charge is +1 unit of charge. The forces on a test charge placed midway between two identical charges Q_1 and Q_2 are

$$\vec{F}_1 = \frac{Q_1}{r_1^2} \hat{r}_{12}$$

$$\vec{F}_2 = \frac{Q_2}{r_2^2} \hat{r}_{21} = \frac{-Q_2}{r_2^2} \hat{r}_{12}$$

Where the unit vector $\hat{r}_{12}$ points from Q_1 to Q_2 , r_1, r_2 are the distances between the test charge and Q_1 and Q_2, and $\vec{F}_1$ and $\vec{F}_2$ are equal in magnitude but opposite in direction. The net force is therefore zero at P;

$$F = F_1 + F_2 = 0 \ .$$

The force on a unit charge gives the electric field strength at that point, then the electric field $\vec{E}$ at P is also zero.
Although the electric field at P is zero, this does not imply that the electric potential is also zero. The total potential $\Phi_{E\ total}$ is the sum (the algebraic sum since potential is a scalar) of the potentials due to Q_1 and Q_2 :

$$\Phi_{E,1} = \frac{Q_1}{r_1} = \frac{5}{50} = 0.1 \ \text{statV}$$

$$\Phi_{E,2} = \frac{Q_2}{r_2} = \frac{5}{50} = 0.1 \ \text{statV}$$

Therefore,

$$\Phi_{E,total} = \Phi_{E,1} + \Phi_{E,2} = 0.2 \ \text{statV}$$

Notice that if either Q_1 or Q_2 is changed from +5 statC to -5 statC, the electric potential will vanish but the electric field will not. Therefore, the fact that either the field or the potential is zero in any particular case does not necessarily mean that the other quantity will also be zero; each quantity must be calculated separately.

● **PROBLEM 12-7**

Two point charges + 2q and - q are separated by a distance L. At what point on the line between their centers is the electric field zero?

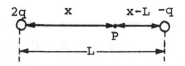

Solution: Suppose that this point is a distance x from the + 2q charge, as shown in the figure.

By definition, the electric field at a point P is

$$E = \frac{K_E q}{r^2},$$

where q is the charge producing the field, r is the distance from q to P, and K_E is a constant ($K=9\times10^9 N\cdot m^2/c^2$).

The field at x due to 2q is

$$E_+ = K_E \frac{2q}{x^2}$$

The electric field E_- due to the negative charge is

$$E_- = - K_E \frac{q}{(x - L)^2}$$

The resultant electric field at the point P is then, by the principle of superposition, equal to the sum of the fields due to the individual charges 2q and - q. Because we want E_{net} at P to be zero, we have

$$E = 0 = E_+ + E_-$$

$$= K_E \frac{2q}{x^2} - \frac{K_E q}{(x - L)^2}$$

or

$$x^2 = 2(x - L)^2$$

$$x^2 = 2x^2 - 4xL + 2L^2$$

$$x^2 - 4xL + 2xL^2 = 0$$

$$x = \frac{4L \pm \sqrt{16L^2 - 8L^2}}{2} = \frac{4L \pm \sqrt{(2\cdot4)L^2}}{2}$$

$$= 2 L \pm \sqrt{2} L$$

$$= 3.41 L \text{ or } 0.588 L$$

All we have done so far is to find two points along the axis where the fields due to +2q and - q are equal in magnitude. We have yet to take account of the vector nature of the fields. At the interior point x = 0.588 L the vectors are in the same direction, so that the fields are added. However at x = 3.41 L the field vectors are in opposite directions, so that the resultant field is zero.

An electric field is set up by two point charges q_1 and q_2, of the same magnitude (12×10^{-9} coul; see diagram) but opposite sign, as shown in the figure. What is the electric intensity at points a, b, and c?

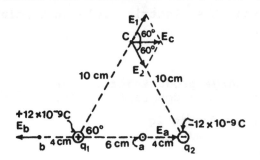

Solution: By definition, the magnitude of the electric field intensity, $\vec{E}$, is

$$E = \frac{kq}{r^2}$$

where q is the charge causing the field, and r is the distance from q to the point at which we wish to calculate $\vec{E}$. ($k = 9 \times 10^9$ N · m²/ c²). If the field is due to more than one charge, then the total field at a point is the vector sum of the fields due to each charge at that point.

At every point, the intensity due to the positive charge is directed radially away from that charge, and the intensity due to the negative charge is radially inward toward the charge.

At point a, the intensity due to each charge is directed toward the right. The resultant intensity $\vec{E}_a$ is also toward the right and its magnitude is the arithmetic sum of the individual intensities. Hence,

$$E_a = \frac{kq_1}{r_1{}^2} - \frac{kq_2}{r_2{}^2}$$

$$E_a = \left(9 \times 10^9 \frac{N \cdot m^2}{C^2}\right)\left(\frac{(12 \times 10^{-9}\ C)}{36 \times 10^{-4}\ m^2} - \frac{(-12 \times 10^{-9}\ C)}{16 \times 10^{-4}\ m^2}\right)$$

$$E_a = 9.75 \times 10^4 \text{ N/C} \qquad \text{toward the right.}$$

At point b, the intensity set up by q_1 is directed toward the left and that set up by q_2 is toward the right. The magnitude of the first is greater than that of the second because q_1 is closer to b than q_2. The resultant intensity $\vec{E}_b$ is toward the left and its magnitude is the difference between the individual intensities. Therefore,

$$E_b = - \frac{kq_1}{(4 \text{ cm})^2} - \frac{kq_2}{(14 \text{ cm})^2}$$

$$E_b = \left(- 9 \times 10^{-9} \frac{\text{N} \cdot \text{m}^2}{\text{C}^2}\right) \left[\frac{12 \times 10^{-9} \text{ C}}{16 \times 10^{-4} \text{ m}^2} - \frac{12 \times 10^{-9} \text{ C}}{196 \times 10^{-4} \text{ m}^2}\right]$$

$E_b = - 6.2 \times 10^4$ N/C, which is toward the left.

At point c, the individual intensities have the directions shown and the resultant intensity $\vec{E}_c$ is their vector sum. Note, from the figure, that the vertical components of $\vec{E}_1$ and $\vec{E}_2$ will cancel, and their horizontal components will reinforce. Hence,

$$E_c = \left|\vec{E}_1\right| \cos 60° + \left|\vec{E}_2\right| \cos 60°$$

$$= \frac{\left|\vec{E}_1\right|}{2} + \frac{\left|\vec{E}_2\right|}{2}$$

$$= \frac{1}{2}\left(\left|\frac{kq_1}{(10 \text{ cm})^2}\right|\right) + \frac{1}{2}\left(\left|\frac{kq_2}{(10 \text{ cm})^2}\right|\right)$$

$$= \frac{1}{2}\left(\left|\frac{\left[9 \times 10^{-9} \frac{\text{N} \cdot \text{m}^2}{\text{C}^2}\right](12 \times 10^{-9} \text{ C})}{100 \times 10^{-4} \text{ m}^2}\right|\right)$$

$$+ \frac{1}{2}\left(\left|\frac{\left[9 \times 10^{-9} \frac{\text{N} \cdot \text{m}^2}{\text{C}^2}\right](- 12 \times 10^{-9} \text{ C})}{100 \times 10^{-4} \text{ m}^2}\right|\right)$$

$= 1.08 \times 10^4$ N/C toward the right.

● PROBLEM 12-9

The square ABCD has a side of 10 cm length. Equal positive charges of +50 statcoulombs are placed at A and B and equal negative charges of - 100 statcoulombs are placed at C and D. Calculate the electric field at P, the center of the square.

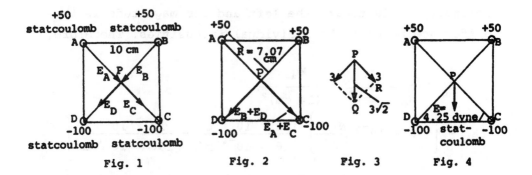

Fig. 1   Fig. 2   Fig. 3   Fig. 4

Solution: P is the point where the two diagonals AC and BD cross. Let AP = BP = CP = DP = R. Then, applying Pythagoras' theorem to the right angle triangle APB,

$$AP^2 + BP^2 = AB^2$$

$$2R^2 = 10^2 \text{ cm}^2$$

$$R^2 = 50 \text{ cm}^2$$

$$R = 7.07 \text{ cm}$$

The charge q_A at A produces a contribution E_A to the field at P given by definition as

$$E_A = \frac{q_A}{R^2}$$

$$= \frac{50 \text{ statcoul.}}{50 \text{ cm}^2}$$

Since $1 \frac{\text{statcoul}}{\text{cm}^2} = 1 \frac{\text{dyne}}{\text{statcoul}}$

$$E_A = 1 \text{ dyne per statcoulomb}$$

Since the charge at A is positive, E_A points directly away from A, (see figure). Similarly, the charge at B produces a contribution

$$E_B = 1 \text{ dyne per statcoulomb}$$

which points directly away from B. The negative charge q_C at C produces a contribution

$$E_C = \frac{q_C}{R^2}$$

$$= \frac{100 \text{ statcoul}}{50 \text{ cm}^2}$$

$$= 2 \text{ dyne per statcoulomb}$$

Since q_C is negative this contribution points directly

175

toward C. Similarly, the charge at D produces a contribution

$$E_D = 2 \text{ dyne per statcoulomb}$$

which points directly toward D.

Adding together E_A and E_C, which point in the same direction, we get a vector of magnitude 3 dyne per statcoulomb pointing toward C. Adding E_B to E_D we get a vector of magnitude 3 dyne per statcoulomb pointing toward D. This is shown in the figure. This figure also gives the triangle of vectors PQR used to add the two vectors shown. Here we are using the parallogram law of vector addition.

The resultant field $E = \vec{PQ}$ is obviously vertically downward and its magnitude is obtained from Pythagoras' theorem.

$$PQ^2 = PR^2 + RQ^2$$

$$E^2 = (3^2 + 3^2)\text{dyne}^2/\text{statcoul}^2$$

$$= 18 \text{ dyne}^2/\text{statcoul}^2$$

$$E = 4.24 \text{ dyne per statcoulomb.}$$

The resultant field at P is therefore 4.24 dyne per statcoulomb pointing in the direction $\vec{AD}$.

● **PROBLEM 12-10**

Show that, for a given dipole, V and E cannot have the same magnitude in MKS units at distances less than 2 m from the dipole. Suppose that the distance is $\sqrt{5}$ m; determine the directions along which V and E are equal in magnitude.

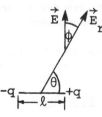

Solution: The expression for the magnitude of the potential due to a dipole is

$$V = \frac{p \cos \theta}{4\pi\epsilon_0 r^2}$$

where p is the dipole moment ($p = q\ell$) of the dipole, r is the distance from the dipole to the point at which we calculate V, and θ is as shown in the figure. $\frac{1}{4\pi\varepsilon_0}$ is a constant equal to $9 \cdot 10^9 N \cdot m^2/c^2$. The magnitude of the electric field intensity is

$$E = \frac{p}{4\pi\varepsilon_0 \, r^3} \sqrt{4 \cos^2 \theta + \sin^2 \theta}$$

If these are to be equal in magnitude,

$$\cos \theta = \frac{\sqrt{4 \cos^2 \theta + \sin^2 \theta}}{r}$$

or $\quad r^2 = \frac{4 \cos^2 \theta + \sin^2 \theta}{\cos^2 \theta} = 4 + \tan^2 \theta$

The minimum value of r^2 occurs when $\tan \theta = 0$. Hence the minimum value of r for V and E to be equal in magnitude occurs for $r^2 = 4$; that is, $r = 2$ m, in MKS units.

If $r = \sqrt{5}$ m, then V and E are equal in magnitude when

$$(\sqrt{5})^2 = \frac{4 \cos^2 \theta + \sin^2 \theta}{\cos^2 \theta}$$

$$5 \cos^2 \theta = 4 \cos^2 \theta + \sin^2 \theta$$

$$\cos^2 \theta = \sin^2 \theta$$

Thus $\theta = 45°$, $135°$, $225°$, or $315°$.

● **PROBLEM 12-11**

Suppose that all of the electrons in a gram of copper could be moved to a position 30 cm away from the copper nuclei. What would be the force of attraction between these two groups of particles?

Solution: The atomic mass of copper is 63.5. Therefore, 1 g of copper contains a number of atoms given by Avogadro's number divided by the mass of 1 mole (that is, 63.5 g):

$$\text{No. atoms} = \frac{6.02 \times 10^{23} \text{ atoms/mole}}{63.5 \text{ g/mole}} = 0.92 \times 10^{22} \text{ atoms/g}$$

The atomic number of copper is 29; in other words, each neutral copper atom contains 29 electrons. Therefore, the number of electrons in 1 g of copper is

No. electrons in 1 g = $29 \times 0.92 \times 10^{22} = 2.7 \times 10^{23}$ electrons

Thus, the total charge on the group of electrons is

$$q_e = 2.7 \times 10^{23} \times (-e)$$
$$= 2.7 \times 10^{23} \times \left(-4.8 \times 10^{-10} \text{ statC}\right)$$
$$= -1.3 \times 10^{14} \text{ statC}$$

A similar positive charge resides on the group of copper nuclei. Hence, the attractive electrostatic force (in the CGS system)

$$F_E = \frac{q_1 q_2}{r^2}$$

where r is the distance between charges q_1 and q_2. Therefore, since the 2 groups of charges with which we are concerned both have magnitude q_e

$$F_E = \frac{q_e^2}{r^2} = \frac{\left|1.3 \times 10^{14} \text{ statC}\right|^2}{(30 \text{ cm})^2}$$
$$= 1.9 \times 10^{25} \text{ dyne}$$

Because the nuclei and electrons have opposite charges, this force is attractive. It is as great as the gravitational force between the Earth and the moon!

● **PROBLEM** 12-12

A shower of protons from outer space deposits equal charges $+q$ on the earth and the moon, and the electrostatic repulsion then exactly counterbalances the gravitational attraction. How large is q?

Solution: If R is the distance between the earth and the moon, the electrostatic force in the CGS system is

$$F_e = \frac{q^2}{R^2}$$

If M_e and M_i are the masses of the earth and the moon respectively, the gravitational force is

$$F_G = \frac{GM_e M_i}{R^2}$$

Since the two forces are equal,

$$\frac{q^2}{R^2} = \frac{GM_e M_i}{R^2}$$

$$q = \sqrt{GM_e M_i}$$

CHAPTER 13

ELECTRIC CIRCUITS

> **Basic Attacks and Strategies for Solving Problems in this Chapter**

The basic element of all electric circuits is resistance, because all elements in a circuit will have some resistance. However, current technology has found some devices which have zero resistance; these are called superconductors. The use of superconductors still needs some development so we still must deal with resistance. Resistance is a slowing down of the flow of energy throughout a circuit. The flow of energy is the movement of electrons which is called a current. The potential or stored energy which will force electrons or current to flow is called the voltage. Voltage, Resistance, and Current are related by Ohms law

$$V = IR.$$

The voltage and currents in a circuit can be explained by Kirchoff's laws. Kirchoff's voltage law states that the sum of all the voltage drops around a closed loop must equal zero. Thus, for the voltages in Figure 1

$$V_1 + V_2 + V_3 + V_4 = 0.$$

Kirchoff's current law states that the sum of all the currents into a node, a point where three or more circuit elements are connected, must equal zero. Therefore, for the circuit of Figure 2, Kirchoff's law tells us that

$$I_1 + I_2 + I_3 = 0.$$

Lastly, in order to find the power used by a circuit element, the voltage

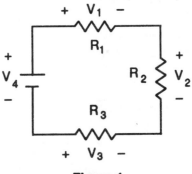

Figure 1

across that element is multiplied by the current through it or $P = VI$, where P is the power in watts.

Electric circuits or parts of electric circuits involving series resistances can be simplified by using the fact that series resistances add up $R_T = \Sigma R_i$.

For example, the resistance of three resistors in Figure 1 can be replaced by one resistor

$$R_T = R_1 + R_2 + R_3.$$

Parallel resistors in a circuit, such as those in Figure 2, will add up with the following reciprocal rule:

$$1/R_T = 1/R_1 + 1/R_2 + 1/R_3.$$

The value of a resistor is determined by its physical dimensions and a characteristic of the material called resistivity. For a conducting wire the resistance is given by

$$R = pL/A,$$

where L is the wire length and A is its cross sectional area. The resistance is temperature dependent $\Delta R = \alpha R \Delta T$ because the resistivity varies with temperature. This variation is known for different materials and is given by the factor α, the temperature coefficient of resistance.

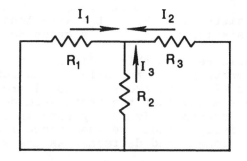

Figure 2

CHAPTER 13

ELECTRIC CIRCUITS

DC CIRCUIT ELEMENTS AND INSTRUMENTS

● PROBLEM 13-1

What is the resistance of a piece of nichrome wire 225 centimeters long with a cross-sectional area of 0.015 square centimeter?

Solution: To solve this problem we use the relation

$$R = \rho \frac{L}{A}$$

Where R = resistance   L = wire length
     ρ = resistivity   A = cross sectional area

This basic relationship tells us that resistance is directly proportional to resistivity and length and inversely proportional to cross sectional area. In the case of a wire this means that the resistance depends on the nature of the substance (which appears in the equation as the resistivity), that the resistance increases as the wire gets longer and decreases as the wire gets thicker.

The resistivity (ρ) for nichrome is 100×10^{-6} ohm-centimeter. The length is 225 centimeters, and the area is 0.015 square centimeter.

Then $R = \dfrac{10^{-4} \text{ ohm-cm} \times 225 \text{ cm}}{0.015 \text{ cm}^2} = 1.5$ ohms.

● PROBLEM 13-2

In order to find how much insulated wire he has left on a bobbin, a scientist measures the total resistance of the wire, finding it to be 5.18 Ω. He then cuts off a

200-cm length and finds the resistance of this to be 0.35 Ω. What was initially the length of wire on the bobbin?

Solution: The resistance of the wire on the bobbin is related to its length by the formula $R_0 = \rho\ell_0/A$. That

is, the resistance is directly proportional to the length (ℓ_0) of the resistor and inversely proportional to the

cross-sectional area A of the resistor. ρ is a constant of proportionality (the resistivity). The cut-off length has the same resistivity and cross-sectional area. Hence its resistance is $R = \rho\ell/A$.

$$\therefore \quad \frac{\ell_0}{\ell} = \frac{R_0}{R} \quad \text{or} \quad \ell_0 = 200 \text{ cm} \times \frac{5.18 \ \Omega}{0.35 \ \Omega} = 2960 \text{ cm}.$$

● **PROBLEM** 13-3

Find the current through the filament of a light bulb with a resistance of 240 ohms when a voltage of 120 volts is applied to the lamp.

Solution: Since we wish to find the current, we use Ohm's Law in the form

$$I = \frac{E}{R} .$$

E = 120 volts,   R = 240 ohms

Therefore

$$I = \frac{120 \text{ volts}}{240 \text{ ohms}} = 0.5 \text{ ampere}.$$

● **PROBLEM** 13-4

What is the resistance of an electric toaster if it takes a current of 5 amperes when connected to a 120-volt circuit?

Solution: This is an application of Ohm's law. Since we wish to find the resistance, we use

$$R = \frac{E}{I} .$$

E = 120 volts,   I = 5 amperes

Therefore

$$R = \frac{120 \text{ volts}}{5 \text{ amperes}} = 24 \text{ ohms}$$

What voltage will send a current of 2 amperes through a bell circuit if the resistance of the circuit is 3 ohms?

<u>Solution:</u> Since we wish to find the voltage, we use Ohm's Law in the form E = IR.

$$I = 2 \text{ amperes}, \qquad R = 3 \text{ ohms}$$

Therefore

$$E = 2 \text{ amperes} \times 3 \text{ ohm} = 6 \text{ volts}.$$

The difference of potential V_1 between the terminals of a resistor is 120 volts when there is a current I_1 of 8.00 amp in the resistor. What current will be maintained in the resistor if the difference of potential is increased to 180 volts?

<u>Solution:</u> Ohm's law indicates that the resistance R will remain the same when the potential difference is increased; hence we can write

$$R = \frac{V_1}{I_1} = \frac{120 \text{ volts}}{8.00 \text{ amp}} = 15.0 \text{ ohms}$$

$$I_2 = \frac{V_2}{R} = \frac{180 \text{ volts}}{15.0 \text{ ohms}} = 12.0 \text{ amp.}$$

How much heat is produced in 5 minutes by an electric iron which draws 5 amperes from a 120-volt line?

<u>Solution:</u> Work is given in joules by

$$W = EIt$$

To convert this to units of heat (calories) we use the conversion factor of $0.239 \frac{\text{calorie}}{\text{joule}}$. This gives us

$$H = \left(0.239 \frac{\text{calorie}}{\text{joule}}\right) EIt$$

$$E = 120 \text{ volts}, \qquad I = 5 \text{ amperes}$$

$$t = 5 \text{ minutes} = 300 \text{ seconds}$$

$$H = \left(0.239 \frac{\text{calorie}}{\text{joule}}\right) \times 120 \text{ volts}$$

$$\times 5 \text{ amperes} \times 300 \text{ seconds}$$

$$= 43,000 \text{ calories approximately.}$$

● PROBLEM 13-8

The voltage across the terminals of a resistor is 6.0 volts and an ammeter connected as in the diagram reads 1.5 amp. (a) What is the resistance of the resistor? (b) What would the current be if the potential difference were raised to 8.0 volts?

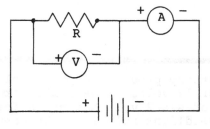

Solution:

(a) $R = \frac{V}{I} = \frac{6.0 \text{ volts}}{1.5 \text{ amp}} = 4.0 \text{ ohms}$

(b) $I = \frac{V}{R} = \frac{8.0 \text{ volts}}{4.0 \text{ ohms}} = 2.0 \text{ amp.}$

In part a of this solution we have used merely the definition of resistance. But in part b we have used Ohm's law, that is, the fact that R is constant.

182

If the cost of electricity is 5 cents per kilowatt-hour, what does it cost to run a motor 2 hours if the motor draws 5 amperes from a 120-volt line?

Solution:

$$E = 120 \text{ volts}, \quad I = 5 \text{ amp}, \quad t = 2 \text{ hours}$$

Work = Power × Time = EI × t

W = EIt = 120 volts × 5 amp × 2 hr

= 1200 watt-hours = 1.2 kw-hr

This is the work done by the motor in the given time period. Multiplying this by the cost per hour we have:

Cost = 1.2 kw-hr × 5¢/kw-hr = 6¢.

A car battery supplies a current I of 50 amp to the starter motor. How much charge passes through the starter in ½ min?

Solution: Current (I) is defined as the net amount of charge, Q, passing a point per unit time. Therefore,

Q = It = (50 amp)(30 sec) = 1500 coul.

An automobile battery produces a potential difference (or "voltage") of 12 volts between its terminals. (It really consists of six 2 volt batteries following one after the other.) A headlight bulb is to be connected directly across the terminals of the battery and dissipate 40 watts of joule heat. What current will it draw and what must its resistance be?

Solution. To find the current, we use the formula P = IV where P is the power dissipated (40 watts), I is the current, and V is the voltage.
    Therefore,

$$I = \frac{P}{V} = \frac{40 \text{ watts}}{12 \text{ volts}} = \frac{40 \text{ joules/sec}}{12 \text{ joules/coulomb}} = 3.33 \text{ coulombs/sec}$$

= 3.33 amps.

The bulb draws 3.33 amps from the battery.
From Ohm's law

$$i = \frac{V}{R}$$

$$R = \frac{V}{I}$$

R ohms = $\frac{12 \text{ volts}}{3.33 \text{ amps}}$

R = 3.6 ohms.

The resistance of the bulb must be 3.6 ohms.

We may also compute the resistance using the formula

$P = \frac{V^2}{R}$. Therefore $R = \frac{V^2}{P} = \frac{(12)^2}{40} = 3.6$ ohms.

This second formula for power may be obtained from the first as follows:

$$P = iV$$

but from Ohm's Law $i = \frac{V}{R}$. Therefore $P = \frac{(V)(V)}{R} = \frac{V^2}{R}$.

● **PROBLEM 13-12**

An electric kettle contains 2 liters of water which it heats from 20°C to boiling point in 5 min. The supply voltage is 200 V and a kWh (kilowatt-hour) unit costs 2 cents. Calculate (a) the power consumed (assume that heat losses are negligible), (b) the cost of using the kettle under these conditions six times, (c) the resistance of the heating element, and (d) the current in the element.

Solution: The heat gained by the water in being raised to the boiling point is given by the expression H = $mc(t_2 - t_1)$ where c is the specific heat of water (the amount of heat required to raise the temperature of the substance 1°C), m is the mass of the water being heated and $(t_2 - t_1)$ is the temperature difference before and after heating.

(a) H = 2×10^3 cm^3 × 1 g·cm^{-3} × 4.18 J·g^{-1}·C deg^{-1}

× (100 - 20)C deg = 6.69×10^5 J.

184

Since heat losses are neglected, the conservation of energy requires that the heat energy generated be equal to the electrical energy consumed by the kettle.

Thus the electric energy E = 6.69 × 10^5 J.

The power is the energy consumed per second, which is thus

$$P = \frac{H}{\tau} = \frac{6.69 \times 10^5 \text{ J}}{5 \times 60 \text{ s}} = 2.23 \times 10^3 \text{ J} \cdot \text{s}^{-1}$$

$$= 2.23 \text{ kW.} \qquad \text{(for IW = 1 J} \cdot \text{s}^{-1}\text{.)}$$

(b) The kettle uses 2.23 kW for 5 min each time the water is boiled. When it is used six times, 2.23 kW is used for 30 min = ½ hr. The cost is thus

2.23 kW × ½ hr × 2 cents · kWh^{-1} = 2.23 cents.

(c) The power P consumed is 2.23 kW and the supply voltage V is 200 V. But P = V^2/R, where R is the resistance of the kettle's heating element.

$$R = \frac{V^2}{P} = \frac{200^2 v^2}{2.23 \times 10^3 \text{ W}} = 17.9 \ \Omega.$$

(d) But one may also write the power as P = IV, where I is the current through the heating element.

$$I = \frac{P}{V} = \frac{2.23 \times 10^3 \text{ W}}{200 \text{ V}} = 11.2 \text{ A.}$$

● **PROBLEM 13-13**

A 12-V automobile battery supplies 20C of charge in 5 s to a stereo tape player. What is the electical current flowing into the device and how much work is done by the battery.

Solution: The charge supplied by the battery, q = 20 C, and the time interval, t = 5 s, are given. The current is, by definition,

$$I = \frac{q}{t} = \frac{20 \text{ C}}{5 \text{ s}} = 4 \text{ A}$$

The potential of the battery, V = 12 V, is also given. However, the potential difference between two points is the work required to move a unit charge from the point at lower potential to that of higher potential. Or

$$V = \frac{W}{q}$$

Then $W = Vq = (12 \text{ V})(20 \text{ C}) = 2.4 \times 10^2 \text{ J}$

The work done by the automobile battery is 240 J.

● **PROBLEM** 13-14

A dynamo driven by a steam engine which uses 10^3 kg of coal per day produces a current I = 200 A at an emf V of 240 V. What is the efficiency of the system if the calorific value of coal is 6.6×10^3 cal·g^{-1}?

Solution: The energy supplied by the coal per second is equal to the product of the calorific value of coal and the mass of coal used, divided by the time it takes to burn the coal. Hence,

$$E_0 = \frac{6.6 \times 10^3 \text{ cal·g}^{-1} \times 10^6 \text{ g}}{24 \times 60 \times 60 \text{ s}} = \frac{4.2 \times 6.6 \times 10^9}{24 \times 60 \times 60} \text{ J·s}^{-1}$$

$$= 3.2 \times 10^5 \text{ W}.$$

The electric power supplied by the dynamo is

$$P = IV = 200 \text{ A} \times 240 \text{ V} = 4.8 \times 10^4 \text{ W}$$

The efficiency of the system is thus

$$\frac{P}{E_0} \times 100\% = \frac{4.8 \times 10^4}{3.2 \times 10^5} \% = 15\%.$$

RESISTANCE-TEMPERATURE CHARACTERISTICS

● **PROBLEM** 13-15

The resistance of a copper wire 2500 cm long and 0.090 cm in diameter is 0.67 ohm at 20°C. What is the resistivity of copper at this temperature?

Solution: The resistivity of a conductor is directly proportional to the cross-sectional area A and its resistance, and inversely proportional to its length ℓ. Therefore, knowing the resistance, we have

$$\rho = R \frac{A}{\ell} = \frac{0.67 \text{ ohm}}{2500 \text{ cm}} \frac{\pi (0.090 \text{ cm})^2}{4}$$

$$= 1.7 \times 10^{-6} \text{ ohm-cm}$$

Resistivity is a characteristic of a material as a whole, rather than of a particular piece of it. For a given temperature, it is constant for the particular medium, as opposed to resistance which depends on the dimensions of the piece.

● PROBLEM 13-16

A copper coil has a resistance of 100 ohms at 20°C. What is its resistance at 50°C if the temperature coefficient of resistivity for copper is 0.0038 ohm per ohm per degree centigrade?

Solution: We are given the resistance of a wire at one temperature, and are asked to calculate its resistance at another temperature given the temperature coefficient of resistivity. The new resistance is given by the old resistance plus a factor proportional to the old resistance, the temperature change, and the constant coefficient for the substance.

R_{20} = 100 ohms, t = 50°C, α = 0.0038 ohm/ohm/°C.

Using $R_t = R_{20} + R_{20} \alpha(t - 20°C)$, we have

R_t = 100 ohms + 100 ohms × 0.0038 ohm/ohm/°C (50° C - 20°C)

= 100 ohms + 11.4 ohms

= 111 ohms, approximately.

● PROBLEM 13-17

The total resistance of a wire wound rheostat when "cold" is 300 ohms. In use it experiences a rise in temperature. How does the current which it draws on a 100 volt line after its temperature has risen 50° C, compare with that drawn at the start when it is "cold"?

Solution: This problem involves a combination of Ohm's Law and the dependence of resistance upon temperature.

$I = \dfrac{V}{R}$ (Ohm's Law)

But $R = R_0(1 + \alpha t)$ where α for metals is .0038/°C

(approx). That is the resistance of the metal increases at a rate directly proportional to the increase in temperature.

When "cold" R_1 = 300 ohms.

$$\therefore \ I_1 = \frac{V}{R_1} = \frac{100}{300} = .333 \text{ ampere}$$

But when "hot" $R_2 = 300[1 + .0038(50)]$

or $R_2 - 300 = 300(.0038)(50)$

$$= 3 \times 3.8 \times 5 \times 10^0 = 57$$

$$\therefore \ R_2 = 357$$

And $I_2 = \dfrac{V}{R_2} = \dfrac{100}{357} = .280 \text{ ampere}$

Thus $I_2 = \dfrac{.280}{.333} I_1 = .84 \ I_1 \text{ (approx).}$

● **PROBLEM 13-18**

A silver wire has a resistance of 1.25 ohms at 0°C and a temperature coefficient of resistance of 0.00375/C°. To what temperature must the wire be raised to double the resistance?

<u>Solution:</u> The change in resistance $R_t - R_0$ is directly proportional to the change in temperature and the original resistance R_0. It is known from experiment that
$$\Delta R = \alpha R_0 \Delta t.$$
Substituting values, we have

$$\Delta t = \frac{\Delta R}{\alpha R_0} = \frac{R_t - R_0}{\alpha R_0}$$

$$t - 0° \ C = \frac{(2.50 - 1.25) \text{ ohms}}{0.00375/C° \times 1.25 \text{ ohms}}$$

since $R_t = 2R_0 = 2(1.25) = 2.50$

$t = 266°C.$

RESISTOR NETWORKS

● **PROBLEM 13-19**

Find the total resistance in the circuit in the figure.

<u>Solution:</u> This problem is simplified by observing that the circuit can be resolved into its component parts. Since resistors R_1 and R_2 are in series, we may take

their sum and consider it as a single resistor (see diagram) with resistance R.

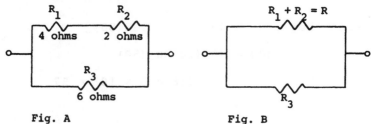

Fig. A   Fig. B

Combining the first two resistances,

$$R = R_1 + R_2 = 4 \text{ ohms} + 2 \text{ ohms} = 6 \text{ ohms}$$

Now we have a simple parallel circuit and can easily solve for the total resistance of the circuit. Letting R' be the total resistance of the circuit we obtain:

$$\frac{1}{R'} = \frac{1}{R} + \frac{1}{R_3} = \frac{1}{6 \text{ ohms}} + \frac{1}{6 \text{ ohms}} = \frac{1}{3 \text{ ohms}}$$

whence
$$R' = 3 \text{ ohms}.$$

● **PROBLEM** 13-20

Consider the simple circuit in the figure grounded at point b. Compute the potentials of points a and c.

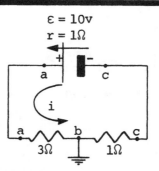

Solution. In this circuit point B is grounded. When dealing with circuits, the grounded point is considered as zero potential and we express potentials relative to this reference level. The direction of current flow is counterclockwise so we will traverse the circuit in this direction. Kirchoff's loop theorem states that the sum of the changes in potential around any closed loop must be equal to zero. Note that this is just a statement of conservation of energy. Applying this theorem gives the following equation:

$$\varepsilon - ir - i(3 \text{ ohms}) - i(1 \text{ ohms}) = 0$$

Observe that although there is 10 volts across the battery by itself, when it is connected to the circuit its internal

189

resistance, r, causes a potential drop equal to -ir.

Substituting 1Ω for r and solving for i, yields 2 amperes as the value for the current.

Since the potential at point b is zero, we start there and proceed to points a or c to find V_a or V_c respectively.

We may go in either direction so long as we take into account the proper sign for the current (negative if counterclockwise, positive if clockwise). Proceeding counterclockwise from b to c yields:

$$V_c = -i(1\Omega) = -2 \text{ volts}$$

Proceeding clockwise from b to a and remembering that in this direction the current is -2 amp, we see that
$V_a = -(-2)(3) = +6 \text{ volts}.$

That is, point a is 6 volts above ground and point c is 2 volts below ground. The potential difference V_{ac} can now be found by subtraction

$$V_{ac} = V_a - V_c = 6 - (-2) = +8 \text{ volts}$$

● **PROBLEM** 13-21

A bell circuit consists of 150 feet of No. 18 wire which has a resistance of 1 ohm, a bell which has a resistance of 5 ohms, and a battery of two dry cells, each having an emf of 1.5 volts. What is the current through the circuit, assuming that the resistance of the battery is negligible?

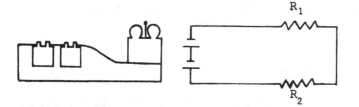

(a) Actual Circuit   (b) Schematic Diagram

Solution: It may be of assistance to draw a diagram (see diagram). Note that

R_1 = resistance of wire (which is represented in the schematic diagram as a resistor in the circuit).

R_2 = resistance of bell in the schematic diagram.

Since the bell and the wire are in series, the total resistance is the sum of 5 ohms and 1 ohm; that is, 6 ohms.

From Ohm's law:

$$I = \frac{E}{R} = \frac{3 \text{ volts}}{6 \text{ ohms}} = 0.5 \text{ amp.}$$

● **PROBLEM 13-22**

A galvanometer has a resistance of 5 ohms with 100 divisions on its face. Maximum deflection of the meter occurs when the current through it is 2 ma.   What series resistance should be used with the galvanometer in order to employ it as a voltmeter of range 0 to 200 volts?

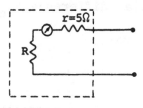

Voltmeter consisting of a galvanometer and resistor in series

Solution: The maximum voltage we need to read is 200 volts. We therefore want maximum deflection to occur when the voltage across the voltmeter is 200 volts. This occurs when the current through the galvanometer is 2ma or 0.002 amp. To accomplish this, we can put a resistor R in series with the galvanometer. The total resistance in the circuit, R + r (see figure), must then be, by Ohm's Law,

$$R + r = \frac{V}{I} = \frac{200 \text{ volts}}{0.002 \text{ amp}} = 100,000 \text{ ohms}$$

and   R = 100,000 - 5 = 99,995 ohms

Since the voltage across the terminals is proportional to the current flowing through the galvanometer, each division of the meter corresponds to

$$\frac{200 \text{ volts}}{100 \text{ divisions}} = 2 \text{ volts/division.}$$

● **PROBLEM 13-23**

Compute the resistance across the terminals in figure A.

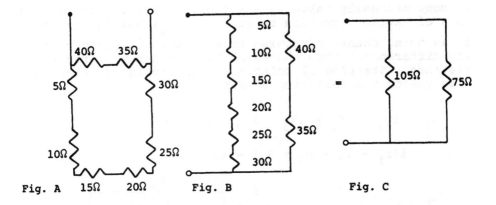

Fig. A 15Ω 20Ω   Fig. B   Fig. C

Solution: First we regroup the resistors to simplify our calculations. We are allowed to do this as long as we do not change the orientation of the resistors with respect to each other and to the terminals. An equivalent arrangement is shown in figure B.

In figure C we sum the resistors in series. We are left with two resistances in parallel which we find from the formula:

$$\frac{1}{R_T} = \frac{1}{R_1} + \frac{1}{R_2} = \frac{1}{105} + \frac{1}{75} = \frac{12}{525} = \frac{4}{173}$$

where R_T is the total resistance across the terminals. Thus:

$$R_T = \frac{173}{4} = 43.25$$

● **PROBLEM 13-24**

In the figure ε_1 = 12 volts, r_1 = 0.2 ohm; ε_2 = 6 volts, r_2 = 0.1 ohm; R_3 = 1.4 ohms; R_4 = 2.3 ohms; compute (a) the current in the circuit, in magnitude and direction, and (b) the potential difference V_{ac}.

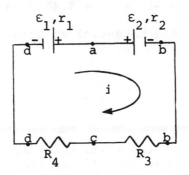

Solution: (a) From conservation of energy we know that the sum of the changes in potential (voltage changes) around any closed loop must equal zero. Therefore the current (which

192

is conventionally taken as the flow of positive charge) is
in a clockwise direction because $\epsilon_1 > \epsilon_2$; but let us choose
it as going counterclockwise to show that it doesn't make
any difference. Note that each battery has an internal resistance. Starting at point A and traversing counterclockwise yields the following equation:

$$-\epsilon_1 - ir_1 - iR_4 - iR_3 - ir_2 + \epsilon_2 = 0$$

$$i(r_1 + r_2 + R_3 + R_4) = \epsilon_2 - \epsilon_1$$

$$i = \frac{\epsilon_2 - \epsilon_1}{(r_1 + r_2 + R_3 + R_4)} = \frac{-6}{4}$$

$$= -1.5 \text{ amp.}$$

The negative value for the current merely means that we
chose the wrong direction (i.e., the current flows clockwise)
   (b) We may use either a clockwise or counterclockwise
path from point A to point C to find V_{AC}. Since we are only
concerned with differences in potential, let us assume a
zero potential of A and then traverse the loop clockwise
from A to C. Taking into account the clockwise flow of current this yields,

$$-\epsilon_2 - ir_2 - iR_3 = -6 - (1.5)(.1) - (1.5)(1.4)$$

$$= -8.25 \text{ volts}$$

This means that the potential is 8.25 volts lower at point
C than at point A. If we go from point A to point C in a
counterclockwise direction we must remember to use the
negative value for the current. This path yields:

$$-\epsilon_1 - ir_1 - iR_4 = -12 - (-1.5)(.2) - (-1.5)(2.3)$$

$$= -12 + .3 + 3.45 = -8.25 \text{ volts.}$$

Again, we see that the potential at point C is 8.25 volts
lower than that at point A.

● **PROBLEM 13-25**

Two cells, one of emf 1.2 V and internal resistance
0.5 Ω, the other of emf 2 V and internal resistance
0.1 Ω, are connected in parallel as shown in the
figure and the combination connected in series with
an external resistance of 5 Ω. What current passes
through this external resistance?

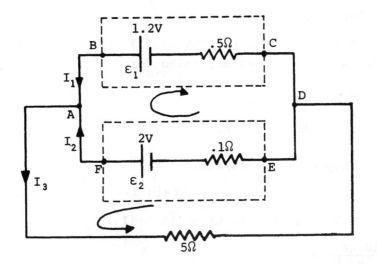

The diagram is labeled and current values have been inserted in each part of the circuit. Applying Kirchhoff's current law to point A, we have

$$I_1 + I_2 = I_3 \qquad\qquad\qquad (1)$$

Note that in the figure, boxes have been drawn representing the 2 batteries in the circuit. The given voltages, ε_1 and ε_2, are the voltages of the batteries assuming zero internal resistance. (The terminal voltages are V_{BC} and V_{FE}, not ε_1 and ε_2.)

Applying Kirchhoff's voltage law to the closed circuit containing both cells, and then to the closed circuit through the lower cell and the external resistance (see figure for the directions in which the loops are traversed) we have

$$+ \varepsilon_2 - \varepsilon_1 + (.5 \ \Omega)I_1 - (.1 \ \Omega)(I_2) = 0$$

and $\quad + \varepsilon_2 - (5 \ \Omega)(I_3) - (.1 \ \Omega)(I_2) = 0$

Hence, $\quad \varepsilon_2 - \varepsilon_1 = (2 - 1.2)V$

$$= (.1 \ \Omega)(I_2) - (.5 \ \Omega)(I_1)$$

$$\varepsilon_2 = 2V = (5 \ \Omega)(I_3) + (.1 \ \Omega)(I_2)$$

or, upon multiplication of both sides of each equation by 10,

$$8 \ V = (1 \ \Omega)(I_2) - (5 \ \Omega)(I_1) \qquad\qquad (2)$$

$$20 \ V = (1 \ \Omega)(I_2) + (50 \ \Omega)(I_3) \qquad\qquad (3)$$

Substituting equation (1) in (3)

$$20 \ V = (1 \ \Omega)(I_2) + (50 \ \Omega)(I_1 + I_2)$$

$$20 \ V = (51 \ \Omega)(I_2) + (50 \ \Omega)I_1 \qquad\qquad (4)$$

194

Multiplying (2) by 10,

$$80 \text{ V} = (10 \text{ } \Omega)(I_2) - (50 \text{ } \Omega)(I_1) \qquad (5)$$

Adding (4) and (5), we may solve for I_2

$$100 \text{ V} = (61 \text{ } \Omega)I_2$$

and

$$I_2 = \frac{100 \text{ V}}{61 \text{ } \Omega} = 1.64 \text{ A} \qquad (6)$$

since 1 ampere = 1 volt/ohm.

Substituting (6) in (3), we obtain I_3,

$$20 \text{ V} = (1 \text{ } \Omega)(1.64 \text{ A}) + (50 \text{ } \Omega)(I_3)$$

$$\frac{18.46 \text{ V}}{50 \text{ } \Omega} = I_3$$

or

$$I_3 \approx .37 \text{ A.}$$

● **PROBLEM 13-26**

Two devices, whose resistances are 2.8 and 3.5Ω, respectively, are connected in series to a 12-V battery. Compute the
current in either device and the potential applied to each.

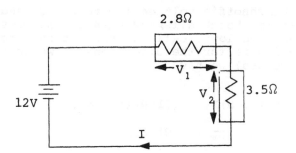

Series Resistance

<u>Solution</u>: Resistances in series add. The equivalent re-
sistance of the two devices is given by

$$R = 2.8\Omega + 3.5\Omega = 6.3\Omega.$$

The current supplied by the battery can be computed using
Ohm's law,

$$I = \frac{V}{R} = \frac{12 \text{ V}}{6.3\Omega} = 1.9 \text{ A.}$$

This current I flows through both devices since they are
in series. Ohm's law may be applied to calculate the
potential applied to each device: (see figure)

$$V_1 = IR_1 = (1.9 \text{ A})(2.8\Omega) = 5.3V$$

$$V_2 = IR_2 = (1.9 \text{ A})(3.5\Omega) = 6.7V.$$

Note that the sum of these potentials is equal to the battery potential, 12V.

● PROBLEM 13-27

Suppose that three devices are connected in parallel to a 12-V battery. Let the resistances of the devices be $R_1 = 2\Omega$, $R_2 = 3\Omega$, and $R_3 = 4\Omega$. What current is supplied by the battery and what is the current in each device?

Solution: Since the resistors are in parallel, we have for the equivalent resistance R,

$$\frac{1}{R} = \frac{1}{R_1} + \frac{1}{R_2} + \frac{1}{R_3} = \frac{1}{2\Omega} + \frac{1}{3\Omega} + \frac{1}{4\Omega} = \frac{13}{12}\Omega^{-1}.$$

The equivalent resistance, therefore, is

$$R = \frac{12}{13}\Omega = 0.92\Omega.$$

The voltage across each device is 12 volts since they are in parallel to the battery. Therefore, using Ohm's law and the figure,

$$I_1 = \frac{V}{R_1} = \frac{12 \text{ V}}{2\Omega} = 6 \text{ amp}$$

$$I_2 = \frac{V}{R_2} = \frac{12 \text{ V}}{3\Omega} = 4 \text{ amp}$$

$$I_3 = \frac{V}{R_3} = \frac{12 \text{ V}}{4\Omega} = 3 \text{ amp}.$$

The current supplied by the battery is found by applying Kirchoff's node equation at point A. Hence

$$I = I_1 + I_2 + I_3 = (6 + 4 + 3) \text{ amp}$$

$$I = 13 \text{ amp}.$$

Compare the cost of operating 3 lamps in series and
in parallel on a 115 volt circuit, if each lamp has a
resistance of 100 ohms.

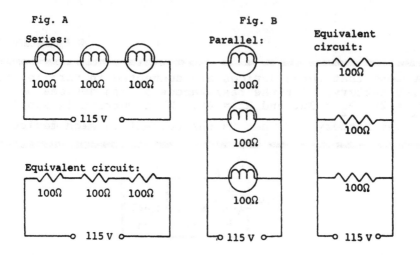

Solution: We calculate the cost of operation for each
configuration (see figures) by calculating the net power
expended by each circuit. Assuming both circuits run for
the same time, the energy used by each can then be found.
The circuit using less energy is the more economical.

For the series circuit, the same current I flows
through each lamp. Each one then uses power

$$P = I^2 R$$

where R is the lamp resistance. Since the resistance
of each lamp is the same, the net power expended in the
series circuit is

$$P_{net} = 3I^2 R \tag{1}$$

Looking at the equivalent circuit in figure (a),
we realize that the net resistance of the series configuration is

$$R_{net} = 3R$$

By Ohm's Law, the current in this circuit is

$$I = \frac{V}{R_{net}} = \frac{V}{3R} \tag{2}$$

Using (2) in (1)

$$P_{net} = \frac{3}{9} \frac{V^2}{R^2} R = \frac{V^2}{3R}$$

Using the given data, the series configuration uses power

$$P_{net} = \frac{(115 \text{ V})^2}{300 \text{ }\Omega} = 44.1 \text{ Watts}$$

For the parallel connection, each lamp has the same voltage V applied across it. Each one uses power

$$P' = \frac{V^2}{R}$$

where R is the lamp resistance. Since all the resistances are equal, the net power expended by the parallel circuit is

$$P'_{net} = \frac{3V^2}{R} = \frac{3(115 \text{ V})^2}{100 \text{ }\Omega} = 396.75 \text{ Watts}$$

If both circuits operate for a time τ, the energies used are

$$E_{series} = P_{net} \text{ } \tau = (44.1 \text{ Watts})\tau$$

$$E_{parallel} = P'_{net} \text{ } \tau = (396.75 \text{ Watts})\tau$$

Hence, the series combination is cheaper to run.

● PROBLEM 13-29

Determine the current in each of the resistors in figure A.

Fig. A

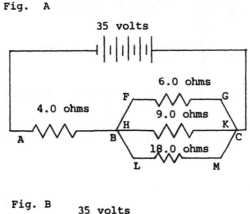

Fig. B

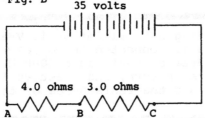

Solution: We find the resistance between points B and C (R_{BC}) by using the relation for resistors R_1, R_2,... in parallel (see figure (A)).

$$\frac{1}{R_{Total}} = \frac{1}{R_1} + \frac{1}{R_2} + \ldots$$

$$\frac{1}{R_{BC}} = \frac{1}{6.0 \text{ ohms}} + \frac{1}{9.0 \text{ ohms}} + \frac{1}{18.0 \text{ ohms}}$$

$$= \frac{6.0}{18.0 \text{ ohms}}$$

$$R_{BC} = \frac{18.0}{6.0} \text{ ohms} = 3.0 \text{ ohms}$$

Using the formula for resistors in series,

$$R_{Total} = R_1 + R_2 + \ldots ,$$

we find the resistance between points A and C in the circuit. (see figure (B))

$$R_{AC} = R_{AB} + R_{BC} = 4.0 \text{ ohms} + 3.0 \text{ ohms}$$

$$= 7.0 \text{ ohms}$$

The current I_t in the circuit is obtained from Ohm's Law

$$I_t = \frac{V_{AC}}{R_{AC}} = \frac{35 \text{ volts}}{7.0 \text{ ohms}} = 5.0 \text{ amp.}$$

The current through each individual resistor is, by Ohm's Law, equal to the voltage across the resistor divided by its resistance. Hence

$$I_{FG} = \frac{V_{FG}}{R_{FG}} = \frac{15 \text{ volts}}{6.0 \text{ ohms}} = 2.5 \text{ amp}$$

$$I_{HK} = \frac{V_{HK}}{R_{HK}} = \frac{15 \text{ volts}}{9.0 \text{ ohms}} = 1.7 \text{ amp}$$

$$I_{LM} = \frac{V_{LM}}{R_{LM}} = \frac{15 \text{ volts}}{18.0 \text{ ohms}} = 0.83 \text{ amp.}$$

Note that $I_t = I_{FG} + I_{HK} + I_{LM}$ by Kirchoff's Current Law.

$$I_t = (2.5 + 1.7 + 0.8) \text{ amp} = 5.0 \text{ amp.}$$

● **PROBLEM 13-30**

A bank of cells having a total emf of 12 V and negligible internal resistance is connected in series with two resistors. A voltmeter of resistance 5000 Ω is connected across the resistors in turn, and measures 4 V and 6 V, respectively. What are the resistances of the two resistors?

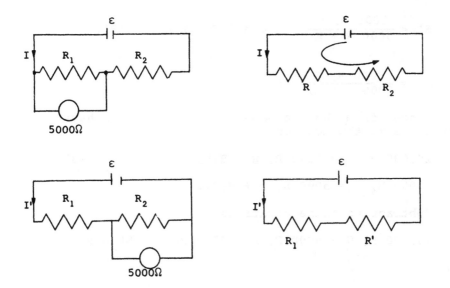

<u>Solution:</u> The voltmeter is connected across R_1 as in diagram (a) and since the resistance of the voltmeter is in parallel with R_1 the circuit is equivalent to that shown in diagram (b), where

$$\frac{1}{R} = \frac{1}{R_1} + \frac{1}{5000\ \Omega} = \frac{5000\ \Omega + R_1}{5000\ \Omega\ R_1}$$

$$R = \frac{5000\ R_1\ \Omega}{5000\ \Omega + R_1} \qquad\qquad (1)$$

Now, the voltmeter measures a 4 V drop across R_1. By Kirchoff's Voltage Law, the net voltage around the circuit shown in figure (b) is zero. Hence, traversing the circuit as shown

$$\varepsilon - IR - IR_2 = 0 \qquad\qquad (2)$$

But we know that the voltage drop across R_1 equals the voltage drop across R, since R_1 and the voltmeter are in parallel. Then

$$IR = 4\ V$$

and, from (2) $IR_2 = \varepsilon - IR = 12\ V - 4\ V = 8\ V$

Therefore, $\dfrac{IR_2}{IR} = \dfrac{8}{4} = 2$

or $R = \frac{1}{2}\ R_2$

Using (1) $R = \dfrac{5000\ R_1\ \Omega}{5000\ \Omega + R_1} = \dfrac{R_2}{2}$

Similarly, from diagrams (c) and (d), showing the second connection of the voltmeter and the equivalent circuit, we have

200

$$R' = \frac{5000\ R_2\ \Omega}{5000\ \Omega + R_2} \qquad \text{and } 6\ V = I'R_1 = I'R'.$$

$$R' = \frac{5000\ R_2\ \Omega}{5000\ \Omega + R_2} = R_1.$$

Hence, from the two equations obtained, we have (by cross multiplication)

$$10{,}000\ R_1\ \Omega = 5000\ R_2\ \Omega + R_1 R_2 \tag{3}$$

and $\quad 5000\ R_2\ \Omega = 5000\ R_1\ \Omega + R_1 R_2.$ (4)

Subtracting these equations,

$$10{,}000\ R_1\ \Omega - 5000\ R_2\ \Omega = 5000\ R_2\ \Omega - 5000\ R_1\ \Omega$$

or

$$15{,}000\ R_1 = 10{,}000\ R_2 \qquad \text{or} \qquad R_1 = \frac{2}{3}\ R_2.$$

Substituting back into equation (3), we get

$$10{,}000 \left(\frac{2}{3}\ R_2\right)\Omega = 5000\ R_2\ \dot{\Omega} + \left(\frac{2}{3}\ R_2\right)(R_2)$$

$$10{,}000\ \Omega = 7500\ \Omega + R_2$$

$$R_2 = 2500\ \Omega$$

and $\qquad R_1 = \frac{2}{3}\ R_2 = \frac{2}{3}\ (2500\ \Omega)$

$$R_1 = 1667\ \Omega$$

• **PROBLEM 13-31**

Five resistors, each of resistance 10 Ω, are connected to form a letter H, a 2-V cell of internal resistance 1.86 Ω being connected across the upper ends and an ammeter of resistance 5 Ω across the lower ends. What current passes through the ammeter?

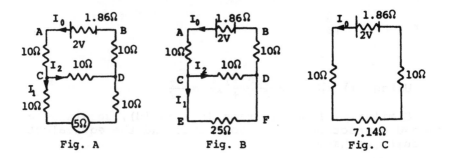

Fig. A   Fig. B   Fig. C

Solution: Because the 5 Ω resistance of the ammeter and the 10 Ω resistance of the lower branch of the circuit in figure (A) are in series, figure (A) is equivalent to figure (B). This follows because the equivalent resistance of n resistors in series is equal to the sum of their individual resistances. The resistances of 10 Ω and 25 Ω are in parallel. Hence the equivalent resistance is R, where

$$\frac{1}{R} = \frac{1}{10 \ \Omega} + \frac{1}{25 \ \Omega} = \frac{35 \ \Omega}{250 \ \Omega^2}$$

$$\therefore \ R = \frac{50}{7} \ \Omega = 7\frac{1}{7} \ \Omega = 7.14 \ \Omega.$$

The circuit is therefore equivalent to the one shown in diagram (C). It is now possible to find the current I_0 in the battery circuit, for, by Ohm's Law

$$I_0 = \frac{\varepsilon}{R} = \frac{2 \ V}{(10 + 10 + 7.14 + 1.86) \Omega} = \frac{2}{29} \ A. \qquad (1)$$

This current splits up into currents I_1 and I_2 through the lower parts of the circuit, as shown in diagrams (A) and (B). Using figure (B), note that branches CD and EF are in parallel. Therefore, the voltage drops across CD and EF are equal. Using Ohm's Law

$$V_{CD} = V_{EF}$$

or $(10 \ \Omega) I_2 = (25 \ \Omega) I_1$

$$\frac{I_1}{I_2} = \frac{R_2}{R_1} = \frac{10 \ \Omega}{25 \ \Omega} = \frac{2}{5}$$

Since no charge can accumulate in the circuit, then $I_1 + I_2 = I_0$. Therefore,

$$I_1 + \frac{25}{10} \ I_1 = I_0$$

$$I_1 = \frac{10}{35} \ I_0 = \frac{10}{35} \times \frac{2}{29} \ A = 0.0197 \ A,$$

where we have used (1). This is the current flowing through the ammeter.

● PROBLEM 13-32

Let the magnitudes and directions of the emf's, and the magnitudes of the resistances in the figure be given. Solve for the currents in each branch of the network.

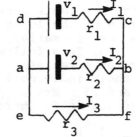

Resistive
Network

Solution: We assign a direction and a letter to each unknown current. The assumed directions are entirely arbitrary. Note that the currents in source 1 and resistor 1 are the same, and require only a single letter I_1. The same is true for source 2 and resistor 2; the current in both is represented by I_2.

At any branch point we may apply Kirchoff's current law, which states that the current entering a branch point must equal the current leaving a branch point.

There are only two branch points, a and b. At point b,

$$\Sigma I = I_1 + I_2 + I_3 = 0 \tag{1}$$

Since there are but two branch points, there is only one independent "point" equation. If the point rule is applied at the other branch point, point a, we get

$$\Sigma I = -I_1 - I_2 - I_3 = 0 \tag{2}$$

which is the same equation with signs reversed.

We now apply Kirchoff's voltage law to the two loops of the figure. This law states that the sum of the voltage drops around any closed loop of a circuit must be zero. Hence, for loop defc,

$$v_1 - I_3 r_3 + I_1 r_1 = 0 \tag{3}$$

and for loop aefb

$$v_2 - I_3 r_3 + I_2 r_2 = 0 \tag{4}$$

We first solve for I_3. Solving (1) for I_1,

$$I_1 = -I_2 - I_3 \tag{5}$$

Substituting this in (3)

$$v_1 - I_3 r_3 + (-I_2 - I_3) r_1 = 0$$

or $\quad v_1 - I_3 r_3 - I_2 r_1 - I_3 r_1 = 0$

$$v_1 - I_3(r_1 + r_3) - I_2 r_1 = 0 \qquad (6)$$

Solving this for I_2

$$I_2 r_1 = v_1 - I_3(r_1 + r_3)$$

$$I_2 = \frac{v_1 - I_3(r_1 + r_3)}{r_1} \qquad (7)$$

Substituting (7) in (4)

$$v_2 - I_3 r_3 + \left[\frac{v_1 - I_3(r_1 + r_3)}{r_1}\right] r_2 = 0$$

Solving for I_3

$$v_2 - I_3 r_3 + \frac{v_1 r_2}{r_1} - I_3 \frac{(r_1 + r_3)}{r_1} r_2 = 0$$

or $\quad I_3 \left[r_3 + \frac{(r_1 + r_3)}{r_1} r_2\right] = v_2 + \frac{v_1 r_2}{r_1}$

Hence

$$I_3 = \frac{\left(v_2 + \dfrac{v_1 r_2}{r_1}\right)}{\left(r_3 + \dfrac{(r_1 + r_3)}{r_1} r_2\right)} \qquad (8)$$

Now, we solve for I_2 by substituting (8) in (4)

$$v_2 - \frac{\left(v_2 + \dfrac{v_1 r_2}{r_1}\right) r_3}{\left(r_3 + \dfrac{(r_1 + r_3) r_2}{r_1}\right)} + I_2 r_2 = 0$$

$$I_2 r_2 = \frac{\left(v_2 + \dfrac{v_1 r_2}{r_1}\right) r_3}{\left(r_3 + \dfrac{(r_1 + r_3) r_2}{r_1}\right)} - v_2$$

$$I_2 = \frac{\left(v_2 + \dfrac{v_1 r_2}{r_1}\right) \dfrac{r_3}{r_2}}{\left(r_3 + \dfrac{(r_1 + r_3) r_2}{r_1}\right)} - \frac{v_2}{r_2} \qquad (9)$$

Substituting (9) and (8) in (5), we may solve for I_1

$$I_1 = \frac{v_2}{r_2} - \frac{\left(v_2 + \dfrac{v_1 r_2}{r_1}\right) \dfrac{r_3}{r_2}}{\left(r_3 + \dfrac{(r_1 + r_3) r_2}{r_1}\right)} - \frac{\left(v_2 + \dfrac{v_1 r_2}{r_1}\right)}{\left(r_3 + \dfrac{(r_1 + r_3) r_2}{r_1}\right)}$$

Hence

$$I_1 = \frac{v_2}{r_2} - \frac{\left(v_2 + \dfrac{v_1 r_2}{r_1}\right)}{\left(r_3 + \dfrac{(r_1 + r_3) r_2}{r_1}\right)} \left(\frac{r_3}{r_2} + 1\right)$$

● **PROBLEM 13-33**

Discuss the operation of (1) a voltmeter across a 12v. battery with an internal resistance $r = 2\Omega$, (2) an ammeter in series with a 4Ω resistor connected to the terminals of the same battery.

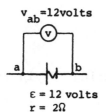

$v_{ab} = 12$volts

$\mathcal{E} = 12$ volts
$r = 2\Omega$

Fig. 1: A source on open circuit.

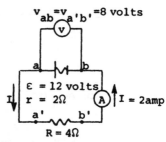

$v_{ab} = v_{a'b'} = 8$ volts

$\mathcal{E} = 12$ volts
$r = 2\Omega$

$I = 2$amp

$R = 4\Omega$

Fig. 2: A source on closed circuit.

Solution: (1) Consider a source whose emf $\mathcal{E}$ is constant and equal to 12 volts, and whose internal resistance r is 2 ohms. (The internal resistance of a commercial 12-volt lead storage battery is only a few thousandths of an ohm.) Figure 1 represents the source with a voltmeter V connected between its terminals a and b. A voltmeter reads the potential difference between its terminals. If it is of the conventional type, the voltmeter provides a conducting path between the terminals and so there is a current in the source (and through the voltmeter). We shall assume, however, that the resistance of the voltmeter is so large (essentially infinite) that it draws no appreciable

205

current. The source is then an open circuit, corresponding to a source with open terminals and the voltmeter reading V_{ab} equals the emf ϵ of the source, or 12 volts.

(2) In Fig. 2, an ammeter A and a resistor of resistance $R = 4\Omega$ have been connected to the terminals of the source to form a closed circuit. The total resistance of the circuit is the sum of the resistance R, the internal resistance r, and the resistance of the ammeter. The ammeter resistance, however, can be made very small, and we shall assume it so small (essentially zero) that it can be neglected. The ammeter (whatever its resistance) reads the current I through it. The circuit corresponds to a source with a 4Ω resistance across its terminals.

The wires connecting the resistor to the source and the ammeter, shown by straight lines, ideally have zero resistance and hence there is no potential difference between their ends. Thus points a and a' are at the same potential and are electrically equivalent, as are points b and b'. The potential differences V_{ab} and $V_{a'b'}$ are therefore equal.

The current I in the resistor (and hence at all points of the circuit) could be found from the relation $I = V_{ab}/R$, if the potential difference V_{ab} were known. However, V_{ab} is the terminal voltage of the source, equal to $\epsilon - Ir$, and since this depends on I it is unknown at the start. We can, however, calculate the current from the circuit equation:

$$I = \frac{\epsilon}{R + r} = \frac{12 \text{ volts}}{4\Omega + 2\Omega} = 2 \text{ amp.}$$

The potential difference V_{ab} can now be found by considering a and b either as the terminals of the resistor or as those of the source. If we consider them as the terminals of the resistor,

$$V_{a'b'} = IR = 2 \text{ amp} \times 4\Omega = 8 \text{ volts.}$$

If we consider them as the terminals of the source,

$$V_{ab} = \epsilon - Ir = 12 \text{ volts} - 2 \text{ amp} \times 2\Omega = 8 \text{ volts.}$$

The voltmeter therefore reads 8 volts and the ammeter reads 2 amp.

CHAPTER 14

MAGNETICS

Basic Attacks and Strategies for
Solving Problems in this Chapter

Magnetism is familiar to all of us from the childhood magnet, which has a north and south pole. The magnetic field lines extend from the north pole to the south pole as shown in Figure 1. Like poles repel and unlike poles attract one another. A magnetic field is produced by the motion of electric charges. So in addition to the electric field surrounding an electron, if that electron is moving, a magnetic field will also be created around the electron.

If another electron is brought close to the electron in motion and crosses its magnetic field, the magnetic field will apply a force on the second electron. The strength and direction of this force is given by

$$\vec{F} = q\vec{v} \times \vec{B}.$$

F *is the force on the electron,* $\vec{v}$ *is the velocity of the electron's motion and* B *is the magnetic field produced. The cross product of* $\vec{v}$ *and* $\vec{B}$ *is given by the right hand rule (see Figure 2). If the vector* $\vec{v}$ *is moved counterclockwise toward* $\vec{B}$ *and if you place your right hand with your fingers curled counterclockwise, the force will be in the direction your thumb is pointing. Remember the force is related by a cross product so if an electron is travelling parallel to the magnetic field then no magnetic force will act on it. For a direction other than parallel to the field, the perpendicular component of the velocity will determine the strength of the force. However, regardless of the electron's motion an electric force will always occur between two electrons.*

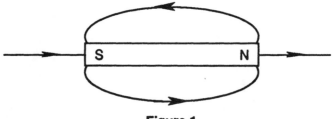

Figure 1

When dealing with problems involving both electric and magnetic forces the two forces can be solved for separately. Then their influence on another object can be summed together. A wire carrying current will also produce a magnetic field because it has a flow of electrons passing through it. To find the magnetic field around the wire, use the formula

$$B = \mu I \ / \ 2\pi r.$$

The direction of the magnetic field is again given by the right hand rule. By holding the wire with your right hand and making sure your thumb is pointing in the direction of the current, your fingers will be curled around the wire in the direction of the magnetic field.

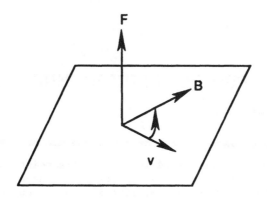

Figure 2

MAGNETICS

MAGNETIC FIELDS, FLUX INTENSITY, PERMEABILITY

What is the magnetic field intensity at a point in air 30 cm away from and on the extension of the line of a bar magnet 10 cm long whose magnetic moments is 400 poles cm, if the point in question is nearer the north pole of the magnet?

Solution: Draw a diagram. Recall that field intensity H is a vector quantity, which with respect to a pole strength m is given by the expression

$$H = \frac{m}{\mu r^2} \text{ which follows directly from Coulomb's Law } F = \frac{mm'}{\mu r^2}$$

where, by definition

$$H = \frac{F}{m'}$$

where m' is a test pole with a north polarity. Hence $H = \frac{m}{\mu r^2}$.

In this problem, the pole strength can be evaluated because the nagnetic moment is given by the defining equation $M = mL$, where M is 400 poles cm, and L is 10 cm.

$$m = \frac{M}{L} = \frac{400}{10} = 40 \text{ poles.}$$

It follows that due to the north pole of the magnet, the field intensity H_1 at P is

$$H_1 = \frac{m}{\mu r^2} = \frac{40 \text{ poles}}{(1)(30\text{cm})^2} = \frac{40}{900} \frac{\text{poles}}{\text{cm}^2} = .044 \text{ oersteds to the}$$

right. Also, the field intensity H_2 due to the south pole is

$$H_2 = \frac{40 \text{ poles}}{1(40\text{cm})^2} = \frac{1}{40} \frac{\text{poles}}{\text{cm}^2}$$

Therefore   H is the vector sum of H_1 and H_2

or

$$\vec{H} = .0\overrightarrow{44} - .0\overleftarrow{25} = .019 \text{ oersteds to the right. This}$$

problem is completely analogous to the problem of finding the electric field intensity at point p, due to two charges, one positive and one negative, at a distance 30 cm and 40 cm from the point P. Coulomb's law for the electrostatic force between charges would be the electrostatic analogue for Coulomb's law for the magnetic force between poles.

● PROBLEM 14-2

A bar with a cross-sectional area of 6 square centimeters and a permeability of 1000 units is placed in a magnetic field of intensity 5 oersteds. What is the total number of lines of magnetic flux in the iron?

Solution: Let

    B = flux density

    μ = magnetic permeability

    H = magnetic field intensity

    B = μH and total flux ϕ = B × area

Since

    H = 5 oersteds,

    B = 1000 × 5 oersteds = 5000 gauss

Then

    the flux ϕ = 5000 gauss × 6cm^2

            = 30,000 lines of flux.

● PROBLEM 14-3

In the figure, a long straight conductor perpendicular to the plane of the paper carries a current i going into the paper. A bar magnet having point poles of strength m at its ends lies in the plane of the paper. What is the magnitude and direction of the magnetic intensity H at point P?

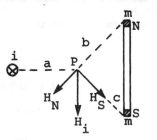

208

<u>Solution</u>: The assumption that the ends of the magnet can be taken to be point sources of magnetic flux is not a realistic one although it greatly simplifies the calculation.

The vectors H_i, H_N, and H_S, as shown in the figure, represent the components of H due respectively to the current, and to the N and S poles of the magnet. Consider first H_i. The flux density B at point P, due to the current i in a long straight conductor at a distance "a" from the conductor is known to be

$$B = \frac{\mu_0}{2\pi} \frac{i}{a} .$$

In free space, the magnetic field strength H is related to B by

$$H = \frac{B}{\mu_0}$$

hence $H_i = \frac{1}{2\pi} \frac{i}{a} .$

Analogous to the electric field, the magnetic field due to a magnetic pole of strength m at a distance r from the magnetic pole is

$$H = \frac{1}{4\pi\mu_0} \frac{m}{r^2} ,$$

therefore, the components H_N and H_S are respectively

$$H_N = \frac{1}{4\pi\mu_0} \frac{m}{b^2}$$

$$H_S = \frac{1}{4\pi\mu_0} \frac{m}{c^2} .$$

The resultant of these three vectors is the magnetic intensity H at the point P.

● PROBLEM 14-4

The current from a dc supply is carried to an instrument by two long parallel wires, 10 cm apart. What is the magnetic flux density midway between the wires when the current carried is 100 A?

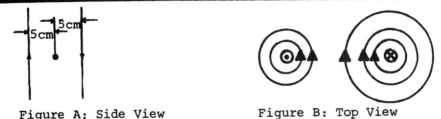

Figure A: Side View   Figure B: Top View

Solution: The magnetic field due to each wire in the diagram at the point midway between them will be into the paper. This may be seen by use of the right hand rule. If the thumb of the right hand points in the direction of current through the wire, then the fingers will curl in the direction of the magnetic field (or magnetic flux density) created by the current. Application of this rule to both current carrying wires indicates that the field of each is into the page (see figures A and B). The effects due to the wires are therefore additive at that point and the total effect is twice the effect of either alone. Hence, midway between the wires the magnetic field due to one wire is

$$B = \frac{\mu_0}{2\pi}\,\frac{I}{r}$$

where the permeability $\mu_0 = 4\pi \times 10^{-7}$ N - A^{-2}, I is the current through the wire, and r is the distance from the point being considered to the wire. Thus

$$B = 2 \times 10^{-7} \text{ N} - \text{A}^{-2} \times \frac{100 \text{ A}}{0.05 \text{ m}} = 4 \times 10^{-4} \text{ Wb} - \text{m}^{-2}$$

The magnetic field due to both wires is then

$$B_T = 2B = 8 \times 10^{-4} \text{ Wb} - \text{m}^{-2}.$$

● **PROBLEM** 14-5

An electron, charged - 1.6 x 10^{-19} coul, moves at some instant of time in the +x-direction with velocity v = 0.8 c. A magnetic field B = 10 W/m^2 is present in the +y-direction. What is the direction and magnitude of the magnetic force?

$$B = 10 \text{W/m}^2$$

Solution: To find the magnetic force acting on a charged particle moving through a magnetic field, one uses the formula

$$\vec{F}_m = q\vec{v} \times \vec{B}$$

where $\vec{F}_m$ is the resulting magnetic force, $\vec{v}$ is the

210

velocity of the particle and $\vec{B}$ is the magnetic field vector.

In this problem $\vec{v}$ is $0.8\ c = 0.8 \times 3 \times 10^8$ m/sec in the +x-direction, $\vec{B}$ is 10 W/m^2 in the +y-direction, and q is $e^- = -1.6 \times 10^{-19}$ coul.

So:

$$\vec{F}_m = \left(-1.6 \times 10^{-19}\ \text{coul.}\right)(0.8)\left(3 \times 10^8\ \text{m/sec}\right)\hat{i}$$

$$\times\ (10\ \text{W/m}^2)\hat{j}$$

$$= -3.84 \times 10^{-10}\ \frac{\text{coul.} - \text{m} - \text{W}}{\text{m}^2 - \text{sec}}\ (\hat{i} \times \hat{j})$$

$$= -3.84 \times 10^{-10}\ \text{N}\ \hat{k}$$

where we used the fact that $\hat{i} \times \hat{j} = \hat{k}$, $\hat{i}$, $\hat{j}$, and $\hat{k}$ being the unit vectors in the +x, +y, and +z-directions, respectively.

● **PROBLEM 14-6**

A particle is projected horizontally with a velocity of 10^4 m · s^{-1} in such a direction that it moves at right angles to a horizontal magnetic field of induction, of magnitude 4.9×10^{-5} Wb · m^{-2}. The particle, which carries a single electronic charge, stays in the same horizontal plane. What is its mass?

Solution: The upward acting magnetic force is $\vec{F} = q(\vec{v} \times \vec{B})$, where q is the charge of the particle, $\vec{v}$ its velocity, and $\vec{B}$ the magnetic induction. Since the motion is at right angles to the direction of the magnetic induction, it follows that the magnitude of $\vec{F}$, $|\vec{F}| = q\ v\ B \sin 90° = q\ v\ B$. Since the particle stays in the same horizontal plane during the motion, the magnetic force on it must, by Newton's Second Law, just balance its weight (= mg). Thus, mg = qvB or m = qvB/g.

$$\therefore\ m = \frac{1.6 \times 10^{-19}\text{C} \times 10^4\ \text{m·s}^{-1} \times 4.9 \times 10^{-5}\ \text{Wb·m}^{-2}}{9.8\ \text{m·s}^{-2}}$$

$$= 8.0 \times 10^{-21}\ \text{kg.}$$

● **PROBLEM 14-7**

The energy of the doubly charged α-particles of mass 6.64×10^{-27} kg emitted from ThC is 6.048 MeV. What is

their velocity and what magnetic field applied perpendicular to a collimated beam of such particles
would bend the beam into a circle of radius 40 cm?

Solution: The energy of the α-particles is 6.048 MeV
= 6.048 MeV × 1.602 × 10⁻¹³ J/ 1 MeV = 9.689 × 10⁻¹³ J.
The energy of the particle refers to its kinetic energy
or KE = ½ mv² = 9.689 × 10⁻¹³ J, or

$$v = \sqrt{\frac{19.378 \times 10^{-13} \text{ J}}{6.64 \times 10^{-27} \text{ kg}}} = 1.709 \times 10^7 \text{ m} \cdot \text{s}^{-1}.$$

In the magnetic field the magnetic force supplies
the centripetal force necessary to keep the particles
moving in a circle. This centripetal force, F, due to
the magnetic field has magnitude F = qvB sin θ where
θ is the angle between $\vec{v}$ and $\vec{B}$. Since we are given that
this angle is 90°, then sin θ = 1. The centripetal
acceleration of a particle with velocity v about a
circle of radius R is a = v²/R. By Newton's second
law, F = mv²/R = qvB or v = qBR/m. Therefore B =
mv/qR.

The α-particles carry twice the electronic charge
(for they contain two positively charged protons and
two neutral neutrons).

$$\therefore B = \frac{6.64 \times 10^{-27} \text{ kg} \times 1.709 \times 10^7 \text{ m} \cdot \text{s}^{-1}}{2 \times 1.602 \times 10^{-19} \text{ C} \times 0.40 \text{ m}}$$

$$= 0.885 \text{ Wb} \cdot \text{m}^{-2}.$$

● **PROBLEM 14-8**

Deuterons with a mass of 3.3 x 10⁻²⁷ kg may have a velocity
of 5 x 10⁷ m/s and an orbit radius of 0.8 m in a cyclotron.
(a) Find the frequency at which the accelerating field
must change. (b) What is the energy of the deuterons in
MeV.

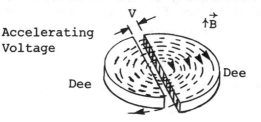

Accelerating
Voltage

Dee

V

$\uparrow\vec{B}$

Dee

Dee

Solution: As shown in the figure, the particles move in
circular orbits in the dees under the influence of the magnetic field and are accelerated across the gap by the electric field. Therefore, the polarity of the electric field
varies with time in such a way that each time the particle
enters the gap, it is accelerated rather than decelerated.

Deuterons travel during each cycle a distance

$$d = 2\pi r = 2 \times \pi \times \left(8 \times 10^{-1} \text{ m}\right) = 5.0 \text{ m}$$

in the cyclotron. The frequency of the electric field should be equal to the frequency of the deuteron's revolutions in the dee.

$$f = \frac{1}{\text{period}} = \frac{\text{particle speed}}{\text{distance traveled during one revolution}}$$

$$= \frac{5 \times 10^7 \text{ m/s}}{5\text{m}} = 1 \times 10^7 \text{ Hz}$$

$$= 10 \text{ MHz}.$$

b) Since the deuteron speed is much less than the speed of light we can use the non-relativistic expression for kinetic energy:

$$K = \frac{1}{2}mv^2 = \left(\frac{1}{2}\right)\left(3.3 \times 10^{-27} \text{ kg}\right)\left(5 \times 10^7 \text{m/s}\right)^2$$

$$= 4.13 \times 10^{-12} \text{ J}$$

Since 1 eV equals 1.6×10^{-19} J, the kinetic energy may be written

$$K = \frac{4.13 \times 10^{-12} \text{ J}}{1.6 \times 10^{-19} \text{ J/eV}} = 2.58 \times 10^7 \text{ eV} = 25.8 \text{ MeV}$$

● **PROBLEM 14-9**

In one type of mass spectrometer the charged particles pass through a velocity selector before entering the magnetic field. In another the particles pass through a strong electric field before entering the magnetic field. Compare the ratio of the radii of singly charged lithium ions of masses 6 amu and 7 amu in the two cases.

Solution: In the magnetic field, an ion moves in a circle, the centripetal force necessary being provided by the magnetic force on it. If the velocity $\vec{v}$ of the ion is perpendicular to the field of magnetic induction $\vec{B}$, then the magnetic force on the ion of charge q, is

$$F = q v B \qquad (1)$$

Since this is the required centripetal force,

$$F = \frac{mv^2}{R} \qquad (2)$$

where m is the ion's mass, and R is the radius of the circle traversed by the ion. Equating (1) and (2),

$$q v B = \frac{mv^2}{R}$$

or $\quad v = \dfrac{q \; B \; R}{m}$ $\hspace{4cm}$ (3)

When the ions have passed through a velocity selector, both lithium ions have the same velocity in the field. Further, they have the same charge and are in the same magnetic flux density. Thus, using (3), $R_6/m_6 = R_7/m_7$.

$$\frac{R_6}{R_7} = \frac{m_6}{m_7} = \frac{6}{7} = 0.857.$$

If the ions have passed through a strong electric field, they have both acquired the same kinetic energy. But, from equation (3) we have

$$\tfrac{1}{2} \; mv^2 = \frac{q^2 \; B^2 \; R^2}{2 \; m}$$

Therefore, since q and B are the same for both isotopes,

$$\frac{r_6^2}{m_6} = \frac{r_7^2}{m_7} \qquad \text{or} \qquad \frac{r_6}{r_7} = \sqrt{\frac{m_6}{m_7}} = 0.926.$$

● **PROBLEM** 14-10

What is the radius of the cyclotron orbit in a field of magnetic induction of 1 weber/m^2 for an electron traveling with velocity 10^6 m/s in a direction normal to $\vec{B}$? (This radius is termed the gyroradius).

Solution: Before starting this problem, we must recognize what type of motion the electron is executing. Since the electron is a charged particle traveling perpendicular to a uniform magnetic field (a field having the same value over all space), the particle will travel in a circle.

To find the exact radius of this circular motion, we relate the magnetic force acting on the electron to the electron's acceleration via Newton's Second Law, $\vec{F} = m\vec{a}$. The magnetic force for a particle of charge q traveling perpendicular to a magnetic field with velocity $\vec{v}$ is

$$F = qvB \hspace{4cm} (1)$$

Using Newton's Second Law,

$$qvB = ma \hspace{4cm} (2)$$

Then because the motion is circular, we know that the acceleration the electron experiences is centripetal (that is, it always points to the center of the circle) and has the value $\dfrac{v^2}{R}$, where v is the speed of the

214

electron, and R is the radius of its orbit. Substituting this into equation (2), we find

$$qvB = \frac{mv^2}{R} \qquad (3)$$

Solving for R, we obtain

$$R = \frac{mv}{qB} \qquad (4)$$

Now, the charge of an electron is $q = 1.6 \times 10^{-19}$ Coulombs, and its mass is $m = 9.11 \times 10^{-31}$ kilograms. Substituting this information and the values of v and B given in the statement of the problem into (4)

$$R = \frac{(9.11 \times 10^{-31} \text{ kg}) (10^6 \text{ m/s})}{(1.6 \times 10^{-19} \text{ C}) (1 \text{ w/m}^2)}$$

$$R = 5.7 \times 10^{-6} \text{ m}$$

MAGNETIC FORCES

● PROBLEM 14-11

An electron is projected into a magnetic field of flux density $B = 10$ w/m^2 with a velocity of 3×10^7 m/sec in a direction at right angles to the field. Compute the magnetic force on the electron and compare with the weight of the electron.

Solution. The force on the electron in a magnetic field is given by $\vec{F} = q\vec{v} \times \vec{B}$ where $\vec{v}$ is the velocity of the electron and $\vec{B}$ is the flux density of the magnetic field. In this case the velocity is perpendicular to the magnetic field so the force may be computed by a straightforward multiplication instead of taking the cross product.
The magnetic force is

$$F = qvB = 1.6 \times 10^{-19} \times 3 \times 10^7 \times 10 = 4.8 \times 10^{-11} \text{ newton}$$

The gravitational force, or the weight of the electron, is

$$F = mg = 9 \times 10^{-31} \times 9.8 = 8.8 \times 10^{-30} \text{ newton.}$$

The gravitational force is therefore negligible in comparison with the magnetic force.

Two long, straight wires, each carrying a current of 9 A in the same direction are placed parallel to each other. Find the force that each wire exerts on the other when the separation distance is 1×10^{-1} m.

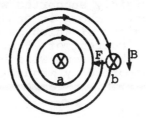

Solution: The currents carried by the wires $i_a = 9$ A, $i_b = 9$ A, and the distance between them, $d = 1 \times 10^{-1}$ m, are given. The first current carrying wire (a) produces a field of induction B at all nearby points around it. The magnitude of B is

$$B = \frac{\mu_0}{2\pi} \frac{i_a}{d} \qquad (1)$$

where i_a is the current through wire a, d is the distance separating the two wires and the permeability constant $\mu_0 = 4\pi \times 10^{-7}$ W/(A · m). The other wire will find itself immersed in the field due to the first wire. The magnetic field it creates, that is its own self field, has no influence on its behavior. The magnetic force on this second current carrying wire (of length ℓ) is

$$\vec{F} = i_b \vec{\ell} \times \vec{B}$$

where i_b is the current through the second wire. Since the wire length is perpendicular to the magnetic field vector B, we then have

$$F = i_b \ell B \qquad (2)$$

F is directed inward toward the first wire. It is perpendicular to both B and to the length vector. Therefore, combining equations (1) and (2) we have

$$F = \frac{\mu_0}{2\pi} \frac{i_a i_b}{d} \ell$$

The force per unit length on a wire is then

$$\frac{F}{\ell} = \frac{\mu_0}{2\pi} \frac{i_a i_b}{d} = 2 \times 10^{-7} \text{ N/A}^2 \frac{i_a i_b}{d}$$

$$= 2 \times 10^{-7} \text{ N/A}^2 \; \frac{(9 \cancel{A})(9 \cancel{A})}{1 \times 10^{-1} \text{ m}} = 1.62 \times 10^{-4} \; \frac{\text{N}}{\text{m}}$$

A long, horizontal, rigidly supported wire carries a current of 50 A. Directly above it and parallel to it is a fine wire, the weight of which is 0.075 N per meter, which carries a current of 25 A. How far above the first wire should the second wire be strung in order for it to be supported by magnetic repulsion?

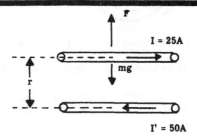

Solution: If the upper wire is to be supported by magnetic repulsion, the magnetic force per unit length (F/ℓ) must just equal the weight of a unit length of the wire (mg/ℓ). Further, the currents in the two wires must be in opposite directions in order for the force between the wires to be one of repulsion. Hence

$$\frac{mg}{\ell} = \frac{F}{\ell}$$

but

$$\frac{F}{\ell} = \frac{\mu_0}{2\pi} \; \frac{I\,I'}{r} \quad \text{(see the figure)}$$

$$\therefore \quad \frac{mg}{\ell} = \frac{\mu_0}{2\pi} \; \frac{I\,I'}{r}$$

$$r = \frac{\mu_0 \ell I I'}{2\pi mg} = \frac{2 \times 10^{-7} \text{ N} \cdot \text{A}^{-2} \times 50\text{A} \times 25 \text{ A}}{0.075 \text{ N} \cdot \text{m}^{-1}}$$

$$= 0.33 \times 10^{-2} \text{ m} = 0.33 \text{ cm}.$$

The wires must therefore be very thin in order to allow their centers to be so close together.

Find the force on an electrically charged oil drop when it moves at a speed of 1×10^2 m/s across a magnetic field whose strength is 2 T. Assume that the charge on the oil-drop is 2×10^{-17} C.

<u>Solution:</u> The speed of the particle, $v = 1 \times 10^2$ m/s, the field strength, $B = 2$ T, and the charge, $q = 2 \times 10^{-17}$ C, are given.

The force on the drop due to its motion through the magnetic field is given by

$$\vec{F} = \vec{q}\ \vec{v} \times \vec{B} \tag{1}$$

Since the drop moves across the magnetic field, the angle between $\vec{v}$ and $\vec{B}$ is $90°$. Equation (1) then reduces to

$$|\vec{F}| = qvB = (2 \times 10^{-17}\text{C})(1 \times 10^2\text{ m/s})(2\text{ T}) = 4 \times 10^{-15}\text{ N}$$

The force acts in a direction perpendicular to both $\vec{B}$ and to $\vec{v}$. This force is very small compared with the weight of even a very small oil drop.

● **PROBLEM** 14-15

A rectangular coil 30 cm long and 10 cm wide is mounted in a uniform field of flux density 8.0 X 10^{-4} nt/amp –m. There is a current of 20 amp in the coil, which has 15 turns. When the plane of the coil makes an angle of 40° with the direction of the field, what is the torque tending to rotate the coil?

Plane of coil

<u>Solution:</u> The torque on a circuit in a field of magnetic induction, $\vec{B}$, is

$$\vec{T} = \vec{\mu} \times \vec{B} \tag{1}$$

where $\vec{\mu}$ is the magnetic moment of the circuit. (This is the property of the circuit which causes the torque to be exerted.) The magnitude of the magnetic moment is

$$\mu = NIA \tag{2}$$

where N is the number of turns in the circuit, I is the current in the circuit, and A is the area it encloses.

The direction of $\vec{\mu}$ is given by the right hand rule: wrap the fingers of your right hand around the circuit in the direction of the current, and the direction in which your thumb points will then be the sense of $\vec{\mu}$. Since we only want the magnitude of $\vec{T}$, we write

$$T = \mu B \sin \theta \qquad\qquad (3)$$

where T, μ, B are the magnitudes of $\vec{T}$, $\vec{\mu}$, $\vec{B}$, and θ is the angle between the directions of $\vec{\mu}$ and $\vec{B}$ (see figure). Substituting (2) into (3), we obtain

$$T = NiAB \sin \theta \qquad\qquad (4)$$

However, the data is given in terms of flux density, not in terms of B. But flux density is actually equal to B because

$$\text{Flux density} = \frac{\phi}{A} = \frac{BA}{A} = B$$

where A is the area enclosed by the circuit, and ϕ is the flux cutting through the circuit. We still cannot proceed yet, because we do not have θ. The question gives us the angle between the plane of the coil and the direction of $\vec{B}$. (In the figure this is α.) The angle we need, θ, is $90° - \alpha = 50°$. Inserting the given data in

(4), we find

$$T = \left[8 \times 10^{-4} \ \frac{nt}{A \cdot m} \right] (15)(20A)(.3m)(.1m)(.77)$$

$$T = .0055 \ nt \cdot m$$

CHAPTER 15

GEOMETRICAL OPTICS

> Basic Attacks and Strategies for
> Solving Problems in this Chapter

Recall that light propagates at speed $c = \upsilon\lambda$ *in a vacuum, or speed* v *= c/n in a medium of index of refraction* n. *Usually, the propagation of light is also represented as a ray moving in a straight line. For many problems in optics, one may use the fact that for a ray of light the angle of incidence is equal to the angle of reflection from a mirrored surface. Hence, the first part of solving an optics problem is always to draw an accurate ray diagram.*

To solve problems involving the propagation of light from one medium (of index of refraction n_i*) to another (of index of refraction* n_r*). Snell's law is used. Refer to Figure 1. Snell's law states that*

$$n_i \sin \theta_i = n_r \sin \theta_r.$$

Hence, given any three of the four variables, one can solve for the other. Note that for a vacuum or near vacuum (sometimes a good approximation for air), the index of refraction is one.

Notice from Figure 1 that it is conceivable to have $\theta_r = 90°$. *When this happens,* θ_i *is called the* critical angle θ_c *given by* $\sin \theta_c = n_r / n_i$. *If the angle of incidence is greater than the critical angle, then we have total internal reflection: the light will not escape from the first medium. This principle is used to transmit pulses of light in fiber optic communication.*

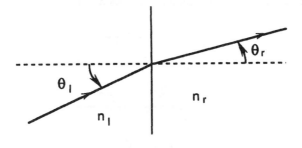

Figure 1

CHAPTER 15

GEOMETRICAL OPTICS

● **PROBLEM 15-1**

How fast does light travel in glass of refractive index 1.5?

<u>Solution:</u> By definition, refractive index n is the ratio of the velocity of light in vacuum (3.00 x 10^{10} cm/sec) to the velocity of light in the medium in question.

Therefore

$$n = \frac{3 \times 10^{10} \text{ cm/s}}{v} = 1.5$$

Therefore

$$v = \frac{3 \times 10^{10} \text{ cm/s}}{1.5}$$

$$= 2.00 \times 10^{10} \text{ cm/sec.}$$

● **PROBLEM 15-2**

An incident wavefront of light makes an angle of 60° with the surface of a pool of water. The speed of light in water is 2.3 × 10^{8} m/s. What angle does the refracted wavefront make with the surface of water?

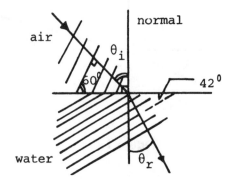

Solution: The angle θ_i between the incident ray and the normal to the surface (as shown in the figure),equals the angle between the incident wavefront and the water surface, and

$$\theta_i = 60°.$$

Snell's Law, relating the angle of incidence, θ_i, to the angle of refraction, θ_r of the light, is

$$n_1 \sin \theta_i = n_2 \sin \theta_r$$

where n_1 and n_2 are the refractive indices of air and water, respectively. Hence

$$\sin \theta_r = \frac{n_1}{n_2} \sin \theta_i$$

But

$$n_1 = \frac{\text{speed of light (vacuum)}}{\text{speed of light (air)}} \qquad n_2 = \frac{\text{speed of light (vacuum)}}{\text{speed of light (water)}}$$

Hence $\quad \sin \theta_r = \left(\dfrac{2.3 \times 10^8 \text{ m/s}}{3 \times 10^8 \text{ m/s}} \right) \sin 60° = .664$

or $\qquad \theta_r = 42°.$

θ_r also equals the angle the refracted wavefront makes with the water surface.

● **PROBLEM 15-3**

Show that the optical length of a light path, defined as the geometrical length times the refractive index of the medium in which the light is moving, is the equivalent distance which the light would have traveled in a vacuum.

Solution: Suppose that light travels a distance ℓ in a medium of refractive index n. The optical length is then

optical length = $n\ell$

and, since n = c/v

optical length = $c\ell/v$

Here c and v are the speeds of light in vacuum and the

medium, respectively.

But light travels with constant velocity in the medium, and hence $\ell/v = t$, where t is the time taken to traverse the light path.

$$n\ell = \frac{c\ell}{v} = ct = \ell_0$$

where ℓ_0 is the distance the light would have traveled at velocity c, that is, in a vacuum. Thus the optical length is the equivalent distance which the light would have traveled in the same time in a vacuum.

● **PROBLEM 15-4**

Describe the phenomena of the critical angle in optics. What is the critical angle for a glass-air interface, if the index of refraction of glass with respect to air is 1.33?

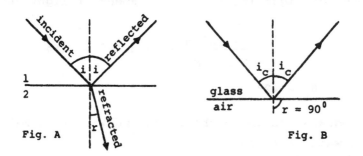

Fig. A   Fig. B

Solution: Consider two media,1 and 2, such that the index of refraction of 1 with respect to 2 is less than unity, as shown in Fig. A. That is, medium 1 is "denser", and the angle of refraction will be greater than the angle incidence.

In general part of the incident ray is reflected and part refracted. As the angle of incidence is increased, the angle of refraction will increase until $r = 90°$. At this critical angle, i_c, (see Fig. B), we have

$$\frac{\sin i_c}{\sin 90°} = \sin i_c = n_{21}$$

At the critical angle, and for values of i greater than i_c, refraction cannot occur and all the energy of the incident beam appears in the reflected beam. This phenomenon is called total internal reflection.

The index of refraction of air with respect to glass is

$$\frac{1}{1.33} = 0.75.$$

The critical angle for a glass-air interference is therefore

$$\sin i_c = 0.75$$

or

$$i_c = 48.6°$$

Thus, for angles of incidence $\geq 48,6°$, total internal reflection will occur for a glass-air combination similar to the one shown in the figure.

● **PROBLEM** 15-5

What is the critical angle between carbon disulfide and air?

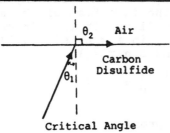

Critical Angle

Solution. Carbon disulfide is a more optically dense material than air. Therefore, as a beam of light passes from carbon disulfide to air, the angle of refraction is larger than the angle of incidence. There is an angle of incidence smaller than 90° for which the angle of refraction is equal to 90°, meaning that the beam of light emerges parallel to the boundary between the two mediums. This angle of incidence is called the critical angle. If the angle of incidence is greater than this value, the light will not escape from the carbon disulfide. It will be reflected back into the carbon disulfide following the regular law of reflection. Solving for the critical angle θ_1, let θ_2 be 90°. The index of refraction for carbon disulfide is 1.643 and for air it is 1.00 Using Snell's law

$$n_1 \sin \theta_1 = n_2 \sin \theta_2$$

$$1.643 \sin \theta_1 = 1.00 \sin 90°$$

$$\sin \theta_1 = \frac{1.00}{1.643} = 0.608$$

$$\theta_1 = 37.4°.$$

● **PROBLEM** 15-6

What is the critical angle of incidence for a ray of light passing from glass into water. Assume $n_{glass} =$ 1. 50 and $n_{water} = 1.33$

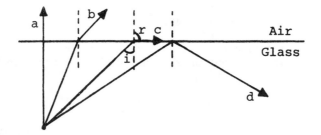

Solution: When light passes from a more optically dense to a less optically dense medium, there is an angle of incidence i, called the critical angle, at which the light ray (ray c of the diagram) will be refracted parallel to the interface of the media. The angle of refraction r will be 90° in this case. Therefore, by Snell's Law, $n_1 \sin i = n_2 \sin r$. Also critical angle of incidence means $\sin r = 1$.

$$\therefore \quad \sin i = \frac{n_2}{n_1} = \frac{1.33}{1.50} = .887$$

$$\therefore \quad i_c = 62° \text{ (approx)}.$$

● **PROBLEM** 15-7

A beam of light in air falls on a glass surface at an angle of incidence of 20.0°. Its angle of refraction in the glass is 12.4°. What is the index of refraction of the glass?

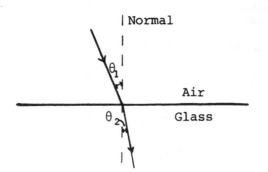

Solution. Since the beam of light passes obliquely from an optically less dense medium, air, to an optically denser medium, glass, the angle of incidence is larger than the angle of refraction. The equation for indices of refraction is

$$\frac{\sin \theta_1}{\sin \theta_2} = \frac{n_2}{n_1}.$$

224

Since the index of refraction for air is approximately one, this reduces to

$$n_2 = \frac{\sin \theta_1}{\sin \theta_2} = \frac{\sin 20.0°}{\sin 12.4°} = \frac{0.342}{0.215} = 1.58.$$

A ray of light in water is incident on a plate of crown glass at an angle of 45°. What is the angle of refraction for the ray in the glass?

<u>Solution.</u> The indices of refraction are inversely proportional to the sine of their respective angles, or, by Snell's law,

$$n_g \sin \theta_g = n_w \sin \theta_w.$$

From a table,

$$n_g = 1.517$$

$$n_w = 1.333.$$

Substituting these values in the equation above,

$$1.517 \sin \theta_g = 1.137 \sin 45°.$$

Solving for θ_g, the angle of refraction in the glass,

$$\sin \theta_g = \frac{1.333 \times 0.707}{1.517} = 0.624$$

$$\theta_g = 38.6°.$$

Notice that θ_g is less than θ_w. This occurs because the angle of incidence is greater than the angle of refraction when passing from an optically less dense medium, water, to an optically denser medium, glass.

CHAPTER 16

LENSES AND OPTICAL INSTRUMENTS

> **Basic Attacks and Strategies for Solving Problems in this Chapter**

The optics of thin lenses may be understood using Snell's law. Again, one must always draw a careful ray diagram in attacking the problem. From Snell's law we can derive a relation called the thin lens equation

$$1/s + 1/s' = 1/f$$

where $1/f \equiv (n-1)(1/R_1 - 1/R_2)$ is the reciprocal of the focal length.

This thin lens equation applies to both concave *(diverging) and* convex *(converging) lenses. Convex lenses have positive focal length (see Figure 1 for a typical ray diagram), whereas concave lenses have f < 0. The object seen by the lens is said to be real if the object distance is positive. The image is said to be real if the image distance is positive. Otherwise, the object / image is called* virtual. *The image is erect if the magnification is positive; inverted if $m_1 < 0$.*

The simple microscope *consists of one lens placed near the eye with the object just inside the focal point of the lens and the image at the near point of the eye. Using the thin lens equation, we have 1/s = 1/f + 1/25 or for the magnification*

$$m_1 = h'/h = -s'/s = 1 + 25/f.$$

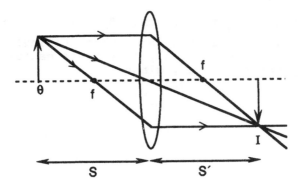

Figure 1

When the eye is relaxed, the object is at the focal point of the lens and the image is at infinity. In that case, we obtain a smaller magnification $m_1 = 25/f$.

The compound microscope consists of two lenses, an objective and an eyepiece. The two lenses are separated by a distance l very much greater than f_e or f_0 : $1 >> f_0, f_e$. The object is placed just outside the focal length of the objective forming an image close to the focal length of the eyepiece. The eyepiece serves as a simple magnifier for this first image. The net magnification is thus $m_1 = m_0 m_e = -l/f_0 \cdot 25/f_e$.

The telescope also makes use of an objective and an eyepiece separated by a distance l. But here, we have $l = f_0 + f_e$. The first image is formed at the focal point of the objective because the object is at ∞. The magnification is then $m_1 = -f_0/f_e$. Hence, it is essential for the telescope that the objective focal length be greater than the eyepiece focal length.

CHAPTER 16

LENSES AND OPTICAL INSTRUMENTS

An object is 24 inches from a convex lens whose focal length is 8 inches. Where will the image be?

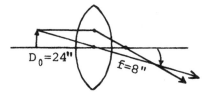

<u>Solution:</u> The use of a ray diagram is helpful here.

We can see that the image is real (on the far side of the lens and inverted).

We then solve mathematically:

D_0 is 24 inches and f is 8 inches. Substituting in

$$\frac{1}{D_0} + \frac{1}{D_I} = \frac{1}{f}$$

$$\frac{1}{24 \text{ in.}} + \frac{1}{D_I} = \frac{1}{8 \text{ in.}}$$

Solving

$$D_I = 12 \text{ in.}$$

Hence

$$D_I = 12 \text{ in.}$$

which means that the image is 12 inches from the lens on the side away from the object.

If an object is in a position 8 cm in front of a
lens of focal length 16 cm, where and how large is the
image? (See figure.)

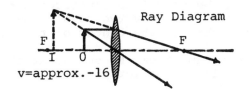

Ray Diagram

v=approx.-16

Solution: We refer here to the relationship

$$\frac{1}{0} + \frac{1}{i} = \frac{1}{f}$$

Here, the image distance, i, is the unknown. The object
distance, 0, is 8 cm, while the focal length, f, is
16 cm. Thus,

$$\frac{1}{0} + \frac{1}{i} = \frac{1}{f}$$

$$\frac{1}{8 \ cm} + \frac{1}{i} = \frac{1}{16 \ cm}$$

$$\frac{1}{i} = \frac{1}{16 \ cm} - \frac{1}{8 \ cm}$$

$$\frac{1}{i} = - \frac{1}{16 \ cm}$$

$$i = - 16 \ cm$$

This means that the image is 16 cm in front of the lens.

To calculate the image size, we first calculate
the magnification. Thus,

$$m = \frac{-i}{0} = \frac{+16}{8} = 2$$

This means that the image is erect, therefore virtual,
and twice as large as the object, or 16 cm high.

An object is 4 inches from a concave lens whose focal
length is - 12 inches. Where will the image be?

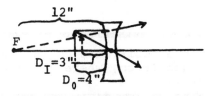

Solution: It may be useful to construct a ray-diagram first (see diagram). We draw two rays - one parallel to the axis and one through the center of the lens.

From the diagram it can be seen that the image is virtual and that it is smaller than the object.

We now attempt a mathematical solution:

D_0 is 4 inches and f is - 12 inches. Substituting in

$$\frac{1}{D_0} + \frac{1}{D_I} = \frac{1}{f}$$

$$\frac{1}{4 \text{ in.}} + \frac{1}{D_I} = \frac{1}{- 12 \text{ in.}}$$

Solving D_I = - 3 in. Hence D_I = - 3 in.

which means that since D_I is negative, the image is 3 inches from the lens on the same side on the lens as the object and is virtual.

● **PROBLEM 16-4**

A converging lens with a focal length of 3 m forms an image of an object placed 9 m from it. Find the position of the image and the magnification.

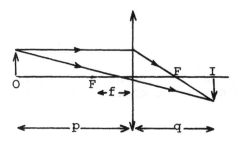

Solution: The simple lens equation for the converging lens of this problem is

$$\frac{1}{f} = \frac{1}{p} + \frac{1}{q}$$

where f, p and q are respectively the focal length of the lens and the distances of the object and the image from the lens. The image is real and inverted (see the figure). Substituting the given values in the above equation, we get

$$\frac{1}{q} = \frac{1}{f} - \frac{1}{p} = \frac{1}{3m} - \frac{1}{9m} = \frac{2}{9}m^{-1} \qquad \text{and}$$

$$q = \frac{9}{2}m = 4.5m.$$

Since the value of q is positive, the image occurs on the right side of the lens. The magnification M is

$$M = \frac{q}{p} = \frac{4.5\ m}{9\ m} = 0.5$$

so the image is one-half as high as the object.

● **PROBLEM** 16-5

A converging lens of 5.0 cm focal length is used as a simple magnifier, producing a virtual image 25 cm from the eye. How far from the lens should the object be placed? What is the magnification?

<u>Solution.</u> The image produced is virtual, on the same side of the lens as the object. Therefore, the distance q of the image from the lens is negative. Using the general lens equation

$$\frac{1}{p} + \frac{1}{q} = \frac{1}{f}; \quad \frac{1}{p} = \frac{1}{f} - \frac{1}{q}.$$

Solve for p and substitute values.
$$p = \frac{fq}{q - f} = \frac{5.0\ cm\,(-25\ cm)}{-25\ cm - 5.0\ cm} = 4.2\ cm.$$

Using absolute values to find the magnification,

$$M = \left|\frac{q}{p}\right| = \left|\frac{-25\ cm}{4.2\ cm}\right| = 5.9.$$

Since the image is on the same side of the lens as the object, the light has been focused in a way that produces an erect image. In a real image, which is seen on the opposite side of the lens in relation to the object, the object is inverted.

The length of a microscope tube is 10 centimeters. The focal length of the objective is 0.5 centimeters and the focal length of the eyepiece is 2 centimeters. What is the magnifying power of the microscope?

Solution: The magnification of this compound microscope is equal to the product of the magnifications of its component lenses or

$$M = M_1 \times M_2$$

which in this case is

$$\frac{25 \text{ cm}}{f_0} \times \frac{10 \text{ cm}}{f_E} .$$

We use 25 cm since in most cases we want the image to be formed at that distance from the ocular. Therefore, the solution is:

$$\frac{25L}{f_0 f_E} = \frac{25 \times 10}{0.5 \times 2} = 250$$

The lens system of a certain portrait camera may be taken as equivalent to a thin converging lens of focal length 10.0 in. How far behind the lens should the film be located to receive the image of a person seated 50.0 in. from the lens? How large will the image be in comparison with the object?

Solution. The general equation for thin lenses states

$$\frac{1}{p} + \frac{1}{q} = \frac{1}{f}$$

where p is the distance of the object, in this case the person, in front of the lens, and q is the distance between the image formed and the lens. The focal length is represented by f. All distances are measured with respect to the optical center of the lens. This center is defined as the point through which light can pass without being bent. Since the lens is a converging one, it is convex. This means that it is thicker at the center than at the edges. Substitute values in the above equation noting that q is positive when it is on the opposite side of the lens in relation to the object.

$$\frac{1}{q} = \frac{1}{10} - \frac{1}{50} = \frac{50 - 10}{(10)(50)} = \frac{4}{50}$$

$$q = \frac{50}{4} = 12.5 \text{ in.}$$

To find the magnification M, the equation $M = \frac{q}{p}$ can be used. Substituting,

$$M = \frac{12.5 \text{ in.}}{50.0 \text{ in.}} = 0.250.$$

The image will be one-fourth as large as the object.

● **PROBLEM** 16-8

A certain farsighted person has a minimum distance of distinct vision of 150 cm. He wishes to read type at a distance of 25 cm. What focal-length glasses should he use?

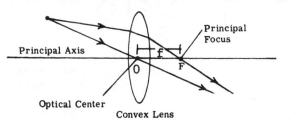

Optical Center
Convex Lens

<u>Solution</u>. The principal axis is the line passing through the centers of curvature of the faces of the lens. The optical center is the point in the lens through which light can pass without being bent. All rays of light parallel to the principal axis pass through F, the point of principal focus. The distance f between F and the optical center is called the focal length of the lens. It is positive for converging, convex lenses, negative for concave, diverging lenses.

Since the person cannot see clearly objects closer than 150 cm, the lens must form a virtual image at that distance. Since the image is formed on the same side of the lens as the object, its distance q from the lens is negative.

$$p = 25 \text{ cm}$$

$$q = -150 \text{ cm.}$$

Substituting in the general equation for lenses,

$$\frac{1}{p} + \frac{1}{q} = \frac{1}{f}$$

$$\frac{1}{25 \text{ cm}} + \frac{1}{-150 \text{ cm}} = \frac{1}{f}$$

$$f = 30 \text{ cm.}$$

Since f is positive, this lens is converging and is convex.

A microscope has an objective lens of 10.0 mm focal length and an eyepiece of 25.0 mm focal length. What is the distance between the lenses, and what is the magnification if the object is in sharp focus when it is 10.5 mm from the objective?

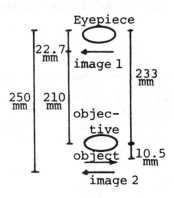

Solution: This is a compound microscope which uses converging lenses to produce large magnification. A short-focus lens, the objective, is placed near the object. It produces a real, inverted and magnified image. The eyepiece further magnifies this inverted image and produces a virtual image 250 mm from the eyepiece. This is the distance of most distinct vision.

Considering the image produced by the objective, we use the optics equation

$$\frac{1}{p} + \frac{1}{q} = \frac{1}{f}$$

p represents the distance of the object from the objective lens, q the distance of image 1 from the lens, and f is the focal length. Substituting,

$$\frac{1}{10.5 \text{ mm}} + \frac{1}{q} = \frac{1}{10.0 \text{ mm}}$$

$$q = 210 \text{ mm}$$

Therefore image 1 is 210 mm from the objective lens, and is real.

The eyepiece magnifies image 1 and produces a second virtual image 250 mm from the lens so as to provide most distinct vision. Since image 2 is virtual, on the same side of the lens as image 1, the distance q' of image 2 from the eyepiece is negative. Using the optics equation again,

$$\frac{1}{p'} + \frac{1}{q'} = \frac{1}{f'}$$

$$\frac{1}{p'} + \frac{1}{-\ 250\ \text{mm}} = \frac{1}{25.0\ \text{mm}}$$

$$p' = 22.7\ \text{mm}$$

Therefore the eyepiece is 22.7 mm from image 1. The distance between lenses is

$q + p' = 210\ \text{mm} + 22.7\ \text{mm} = 233\ \text{mm} = 23.3\ \text{cm}$
To find the magnification, first find the magnification produced by each lens using the equation

$$M = \frac{q}{p}$$

Magnification by objective:

$$M_0 = \frac{210\ \text{mm}}{10.5\ \text{mm}} = 20.0$$

Magnification by eyepiece:

$$M_e = \frac{-\ 250\ \text{mm}}{22.7\ \text{mm}} = -\ 11.0$$

Total magnification:

$M = M_e M_0 = -\ 11.0 \times 20.0 = -\ 220$

● **PROBLEM** 16-10

A projector with a lens of 40 cm focal length illuminates an object slide 4.0 cm long and throws an image upon a screen 20 m from the lens. What is the size of the projected image?

Solution: We use the lens formula $\frac{1}{p} = \frac{1}{f} - \frac{1}{q}$ where p is the object distance, f is the focal length of the lens, and q is the image distance. Upon substitution of the given values in the formula, we have

$$\frac{1}{p} = \frac{1}{40\ \text{cm}} - \frac{1}{20\ \text{m}}$$

In order to do the subtraction, we must change 20 m to centimeters. Since $1\ \text{m} = 10^2\ \text{cm}$, 20 m = 2000 cm and

$$\frac{1}{p} = \frac{1}{40\ \text{cm}} - \frac{1}{2000\ \text{cm}}$$

$$\frac{1}{p} = \frac{2000\ \text{cm} - 40\ \text{cm}}{8000\ \text{cm}^2} = \frac{1960}{80000\ \text{cm}}$$

$$p = \frac{80000 \text{ cm}}{1960} = 40.8 \text{ cm}$$

This is the object distance.

The magnification M of the lens is defined as

$$M = \frac{q}{p} = \frac{2000 \text{ cm}}{40.8 \text{ cm}} = 49.$$

Given, then, an object 4 cm long, the size of its projected image is

Image length = M × object length

$$= 49 \times 4 \text{ cm} \approx 200 \text{ cm}$$

● **PROBLEM 16-11**

The frames in a home movie must be magnified 143 times before the picture formed on a screen 12 ft from the projection lens is large enough to please the family watching. What distance must the film be from the lens and what is the focal length of the lens?

Solution: The magnification produced by the lens is given by

$$m = -\frac{s'}{s} = -\frac{12 \text{ ft}}{s} = -143.$$

where s' and s are the image and object distance, respectively. (The image must be inverted that is, the magnification is negative, since s must be positive (see figure)). Thus the film-to-lens distance is

$$s = \frac{12}{143} \text{ ft} = \frac{144}{143} \text{ in.} = 1.007 \text{ in.}$$

Applying the lens formula, we can obtain the focal length, since

$$\frac{1}{f} = \frac{1}{s} + \frac{1}{s'} = \frac{143}{12 \text{ ft}} + \frac{1}{12 \text{ ft}} = \frac{144}{12 \text{ ft}}$$

$$f = \frac{12}{144} \text{ ft} = 1 \text{ in.}$$

When an object is placed 20 in. from a certain lens, its virtual image is formed 10 in. from the lens. Determine the focal length and character of the lens.

Solution. Since the image is virtual, on the same side of the lens as the object, its distance from the lens, q, is negative. Substitution in the general equation for lenses yields

$$\frac{1}{p} + \frac{1}{q} = \frac{1}{f}$$

$$\frac{1}{20 \text{ in}} + \frac{1}{-10 \text{ in}} = \frac{1}{f}$$

$$\frac{1}{f} = \frac{-10 \text{ in} + 20 \text{ in}}{(20 \text{ in}) \times (-10 \text{ in})} = -\frac{10}{200 \text{ in}}$$

$$f = -20 \text{ in.}$$

The negative sign for the focal length indicates that the lens is diverging. Diverging lenses are concave.

CHAPTER 17

ATOMIC/MOLECULAR STRUCTURE

**Basic Attacks and Strategies for
Solving Problems in this Chapter**

When examining the structure of an atom, the most simple structure to start from is the hydrogen atom. The basic model is a single proton orbited by a single electron. This idea was first developed by Niels Bohr in 1913. Even though this seems like a simple model, it is still used today to describe the operation of many modern chemical analysis techniques.

Bohr went on to describe the different energy states than an electron can occupy because it was found that an electron can change from one orbit to a different one. When this orbit or energy state change occurs, energy is given off. One example of this energy given off is light. This is explained by Plank's hypothesis

$$E = h\upsilon.$$

E is the energy lost by the electron, h is a universal constant and υ is the frequency of the light emitted. Note here that not all the light emitted is visible light that we can see. Only a small range of energies will produce light. Other energies can produce ultraviolet or infrared waves depending on how far the electron moved.

In order to describe what is meant by how an electron moved, I will have to clear up where an electron is positioned in an atom. The electron does not travel around the nucleus in an orbit like the earth, nor does it travel in a continuous path like a normal object. Previously, I used orbit to simplify my explanation. For different energy states, an electron has a certain volume of space around the nucleus where it can be found. These volumes of space have different shapes and are called orbitals. How the electron travels from one orbital to another is not yet explained. It is known that it does move from one orbital to another and energy is given off in the process. Even though we cannot exactly track the electron's movement, its position has been mathematically determined from a formula called the Schrodinger Wave equation.

In order to solve these problems involving atomic structures the formulas used are simple, however, the way the formulas were developed *and proved is the difficult part. Many formulas were developed before any experimental techniques could be used to prove them. For example, Einstein's relation $E = mc^2$, which states that an object's mass can also be described as an amount of energy, wasn't proven until we experienced the power of an atomic explosion from just a little quantity of matter.*

CHAPTER 17

ATOMIC/MOLECULAR STRUCTURE

● **PROBLEM** 17-1

How many nuclei are there in 1 kg of aluminum?

Solution: The mass m of a single aluminum atom $^{27}_{31}Al$, is 26.98153 amu. 1 a.m.u. corresponds to the mass of a proton or 1.66 x 10^{-27} kg, therefore

$$m = (26.98 \text{ amu})\left(1.66 \times 10^{-27} \frac{kg}{amu}\right) = 4.48 \times 10^{-26} kg$$

This mass value is also approximately equal to the mass of an aluminum nucleus since the electron mass is so much smaller than the mass of the atom. Therefore, the number of aluminum nuclei is

$$N = \frac{1.0 \text{ kg}}{4.48 \times 10^{-26} \text{ kg/nuclei}} = 2.23 \times 10^{25} \text{ nuclei.}$$

● **PROBLEM** 17-2

Natural boron is made up of 20 per cent ^{10}B and 80 per cent ^{11}B. What is the approximate atomic weight of natural boron on the scale of 16 units for ^{16}O (chemical scale)?

Solution. The scale of 16 units for ^{16}O means that the superscript represents the atomic weight of the atom. Therefore:

atomic weight of ^{10}B = 10

atomic weight of $^{11}B = 11$

average atomic weight of boron (natural)

$$= \frac{20 \times 10 + 80 \times 11}{100} = 10.8.$$

A cube of copper metal has a mass of 1.46×10^{-1} kg. If the length of each edge of the cube is 2.5×10^{-2} m and a copper atom has a mass of 1.06×10^{-25} kg, determine the number of atoms present in the sample and then estimate the size of a copper atom. Although the actual crystal structure is more complex, assume a simple cubic lattice.

Solution: The number of atoms, N, is found in the following manner:

Mass of N atoms = (Mass of 1 atom)(number of atoms, N)

$$1.46 \times 10^{-1} \text{ kg} = \left(1.06 \times 10^{-25} \frac{\text{kg}}{\text{atom}}\right)(\text{N atoms})$$

$$N = \frac{1.46 \times 10^{-1} \text{ kg}}{1.06 \times 10^{-25} \frac{\text{kg}}{\text{atom}}} = 1.38 \times 10^{24} \text{ atoms.}$$

Let us assume that each copper atom may be represented by a sphere whose diameter is d. If the atoms are touching one another, there will be the same number, say n, along each edge of the cube. The total number of atoms N is related to n by the volume relationship

$$n^3 = N = 138 \times 10^{24}.$$

The number of atoms along one edge is then approximately

$$n = 1.1 \times 10^8 \text{ atoms}$$

This number is approximate due to the inaccuracy of the initial assumption that each atom has the shape of a sphere. Also,

Length of an edge of the cube = (diameter, d, of one copper atom)(number, n, of atoms along an edge)

Then $nd = 2.5 \times 10^{-2}$ m. Therefore, the diameter of a copper atom is approximately

$$d = \frac{2.5 \times 10^{-2} \text{ m}}{1.1 \times 10^{8}} = 2.27 \times 10^{-10} \text{ m}$$

This value agrees reasonably well with the value of 2.56×10^{-10} m obtained using other methods.

● **PROBLEM 17-4**

What is the energy of a photon of green light (frequency = 6×10^{14} vps)?

<u>Solution</u>: Planck's hypothesis states that $E = h\upsilon$, where υ is the frequency of the radiation, and h is Planck's constant. Therefore,

$$E = (6.63 \times 10^{-34} \text{ joule-sec})(6 \times 10^{14} \text{ vps})$$

$$E = 3.98 \times 10^{-19} \text{ joules.}$$

● **PROBLEM 17-5**

What is the energy content of 1 gm of water?

<u>Solution.</u> If the mass of the gram of water was completely converted to energy, the amount of energy released would be

$$E = mc^2$$

$$= 1 \times 10^{-3} \times \left(3 \times 10^8\right)^2$$

$$= 9 \times 10^{13} \text{ joules}$$

● **PROBLEM 17-6**

If the average distance the free electrons travel between collisions in copper is 4×10^{-8} m, how many collisions per second do the electrons make? What is the time between collisions? The average electron speed in copper is 1.21×10^6 m/s.

<u>Solution:</u> The number of collisions per second, N, is,

$$N = \frac{v}{\ell} = \frac{1.21 \times 10^6 \text{ m/s}}{4 \times 10^{-8} \text{ m/collision}} = 3.0 \times 10^{13} \text{ collisions/s}$$

The average time t between collisions is
$$t = \frac{1}{N} = \frac{1}{3.0 \times 10^{13}} \ s = 3.3 \times 10^{-14} \ s \ .$$

● PROBLEM 17-7

Find the energy equivalent to 1 amu.

Solution: The atomic mass unit is 1/12 of the mass of a C_6^{12} atom and is equal to 1.660×10^{-24} gm. The amount of energy released by the conversion of this mass to energy is,

$$E = \Delta mc^2 = 1.660 \times 10^{-24} \ gm \ \times \ \left(2.998 \times 10^{10} \ cm/sec\right)^2$$

$$= 14.94 \times 10^{-4} \ erg = 14.94 \times 10^{-11} \ joule$$

Converting to units of electron volts, since the energies on the molecular level are small,

$$1 \ Mev = 10^6 \ volts \ x \ 1.602 \times 10^{-19} \ coul$$

$$= 1.602 \times 10^{-13} \ joule$$

$$1 \ amu = \frac{14.94 \times 10^{-11}}{1.602 \times 10^{-13}} \ Mev$$

$$= 931 \ Mev$$

● PROBLEM 17-8

Calculate the mass of the electron by combining the results of Millikan's determination of the electron charge q and J.J. Thomson's measurement of q/m.

Solution: The charge of the electron, $q = 1.6 \times 10^{-19} C$,

239

and the ratio of charge to mass, $q/m = 1.76 \times 10^{11}$ C/kg, are known.

$$\frac{q}{m} = 1.76 \times 10^{11} \frac{C}{kg} \text{ but } q = 1.6 \times 10^{-19} \text{ C}$$

Therefore,

$$m = \frac{1.6 \times 10^{-19} \not{C}}{1.76 \times 10^{11} \not{C}/kg} = 9.1 \times 10^{-31} kg$$

The mass of the electon is about $9.1 \times 10^{-31} kg$.

CHAPTER 18

RADIATION

Basic Attacks and Strategies for Solving Problems in this Chapter

Radiation is pervasive in the world around us in various forms: light (4000 – 8000 Å photons), radio waves, black-body photons, cosmic ray particles, etc. Many forms of radiation, expecially particles, follow an exponential law

$$N = N_0 e^{-\lambda t}$$

where λ is the decay constant.

This exponential decay can be related to the half-life $t_{1/2}$ *since*

$$N_0/2 = N_0 e^{-\lambda t_{1/2}}.$$

Using the natural logarithm gives

$$t_{1/2} = \ln 2 / \lambda.$$

In a typical nuclear reaction $I + T \rightarrow R + E$ where an incident particle interacts with a target particle to produce an emitted particle and a residual particle, one can define a Q–value

$$Q = (m_I + m_T - m_I - m_R)c^2.$$

If $Q > 0$, then the reaction is exoergic; for $Q < 0$, it is endoergic or requires energy. This approach is useful in the radioactive decay of one particle by taking $m_I = 0$.

When dealing with nuclear reactions, the key is to keep track of which particles are emitted and how much of the mass of the elements involved changes. Each particle in a reaction is assigned a symbol with a superscript giving the mass number and a subscript for the atomic number. Also some reactions will involve the loss of energy in the form of gamma rays. In this case, the particles involved do not change mass, but instead change in energy.

CHAPTER 18

RADIATION

● PROBLEM 18-1

The half-life of radon is 3.80 days. After how many days will only one-sixteenth of a radon sample remain?

Solution. A half-life of 3.80 days means that every 3.80 days, half the amount of radon present decays. Since one-sixteenth is a power of one-half, this problem can be solved by counting . After 3.80 days, one-half the original sample remains. In the next 3.80 days, one-half of this decays so that after 7.60 days one-fourth the original amount remains. After 11.4 days, one-eighth the original amount remains, and after four half-lives (15.2 days), one-sixteenth the original amount remains.

As an alternate solution, the formula for decaying matter can be used.

$$\frac{N}{N_0} = e^{-\lambda t} \quad (\tfrac{1}{2})$$

λ is an experimental constant which can be determined from the half life. Therefore, for $\frac{N}{N_0} = \frac{1}{2}$,

$$\ln \frac{N}{N_0} = -\lambda t \quad (\tfrac{1}{2})$$

$$\lambda = \frac{\ln \frac{N_0}{N}}{t_{(\tfrac{1}{2})}} = \frac{\ln 2}{t_{(\tfrac{1}{2})}} = \frac{0.693}{3.80 \text{ days}} = 0.182/\text{day}.$$

We want $N/N_0 = 1/16 = e^{-\lambda t} = e^{-0.182t}$.

$$-0.182t = \ln 1/16 = -2.77$$

$$t = 15.2 \text{ days.}$$

How much energy is required to break up a C^{12} nucleus into three α particles?

Solution: This reaction is

$$C^{12} \rightarrow He^4 + Be^8$$

$$Be^8 \rightarrow 2He^4$$

Energy is required since the mass of the three α particles is greater than the mass of the C^{12} nucleus. This is so because the C^{12} nucleus can be considered to be a system of bound α particles, and work must be done (energy must be added) to break up a bound system into its constituent parts. The additional mass of the products comes from energy-mass conversion. To find the additional energy required, calculate the change in mass. By definition, the atomic mass of C^{12} is 12 AMU (exactly). And,

$$3 \times m(He^4) = 3 \times (4.002\ 603 \text{ AMU}) = 12.007\ 809 \text{ AMU}$$

Therefore, the energy required is

$$\varepsilon = \left[3 \times m(He^4) - m\ C^{12} \right] \times c^2$$

$$= (12.007\ 809 \text{ AMU} - 12 \text{ AMU}) \times c^2$$

$$= (0.007\ 809 \text{ AMU}) \times (931.481 \text{ MeV/AMU})$$

$$= 7.274 \text{ MeV.}$$

The gold leaves of the machine in the figure periodically diverge and then collapse. Describe how this perpetual-motion machine operates and explain why it is not a perpetual-motion machine.

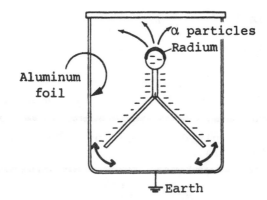

α particles
Radium
Aluminum foil
Earth

Solution: Radium atoms are radioactive and have a half-life of 1,622 years. For radium

$$^{226}_{88}Ra \longrightarrow {}^{222}_{86}Rn + {}^{4}_{2}He \qquad (1)$$

The alpha particle (the $^{4}_{2}He$ nucleus) with 2 quanta of positive charge, is ejected with a kinetic energy of 4.77 MeV and escapes from the surface of the metal. Therefore, if a piece of radium is placed on an electroscope stem, the electroscope becomes negatively charged. This is due to the fact that only a part of the radium atom is emitted as an alpha particle. The number of electrons around the radium nucleus remains the same. Thus, for each alpha particle that escapes 2 quanta of negative charge are left on the electroscope mount and gold leaves. As radium atoms decay, the leaves slowly diverge due to the mutual repulsion of the negative charge on the two foil strips. At the instant they touch the grounded metal surface of the container, the negative charge migrates from the leaves. The gravitational forces cause the leaves to collapse to their original position. The leaves immediately begin to diverge again, repeating the cycle over and over until there are no more radium nuclei present. Since the half-life of radium is 1,622 years, the machine would "run" for many years without any apparent slowing down. From today's perspective, though, we see that the energy source is derived from the nuclear energy released in the nuclear reaction described in (1). This energy is converted to mechanical motion of the gold leaves. Therefore, the device is not a perpetual-motion machine.

● **PROBLEM** 18-4

A uranium nucleus under certain conditions will spontaneously emit an alpha particle, which consists of two protons and two neutrons. If the nucleus was initially at rest and the speed of the emitted alpha particle is 2×10^7 m/s, what is the "recoil" speed of the nucleus?

243

The nuclear mass is 3.9×10^{-25} kg and the alpha-particle mass is 6.7×10^{-27} kg.

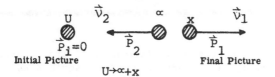

Initial Picture

Final Picture

$U \rightarrow \alpha + x$

Solution: The "nuclear" force responsible for the particle emission is not explained, but this information is not needed if it is recognized that the total momentum of the system is zero. The mass of the recoiling nucleus $m_1 =$ $= 3.9 \times 10^{-25}$ kg; the mass of the alpha particle $m_2 =$ $= 6.7 \times 10^{-27}$ kg; and the velocity of the alpha particle $v_2 = 2 \times 10^7$ m/s are the known observables.

As shown in the figure, the momentum of the initial state is zero, since the uranium atom is initially at rest. Therefore, the vectorial sum of the momenta of the fragments in the final state is also zero. (We are viewing the α-decay of the uranium atom from the center of mass frame of the motion.)

The speed of fragment x is expected to be smaller than that of the α-particle since x is more massive than α. Both speeds are therefore non-relativistic and we are allowed to use the non-relativistic formulae. From the conservation of momentum, we have

$$\vec{P}_f = \vec{P}_i = 0$$

$$\vec{P}_1 + \vec{P}_2 = 0$$

or

$$m_2 \vec{v}_2 + m_1 \vec{v}_1 = 0$$

Therefore

$$\vec{v}_1 = - \frac{m_2}{m_1} \vec{v}_2$$

We see that $\vec{v}_1$ and $\vec{v}_2$ have opposite directions.   The magnitude of $\vec{v}_1$ is

$$v_1 = \frac{m_2 v_2}{m_1} = \frac{\left(6.7 \times 10^{-27} \text{ kg}\right)\left(2 \times 10^7 \text{ m/s}\right)}{3.9 \times 10^{-25} \text{ kg}} = 3.4 \times 10^5 \text{ m/s}$$

After emission, the alpha particle and nucleus move apart as free particles according to Newton's first law because the force causing the separation quickly becomes negligible.

B^{10} is bombarded with neutrons, and α particles are observed to be emitted. What is the residual nucleus?

Solution: Only α particles (helium nuclei) are observed to be emitted in the reaction. The reaction can be described as follows:

$$^{10}_{5}B + {}^{1}_{0}n \rightarrow {}^{A}_{Z}(X) + {}^{4}_{2}He$$

where the superscript gives the mass number A. It is the total number of protons and neutrons in that nucleus. In a nuclear reaction the total nucleon number and the total charge is conserved, therefore the mass number A of the unknown nucleus must be such that

$$10 + 1 = A + 4.$$

Hence $A = 7$.

The subscripts refer to the atomic numbers, total number of protons in each nucleus. Since the above reaction involves protons and neutrons only, the protons carry the total charge. The conservation of total electric charge in that case reduces to the conservation of the total number of protons. Therefore,

$$5 + 0 = Z + 2$$
or $$Z = 3.$$

The nucleus with $A = 7$, $Z = 3$ is ${}^{7}_{3}Li$.

When a uranium nucleus ${}^{235}_{92}U$ captures a neutron, fission occurs. If one of the fission fragments formed is the krypton nucleus ${}^{95}_{36}Kr$, identify what nuclei are formed as the krypton decays to the stable nucleus ${}^{95}_{42}Mo$ by a succession of β-decays.

Solution: When a nucleus of atomic number Z and atomic weight A decays into another nucleus by emitting an electron, the atomic weight of the new nucleus has the same A but its atomic number is Z + 1,

$$^{A}_{Z}X \rightarrow {}^{A}_{Z+1}Y + e^{-} + \overline{\nu_{e}}. \tag{1}$$

Nucleus X has charge +Ze, where e is the unit charge. The charge of Y is + (Z + 1)e and that of the electron is - e. The neutrino (ν_{e}) is a chargeless particle.

Therefore the total charge of the decay products is

+ (Z + 1)e + (- e) + 0 = + Ze

This is equal to the charge of the initial particle, due to the law of conservation of charge.

By using the decay equation (1) and the periodic table, we find the following intermediate decays for the transition

$$^{95}_{36}Kr \rightarrow {}^{95}_{42}Mo.$$

$$^{95}_{36}Kr \rightarrow {}^{95}_{37}Rb + e^- + \bar{\nu}_e \qquad \text{Rb-rubidium}$$

$$^{95}_{37}Rb \rightarrow {}^{95}_{38}Sr + e^- + \bar{\nu}_e \qquad \text{Sr-strontium}$$

$$^{95}_{38}Sr \rightarrow {}^{95}_{39}Y + e^- + \bar{\nu}_e \qquad \text{Y -yittrium}$$

$$^{95}_{39}Y \rightarrow {}^{95}_{40}Zr + e^- + \bar{\nu}_e \qquad \text{Zr-zirconium}$$

$$^{95}_{40}Zr \rightarrow {}^{95}_{41}Nb + e^- + \bar{\nu}_e \qquad \text{Nb-niobium}$$

$$^{95}_{41}Nb \rightarrow {}^{95}_{42}Mo + e^- + \bar{\nu}_e \qquad \text{Mo-molybdenum}$$

CHAPTER 19

SPECIAL ADVANCED PROBLEMS AND APPLICATIONS

Basic Attacks and Strategies for Solving Problems in this Chapter

---

For solving other problems and advanced problems, one should first use any of the methods from the previous chapters. These include Newton's three laws, Coulomb's law, Kirchoff's laws, and the basic relationships of statics and kinematics. Also of great utility in attacking a problem are the conservation laws: mass, momentum, angular momentum, and energy.

One possible advanced problem is any of the previous problems involving forces applied in three dimensional space. Problems involving x, y, and z components are not very different from problems with only x and y components. The only difference is the addition of another equation. The sum of the forces in all the directions must be satisfied independently.

$$\Sigma\, F_x = 0 \quad \Sigma\, F_y = 0 \quad \Sigma\, F_z = 0$$

Therefore, each equation is solved separately so that math is the same, only the bookkeeping is larger.

The mathematics involved in a problem become more difficult when certain information is left out. The missing information must then be solved for by setting up equations based on the information given and solving the equations simultaneously. This method can be summarized in few easy steps as follows:

1) Find out what information is missing and needs to be solved for. These are your missing variables.

2) Write down whatever equations you can based on the physical laws that apply and the information given.

3) You will need the same number of different equations as the number of variables you have.

4) Then keep substituting one equation into another, until one of the variables is solved for, or use a method for solving a simultaneous equations learned from algebra.

The problems included in this chapter do not require any new physical laws. Once you have fully understood the basic physics of the previous chapters, you will be able to solve all of the advanced problems. Difficult problems are not harder to understand. They only need more care in solving. Each formula must be written clearly and each variable must contain its proper subscript, whether it is in direction x or y, or relates to particle 1 or 2. After you have properly applied the physical laws, the problem is only a simple math exercise.

CHAPTER 19

SPECIAL ADVANCED PROBLEMS AND APPLICATIONS

DISPLACEMENT VECTORS

Consider an airplane trip which takes place in four stages. Each stage is represented by a vector as follows (see figure).

A to B	AB = 120 mi	$\phi_1 = 30°$
B to C	BC = 50 mi	$\phi_2 = 60°$
C to D	CD = 700 mi	$\phi_3 = 210°$
D to E	DE = 400 mi	$\phi_4 = 90°$

The angle describing these vectors is with respect to the positive x-axis. Find the resultant displacement vector.

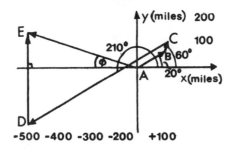

Solution: First we can calculate the x- and y-components.

$$(AB)_x = AB \cos \phi_1 \qquad\qquad (AB)_y = AB \sin \phi_1$$

$$= 120 \cos 30 = 60 \sqrt{3} \text{ mi} \qquad = 120 \sin 30 = 60 \text{ mi}$$

247

$(BC)_x = BC \cos \phi_2$ $(BC)_y = BC \sin \phi_2$

     $= 50 \cos 60 = 25$ mi $= 50 \sin 60$

                                                             $= 25 \sqrt{3}$ mi

$(CD)_x = CD \cos \phi_3$ $(CD)_y = CD \sin \phi_3$

     $= 700 \cos 210$ $= 700 \sin 210$

     $= -350 \sqrt{3}$ mi $= -350$ mi

$(DE)_x = DE \cos \phi_4$ $(DE)_y = DE \sin \phi_4$

     $= 400 \cos 90 = 0$ $= 400 \sin 90$

                                                             $= 400$ mi

These components are summed to find the x and y components of the resultant.

	x-component	y-component
AB	104 mi	60 mi
BC	25 mi	43 mi
CD	- 606 mi	- 350 mi
DE	0 mi	400 mi
Resultant AE	- 477 mi	153 mi

The magnitude of the resultant is therefore, by the Pythagorean theorem:

$$AE^2 = (-477)^2 + (153)^2$$

$$AE = 501 \text{ mi}$$

and its direction is given by the angle ϕ where

$$\sin \phi = \frac{153}{501} = 0.305$$

$$\cos \phi = \frac{-477}{501} = -0.952$$

$$\phi = 17.8°$$

The same thing can be found by making a graph (see figure). The resultant vector, AE, is drawn from the starting point A to the end point E of the trip.

FORCE SYSTEMS IN EQUILIBRIUM

A yule log is being dragged along an icy horizontal path by two horses. The owner keeps the log on the path by using a guide rope attached to the log at the same point as the traces from the horses. Someone in the adjacent woods fires a shotgun, which causes the horses to bolt to opposite sides of the path. One horse now exerts a pull at an angle of 45°, and the other an equal pull at an angle of 30°, relative to the original direction. What is the minimum force the man has to exert on the rope in order to keep the log moving along the path?

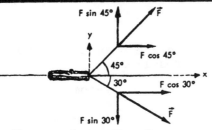

Solution: The figure shows the forces exerted on the log by the horses at the moment they bolt. These forces can be resolved into components along the path and at right angles to the path. Thus the total forces in the x- and y-directions are

$$\Sigma \vec{F}_x = F \cos 45° \; \hat{\imath} + F \cos 30° \; \hat{\imath}$$

and $\Sigma \vec{F}_y = F \sin 45° \; \hat{\jmath} - F \sin 30° \; \hat{\imath}$

where F is the magnitude of the force that each horse exerts.

To keep the log on the path the man must counteract the unbalanced force in the y-direction, $\Sigma \vec{F}_y$, by an equal and opposite force $- \Sigma \vec{F}_y$. We çan see that any force he may have exerted to keep the log moving along the path, exerted in other than the y-direction of the figure, would not have been the minimum force possible. Any otherwise directed force would have an x-component as well as $- \Sigma \vec{F}_y$. But the latter alone could keep the log moving along the path. The magnitude of the result-ant force would then have a greater magnitude than $- \Sigma \vec{F}_y$. Hence the minimum force he must exert has magnitude

$$P_y = F(\sin 45° - \sin 30°) = F \left(\frac{1}{\sqrt{2}} - \frac{1}{2} \right)$$

$$= 0.207 \; F,$$

and must be directed in the negative y-direction, i.e.,
at right angles to the path.

In the above analysis, frictional forces have been
ignored. The frictional force acting along the path does
not affect the solution. The frictional force trying to
prevent motion at right angles to the line of the path
reduces the magnitude of the force the man need apply.
It is, however, assumed that on an icy path this
frictional force is small in comparison with F, and
its effect is therefore ignored.

VECTOR COMPONENTS OF VELOCITY AND ACCELERATION

● PROBLEM 19-3

The total speed of a projectile at its greatest height,
v_1, is $\sqrt{\frac{6}{7}}$ of its total speed when it is at half its
greatest height, v_2. Show that the angle of projection
is $30°$.

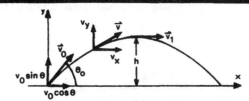

Solution: When a particle is projected as shown in
the figure, the component of the velocity in the x-
direction stays at all times the same, $v_x = v_0 \cos \theta_0$,
since there is no acceleration in that direction,
owing to the fact that there is no horizontal component of force acting on the projectile.

In the y-direction, the upward velocity is
initially $v_0 \sin \theta_0$ and gradually decreases, due to
the acceleration g acting downward. At its greatest
height h, the upward velocity is reduced to zero. The
kinematic relation for constant acceleration which
does not involve time is used to find the greatest
height of the trajectory. It is

$$v_f^2 = v_i^2 + 2as \qquad (1)$$

In this case $v_f = 0$, v_i, the initial velocity, is
$v_0 \sin \theta_0$, $a = -g$ and $s = h$. Then

$$0 = (v_0 \sin \theta_0)^2 - 2gh \quad \text{or} \quad h = \frac{(v_0 \sin \theta_0)^2}{2g}.$$

250

The total velocity at the highest point is thus the x-component only. That is, $v_1 = v_0 \cos \theta_0$. At half the greatest height, $h/2 = (v_0 \sin \theta_0)^2/4g$, the velocity in the y-direction, v_y, is obtained from the equation (1) with $v_f = v_y$, $v_i = v_0 \sin \theta_0$, a = - g, and s = h/2.

$$v_{y^2}^2 = (v_0 \sin \theta_0)^2 - 2g \frac{h}{2}$$

$$= (v_0 \sin \theta_0)^2 - \tfrac{1}{2}(v_0 \sin \theta_0)^2$$

$$= \tfrac{1}{2}(v_0 \sin \theta_0)^2. \tag{2}$$

In addition, there is also the ever-present x-component of the velocity $v_0 \cos \theta_0$. Hence the total velocity at this point is obtained by the Pythagorean theorem,

$$v_2^2 = v_x^2 + v_{y^2}^2 = (v_0 \cos \theta_0)^2 + \tfrac{1}{2}(v_0 \sin \theta_0)^2$$

$$= (v_0 \cos \theta_0)^2 + \tfrac{1}{2}v_0^2(1 - \cos^2 \theta_0)$$

$$= \tfrac{1}{2}v_0^2 + \tfrac{1}{2}(v_0 \cos \theta_0)^2. \tag{3}$$

Here we used the trigonometric identity $\sin^2 \theta + \cos^2 \theta = 1$. However, we are given that $v_1 = \sqrt{\frac{6}{7}} v_2$ or $\frac{v_1^2}{v_2^2} = \frac{6}{7}$.

Therefore, $\dfrac{(v_0 \cos \theta_0)^2}{\tfrac{1}{2}v_0^2 + \tfrac{1}{2}(v_0 \cos \theta_0)^2} = \dfrac{6}{7}$;

or $\quad 7(v_0 \cos \theta_0)^2 = 3v_0^2 + 3(v_0 \cos \theta_0)^2$,

or $\quad 4 \cos^2 \theta_0 = 3$. One can therefore say that

$$\cos \theta_0 = \frac{\sqrt{3}}{2} \qquad \text{or} \qquad \theta_0 = 30°.$$

CURVILINEAR DYNAMICS

● PROBLEM 19-4

The owner of a car and a helpful passer-by attempt to pull the former's car from the field into which it has skidded. They attach two ropes to the front of the chassis symmetrically, each rope being 1 ft from the center point, C, and exert pulls of 200 lb and 150 lb in parallel directions, both at an angle of 30° to the

251

horizontal (see the figure). To what point of the chassis must a tractor be attached and what horizontal force must it exert to produce an equivalent effect?

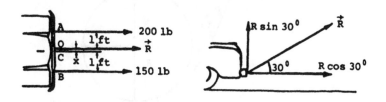

Solution: The resultant force of the two pulls exerted by the men must be $\vec{R}$ of magnitude $(200 + 150)$ lb = 350 lb, in the same direction as either of the forces, i.e., at 30° to the horizontal. Only the horizontal component of this force is doing useful work in pulling the car from the field. This component has magnitude R cos 30 = 350 lb × $\sqrt{3}/2$ = 303.1 lb. This is the force that the tractor must exert.

The point of attachment of the tractor must be the point O at which the line of action of the resultant $\vec{R}$ cuts the front of the chassis. The forces that the two men exert on the chassis produce a net torque τ about the center point C. The point of action O of $\vec{R}$ must lie at a distance from C, along the front of the chassis, such that $\vec{R}$ produces a net torque equal to τ:

$$\tau = (150 \text{ lb})(1 \text{ ft}) - (200 \text{ lb})(1 \text{ ft}) = (350 \text{ lb})x$$

$$x = \frac{-50 \text{ ft-lb}}{350 \text{ lb}} = -\frac{1}{7} \text{ ft}$$

where x is the distance of O from C. All counterclockwise torques are taken as positive. Since x is negative, we see that R produces a clockwise torque about C. This tells us that O must be to the left of C (above C in the figure).

Thus the point of attachment of the tractor is 6/7 ft from A, that is, 1/7 ft from the center point of the front of the chassis.

KINETIC AND POTENTIAL ENERGY

● PROBLEM 19-5

(a) From what height above the bottom of the loop must the car in the figure start in order to just make it around the loop? (b) What is the velocity of the car at point A and at point B?

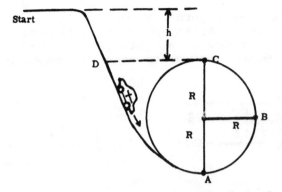

Solution: (a) For the car to just make it around the loop, its speed at the highest point of the loop must be such that the force of gravity on it is sufficient to provide the centripetal force needed to keep it in a circular path. For this to be the case,

$$F_{centripetal} = \frac{mv_C^2}{R} = mg$$

or the velocity must be given by

$$v_C = \sqrt{Rg} \qquad (1)$$

at point C. Neglecting friction, we use conservation of energy and note that the velocity of the car at point D must be the same as at point C, since both correspond to the same net change in potential energy relative to the starting point. The change in potential energy equals the change in kinetic energy and is proportional to the square of the velocity. The change in potential energy from the starting point to point D equated to the corresponding change in kinetic energy yields:

$$mgh = \tfrac{1}{2}m(v_D - v_0)^2 = \tfrac{1}{2}mv_D^2$$

$$v_D = \sqrt{2gh} \qquad (2)$$

where h is the vertical height of the starting point above points C and D (as shown in figure), and v_0 is the initial velocity of the car, which is zero at the starting point. Equating equations (1) and (2),

$$\sqrt{Rg} = \sqrt{2gh}$$

we have

$$h = R/2 \ .$$

This indicates that the starting point must be $2R + R/2 = (5/2)R$ above the bottom of the loop in order for the car to have just enough energy to make it around the loop.

(b) Equating the change in potential energy to the kinetic energy of the car at the point in question, as we did in part (a), we find for point A

$$mg(h + 2R) = \tfrac{1}{2}mv_A^2$$

$$\frac{5}{2} Rg = \tfrac{1}{2}v_A^2$$

$$v_A = \sqrt{5 \ gR}$$

For point B,

$$mg(h + R) = \tfrac{1}{2}mv_B^2$$

$$\frac{3}{2} gR = \tfrac{1}{2}v_B^2$$

$$v_B = \sqrt{3gR}$$

253

LINEAR MOMENTUM

A space probe explodes in flight into three equal portions. One portion continues along the original line of
flight. The other two go off in directions each inclined
at 60° to the original path. The energy released in the
explosion is twice as great as the kinetic energy possess-
ed by the probe at the time of the explosion. Determine
the kinetic energy of each fragment immediately after the
explosion.

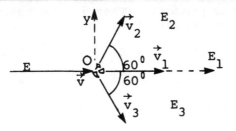

Solution: Take the direction in which the probe is moving immediately prior to the explosion as the positive
x-direction and the point at which the explosion takes
place as the origin of coordinates. Let M be the mass of
the probe and let the quantities applicable to the probe
and its fragments be given subscripts as in the diagram.

Momentum must be conserved in the x-direction, the
y-direction, and the z-direction independently. It
follows that $\vec{V}_1$, $\vec{V}_2$, $\vec{V}_3$, and $\vec{V}$ must be coplanar and that

$$MV = \frac{1}{3} MV_1 + \frac{1}{3} MV_2 \cos 60° + \frac{1}{3} MV_3 \cos 60° \qquad \text{and}$$

$$\frac{1}{3} MV_2 \sin 60° = \frac{1}{3} MV_3 \sin 60°.$$

From the second of these equations $V_3 = V_2$, and thus the
first equation becomes

$$MV = \frac{1}{3} MV_1 + \frac{1}{3} MV_2 \cos 60° + \frac{1}{3} MV_2 \cos 60°$$

$$= \frac{1}{3} MV_1 + \frac{2}{3} MV_2 \cos 60°$$

$$= \frac{1}{3} MV_1 + \frac{2}{3} MV_2 (\tfrac{1}{2}) = \frac{1}{3} MV_1 + \frac{1}{3} MV_2$$

But $E = \tfrac{1}{2} MV^2 = \dfrac{M^2V^2}{2M}$ or $MV = \sqrt{2ME}.$

Similarly,

$$E_1 = \tfrac{1}{2} \left(\tfrac{1}{3}M\right) V_1^2 = \frac{M^2V_1^2}{(3)(2M)} = \left(\frac{3 \, M^2V_1^2}{2M}\right)\left(\frac{1}{9}\right) \qquad \text{or}$$

254

$$\frac{1}{3} MV_1 = \sqrt{\frac{2}{3} ME_1}$$

and $\quad \frac{1}{3} MV_2 = \sqrt{\frac{2}{3} ME_2}$

The first equation thus becomes

$$\sqrt{2ME} = \sqrt{\frac{2}{3}ME_1} + \sqrt{\frac{2}{3} ME_2} \quad \text{or} \quad \sqrt{3E} = \sqrt{E_1} + \sqrt{E_2}.$$

$$\therefore \quad 3E = E_1 + E_2 + 2\sqrt{E_1 E_2} .$$

The original kinetic energy of the probe plus the energy released by the explosion must equal the sum of the kinetic energies of the fragments, since no energy can be lost in the process. (That is, we assume an elastic "collision." occurs.) Hence

$$E + 2E = 3E = E_1 + E_2 + E_3 = E_1 + 2E_2.$$

$$\therefore \quad E_1 + 2E_2 = E_1 + E_2 + 2\sqrt{E_1 E_3} \quad \text{or} \quad E_2 = 2\sqrt{E_1 E_2}.$$

$$\therefore \quad E_2^2 = 4E_1 E_2 \quad \text{or} \quad E_2 = 4E_1.$$

Thus, $\quad 3E = E_1 + 2E_2 = E_1 + 8E_1 \quad \text{or} \quad E_1 = \frac{1}{3} E.$

$$\therefore \quad E_2 = \frac{4}{3} E.$$

Thus the fragment that continues in the line of flight has one-third of the original kinetic energy. The other fragments each have four-thirds of the original kinetic energy. The sum of these kinetic energies is three times the original kinetic energy, as required by the conservation principle.

ANGULAR MOMENTUM

A small ball swings in a horizontal circle at the end of a cord of length ℓ_1 which forms an angle θ_1 with the vertical. The cord is slowly shortened by pulling it through a hole in its support until the free length is ℓ_2 and the ball is moving at an angle θ_2 from the vertical. a) Derive a relation between ℓ_1, ℓ_2, θ_1, and θ_2. b) If $\ell_1 = 600$ mm, $\theta_1 = 30°$ and, after shortening, $\theta_2 = 60°$, determine ℓ_2.

Solution: In the system shown, ℓ_n is the cord length, θ_n is the cone angle cut out by the cord as it revolves, r_n is the distance from the mass to the axis of rotation, and v_n is the velocity of the mass.

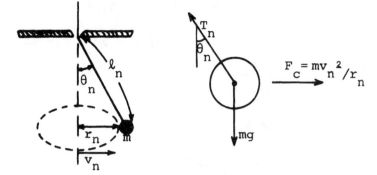

To find the relationship between ℓ_1, ℓ_2, θ_1 and θ_2 when the cord is shortened from ℓ_1 to ℓ_2, one should first analyze a free body diagram of the particle.

Since the particle is in a circular motion, the inward component of T must supply the centripetal force, $m \, v_n^2/r_n$.

$$T_n \sin \theta_n = \frac{m \, v_n^2}{r_n} \qquad (1)$$

Also, the vertical component of T must balance the weight.

$$T_n \cos \theta_n = m \, g \qquad (2)$$

Dividing (1) by (2) yields:

$$\text{Tan } \theta_n = \frac{m \, v_n^2}{m \, g \, r_n} = \frac{v_n^2}{g \, r_n} \qquad (3)$$

One more relationship is needed to solve the problem. Since no external torques act on the system, angular momentum L is conserved.

$$L_1 = L_2$$

$$m \, r_1 \, v_1 = m \, r_2 \, v_2$$

$$r_1 \, v_1 = r_2 \, v_2. \qquad (4)$$

If one rearranges (3),

$$g \, r_n^3 \tan \theta_n = r_n^2 \, v_n^2. \qquad (5)$$

From (4), it follows that $(r_1 \, v_1)^2 = (r_2 \, v_2)^2$. (6)

Combining (5) and (6), $g \, r_1^3 \tan \theta_1 = g \, r_2^3 \tan \theta_2$. (7)

Finally, from geometry, $r_n = \ell_n \sin \theta_n$ (8)

Using this relation in (7) and dividing both sides by g produces the desired result.

$$(\ell_1 \sin \theta_1)^3 \tan \theta_1 = (\ell_2 \sin \theta_2)^3 \tan \theta_2.$$

In this problem, $\ell_1 = .6m$, $\theta_1 = 30°$, $\theta_2 = 60°$

Solving for ℓ_2 yields

$$\ell_2 = \sqrt[3]{\frac{(\ell_1 \sin \theta_1)^3 \tan \theta_1}{\sin \theta_2{}^3 \tan \theta_2}}$$

$$\ell_2 = \frac{\ell_1 \sin \theta_1}{\sin \theta_2} \sqrt[3]{\frac{\tan \theta_1}{\tan \theta_2}},$$

and substituting in the numbers yields

$$\ell_2 = \frac{.6 \text{ m } (\sin 30°)}{\sin 60°} \sqrt[3]{\frac{\tan 30°}{\tan 60°}}$$

$$= \frac{.6 \text{ m } (.5)}{(.87)} \sqrt[3]{\frac{.58}{1.73}}$$

$$= .24 \text{ m.}$$

FLUID FORCES

● **PROBLEM** 19-8

A rectangular cistern 6 ft × 8 ft is filled to a depth of 2 ft with water. On top of the water is a layer of oil 3 ft deep. The specific gravity of the oil is .6. What is the absolute pressure at the bottom, and what is the total thrust exerted on the bottom of the cistern?

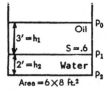

Solution: The total force F acting at the bottom of the cistern is the sum of the weights of the water Wg, the oil W_o, and the air in the atmosphere above the cistern $\left(F_{atm} \right)$. Since

$$\text{Density (d)} = \frac{\text{Mass}}{\text{Volume}} \quad \text{and} \quad \text{Pressure} = \frac{\text{Force}}{\text{Area}}$$

Then

$$F = M_w g + M_o g + F_{atm} = d_w V_w g + d_o V_o g + P_{atm} A$$

257

where V_w and V_0 are the volumes of water and oil respectively, and A is the cross sectional area of the cistern.

$$V_w = h_2 A$$

$$V_0 = h_1 A$$

Therefore $F = (d_w h_2 g + d_0 h_1 g + P_{atm}) A$

$$d_w = \frac{62.4 \text{ slug}}{32 \text{ ft}^3}$$

By definition of specific gravity (or relative density) of oil

$$S_0 = \frac{d_0}{d_w}$$

Since we are given that $S_0 = .6$ we have

$$d_0 = .6 \ d_w = (.6) \left(\frac{62.4 \text{ slug}}{32 \text{ ft}^3} \right)$$

Also $P_{atm} = 14.7 \text{ lb/in}^2 = 14.7 \text{ lb/in}^2 \times 144 \text{ in}^2/1 \text{ ft}^2$
$h_1 = 3$ ft   and $h_2 = 2$ ft

Therefore

$$F = \left[\left(\frac{62.4 \text{ slug}}{32 \text{ ft}^3} \right) (2 \text{ ft}) \ (32 \text{ ft/sec}^2) \right.$$

$$\left. + \ .6 \left(\frac{62.4 \text{ slug}}{32 \text{ ft}^3} \right) (32 \text{ ft/sec}^2) \ + \ (14.7) \ (144) \text{lb/ft}^2 \right] A$$

or $F = (2357 \text{ lb/ft}^2) \ A$

$$P_{bottom} = \frac{F}{A} = 2357 \text{ lb/ft}^2$$

Since $A = 6 \text{ ft} \times 8 \text{ ft}$

$$F = (2357 \text{ lb/ft}^2) \ (6 \times 8 \text{ ft}^2) = 113,000 \text{ lb.}$$

THERMAL ENERGY

● **PROBLEM** 19-9

Water flows at a rate of 2.5 $m^3 \cdot s^{-1}$ over a waterfall of height 15 m. What is the maximum difference in temperature between the water at the top and at the bottom of the waterfall and what usable power is going to waste? The density of water is 10^3 kg $\cdot$ m^{-3} and its specific heat capacity is 10^3 cal $\cdot$ kg^{-1} $\cdot$ C deg^{-1}.

Solution: The water loses potential energy and gains kinetic energy in falling over the waterfall. The maximum possible temperature difference between the water at the top and at the bottom of the falls occurs if all this kinetic energy is converted to heat. The potential energy lost, mgh, is completely converted to heat in this case. The power available is the potential energy lost in a time τ, or

$$P = \frac{mgh}{\tau} = \frac{\rho Vgh}{\tau} \qquad (1)$$

where m is the mass contained in a volume of water V, and ρ is the mass density of water. Note that V/τ is the volume of water passing over the waterfall per unit time. Hence,

$$P = 10^3 \text{ kg} \cdot \text{m}^{-3} \times 2.5 \text{ m}^3 \cdot \text{s}^{-1} \times 9.8 \text{ m} \cdot \text{s}^{-2} \times 15 \text{ m}$$

$$= 3.675 \times 10^5 \text{ W} = 367.5 \text{ kW}.$$

Under the conditions we have assumed, all this power goes into heat.

The rise in temperature, Δt, of a mass of material m, caused by an amount of heat Q is given by the relation

$$Q = mc \, \Delta t$$

where c is the specific heat capacity of the material. Hence

$$\Delta t = \frac{Q}{mc} = \frac{Q/\tau}{cm/\tau}$$

In our case, $P = Q/\tau$ and

$$\Delta t = \frac{P}{cm/\tau} = \frac{P\tau}{mc}$$

Furthermore, m is the mass of water in a volume V, or

$$m = \rho V$$

whence $\quad \Delta t = \frac{\rho Vgh}{\rho Vc} = \frac{gh}{c}$

$$\Delta t = \frac{9.8 \text{ m} \cdot \text{s}^{-2} \times 15 \text{ m}}{4.186 \times 10^3 \text{ J} \cdot \text{kg}^{-1} \cdot \text{C deg}^{-1}} = 0.035° \text{ C}.$$

This is the temperature change experienced by a mass m of water in falling through a distance h.

MOLECULAR CHARACTERISTICS OF GASES

A container with a pressure of 3 atmospheres and a temperature of 200° C. contains 36 gm of nitrogen. What is the average speed of the nitrogen molecules? What is the mean distance between molecules (assuming that the container has a cubic shape), and approximately what distance will a molecule travel before it collides with another?

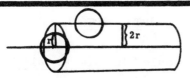

Solution: The number of moles of gas present is the mass of gas present divided by the molecular mass of nitrogen, or

$$n = \frac{36}{28} = 1.29$$

The pressure is

p = 3 atm

= 3 × 1.013 × 10⁵ N/m² = 3.04 × 10⁵ N/m²

$$p = 3 \text{ atm}$$

$$= 3 \times 1.013 \times 10^5 \text{ N/m}^2 = 3.04 \times 10^5 \text{ N/m}^2$$

Thus the volume of the container is by the ideal gas law

$$V = \frac{nRT}{p}$$

$$= \frac{1.29 \text{ moles} \times 8.313 \text{ joules/}^\circ k \times 473^\circ\ k}{3.04 \times\ 10^5 \text{ N/m}^2}$$

$$= \frac{1.29 \text{ moles} \times 8.313 \text{ N-m/}^\circ k \times 473^\circ\ k}{3.04 \times 10^5 \text{ N/m}^2}$$

$$= 16.7 \times 10^{-3} \text{ m}^3$$

That is, the volume is a cube with sides 25.6 cm. The total number of molecules is the number of moles of gas times Avogadro's number, or

$$(1.29 \text{ moles})\left(6.02 \times 10^{23} \frac{\text{molecules}}{\text{moles}}\right)$$

$$= 1.29 \times 6.02 \times 10^{23} \text{ molecules}$$

so that the volume per molecule is

$$\frac{16.7 \times 10^{-3} \text{ m}^3}{1.29 \times 6.02 \times 10^{23}} = 2.15 \times 10^{-26} \text{ m}^3$$

$$= 2.15 \times 10^{-20} \text{ cm}^3$$

This corresponds to a cube with sides 2.8×10^{-7} cm, which is the mean distance between molecules.

The mean square speed is calculated from

$$\tfrac{1}{2} m\overline{v^2} = \frac{3}{2} kT$$

where m is the mass of one molecule of nitrogen, $\overline{v^2}$ is the mean square speed of the molecule, k is Boltzmann's constant, and T is the absolute temperature. Furthermore, since $k = R/N_0$ where R is the gas constant and No is Avogadro's number, and $mN_0 = M$ where M is the mass of one mole of gas, we have:

$$\overline{v^2} = \frac{3kT}{m} = \frac{3RT}{N_0 m} = \frac{3RT}{M}$$

$$\overline{v^2} = \frac{3 \times 8.313 \text{ joule}/^\circ k \text{ mole} \times 473^\circ \text{ k}}{28 \times 10^{-3} \dfrac{kg}{mole}}$$

$$= \frac{3 \times 8.313 \text{ kg-m}^2/\text{s}^2 \, ^\circ k \text{ mole} \times 473^\circ \text{ k}}{28 \times 10^{-3} \text{ kg/mole}}$$

$$= 4.21 \times 10^5 \text{ m}^2/\text{sec}^2$$

Thus the average speed c of a molecule is

$$c = \sqrt{\overline{v^2}} = 6.5 \times 10^2 \text{ m/sec.}$$

When two molecules of radius r collide, their centers are a distance 2r apart. Therefore, a molecule travelling along a straight line will collide with other molecules within a distance 2r of its center (we assume a simplified model in which one molecule moves and the others remain stationary and in which all collisions are elastic). During a time Δt, the molecule which we are following travels a distance $c\Delta t$. Thus, the molecules with which our molecule will collide are all found within a cylinder of base radius 2r and height $c\Delta t$. This cylinder is called the collision cylinder. If N is the number of molecules in volume V, then the density of molecules is N/V. If we multiply the volume of the cylinder by the density of molecules we will have the number of molecules in the cylinder ($4\pi r^2 \, c\Delta t \, N/V$). Dividing this quantity by Δt we have the number of collisions per unit time ($4\pi r^2 c \, N/V$). The average time between collisions is the reciprocal of this, called the mean free time ($V/4\pi r^2 \, cN$). If we multiply this by the average velocity, we have the average distance a molecule travels before colliding with another (the mean free path):

$$L = \frac{cV}{4\pi r^2 cN}$$

$$= \frac{V}{4\pi r^2 N}$$

Substituting our values, we have (in the present case let $r = 1.3 \times 10^{-10}$ m):

$$L = \frac{16.7 \times 10^{-3} \text{ m}^3}{4\pi (1.3 \times 10^{-10} \text{ m})^2 (1.29 \text{ moles}) (6.023 \times 10^{23} \text{ moles}^{-1})}$$

$$= 1.01 \times 10^{-7} \text{ m}$$

ELECTROSTATICS

● **PROBLEM** 19-11

An isolated sphere 10 cm in radius is charged in air to 500 volts. How much charge is required? If this charge is then shared with another isolated sphere of 5 cm radius by connecting them together quickly with a fine wire, what is the final charge on each and what is the final potential of each?

FIGURE A   FIGURE B

$r_1 = 10$ cm.

$V_1 = 500$ V

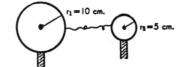

$r_1 = 10$ cm.

$r_2 = 5$ cm.

Solution: Figure A shows the first situation. (We assume both spheres are made of a conducting material.) The potential of a sphere is

$$V = \frac{1}{4\pi\epsilon_0} \frac{q}{R}$$

where ϵ_0 is the permittivity of free space, and q is the charge on the sphere of radius R. Solving for q, and using the given data

$$q = 4\pi\epsilon_0 RV$$

$$q = \frac{(10 \times 10^{-2} \text{m}) (500 \text{ V})}{(9 \times 10^{9} \text{ N} \cdot \text{m}^2/\text{c}^2)} \approx 5.6 \times 10^{-9} \text{ C} \qquad (1)$$

This is the charge needed to raise the sphere of 10 cm radius to 500 V.

In figure B, we show the 2 spheres connected by a fine wire. In this situation, they have equal potentials and

$$V_1 = V_2$$

or $\dfrac{1}{4\pi\epsilon_0}\dfrac{q_1}{R_1} = \dfrac{1}{4\pi\epsilon_0}\dfrac{q_2}{R_2}$

whence $\quad q_1 = \dfrac{R_1}{R_2} q_2 \qquad\qquad\qquad\qquad\qquad$ (2)

Here, the subscript 1, refers to variables involved with the larger sphere, and similarly for the subscript 2 and the smaller sphere. Furthermore, since both spheres share the charge initially on the larger sphere,

$$q_1 + q_2 = q \qquad\qquad\qquad\qquad (3)$$

where q is given by (1). Using (2) in (3), we solve for q_2,

$$\left(\dfrac{R_1}{R_2} + 1\right) q_2 = q$$

$$q_2 = \dfrac{q}{\dfrac{R_1}{R_2} + 1} = \dfrac{q}{2+1} = \dfrac{q}{3}$$

whence $\quad q_2 = \dfrac{5.6}{3} \times 10^{-9}\,C \approx 1.86 \times 10^{-9}\,C$

Furthermore, $\quad q_1 = q - q_2 \approx (5.6 - 1.86) \times 10^{-9}\,C$

$$q_1 \approx 3.74 \times 10^{-9}\,C$$

The final potential of the larger sphere is the same as the final potential of the smaller sphere. Both spheres then have a final potential of

$$V = V_1 = V_2 = \dfrac{q_1}{4\pi\epsilon_0 R_1}$$

$$V \approx \dfrac{(3.74 \times 10^{-9}\,C)\,(9 \times 10^{9}\,N \cdot m^2/c^2)}{(10 \times 10^{-2}\,m)}$$

$$V \approx 336.6\,\text{Volts}$$

ELECTROSTATIC INTERACTION

• PROBLEM 19-12

Consider the array of three charges shown in the diagram. Find the force on charge 1 caused by the other two charges. Calculate the field at the position of 1 due to the other two charges.

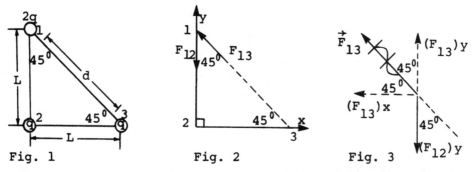

Fig. 1   Fig. 2   Fig. 3

<u>Solution:</u> The force at 1 will be the vector sum of forces caused by charges 2 and 3. The magnitudes of these forces are

$$F_{12} = K_E \frac{(2q)q}{L^2} = K_E \frac{2q^2}{L^2}$$

$$F_{13} = K_E \frac{(2q)q}{d^2}$$

But $d^2 = 2L^2$ (figure 1). Therefore

$$F_{13} = \frac{K_E q^2}{2L^2}$$

F_{12} is an attractive force, and F_{13} repulsive. Their x- and y- components are (figure 3).

$$\left(F_{12}\right)_x = 0$$

$$\left(F_{12}\right)_y = -K_E \frac{2q^2}{L^2}$$

$$\left(F_{13}\right)_x = -K_E \frac{q^2}{2L^2} \cos 45°$$

$$\left(F_{13}\right)_y = K_E \frac{q^2}{2L^2} \sin 45°$$

Thus the resultant force F at 1 is

$$F_x = \left(F_{12}\right)_x + \left(F_{13}\right)_x = -K_E \frac{q^2}{2L^2} \frac{1}{\sqrt{2}} \quad \text{for} \quad \cos 45° = \frac{1}{\sqrt{2}}$$

$$F_y = \left(F_{12}\right)_y + \left(F_{13}\right)_y = -K_E \frac{2q^2}{L^2} + K_E \frac{q^2}{2L^2} \frac{1}{\sqrt{2}} \quad \text{for} \quad \sin 45° = \frac{1}{\sqrt{2}}$$

The magnitude of F is

$$F = \sqrt{F_x^2 + F_y^2} = 1.59 \, K_E \frac{q^2}{L^2}$$

If $q = e$ and $L = 1 \overset{\bullet}{A} = 10^{-10}$ m, then

$$F = 1.59 \times \left(9 \times 10^9 \, \frac{\text{nt-m}^2}{\text{coul}^2}\right) \times \frac{\left(1.6 \times 10^{-19} \, \text{coul}\right)^2}{\left(10^{-10} \, \text{m}\right)^2}$$

$$= 2.24 \times 10^{-8} \, \text{N}$$

The electric field E at position 1 is given by the force at 1 divided by the net charge at 1, 2q:

$$E = \frac{F}{2q} = 1.59 \ K_E \frac{q}{2L^2}$$

$$= \frac{2.24 \times 10^{-8} \ N}{\left(2 \ 1.6 \times 10^{-19} \ coul\right)} = 2.1 \times 10^{11} \ \frac{N}{coul}$$

ELECTRIC CIRCUITS

● PROBLEM 19-13

An enquiring physics student connects a cell to a circuit and measures the current drawn from the cell to be I_1.

When he joins a second, identical cell in series with the first, the current becomes I_2. When he connects the cells in parallel, the current through the circuit is I_3. Show that the relation he finds between the currents is $3I_2I_3 = 2I_1(I_2 + I_3)$. (See figures (a), (b) and (c)).

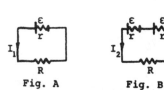

Fig. A   Fig. B

Fig. C

Solution: Let the emf of any of the cells be ε and its internal resistance be r. Let the external circuit have a resistance R. When a single cell is used (see figure (a)) R and r will be in series. Hence, the equivalent circuit resistance R_{eq} is

$$R_{eq} = R + r$$

Ohm's Law yields

$$I_1 = \frac{\varepsilon_{net}}{R_{net}} = \frac{\varepsilon}{R_{eq}} = \frac{\varepsilon}{R + r}$$

If two identical cells are connected in series, their emf's act in the same sense. Hence, again using Ohm's Law (see figure (b))

$$I_2 = \frac{\varepsilon_{net}}{R_{net}} = \frac{2\varepsilon}{R + r}$$

When the cells are connected in parallel, since they are identical, by the symmetry of the arrangement identical currents I_0 must flow through each cell.

265

Further, since no charge accumulates at point A in this circuit, (by conservation of charge)

$$I_3 = I_0 + I_0 = 2I_0$$

Considering the passage of current through either cell, we have

$$V_{AB} = \varepsilon - I_0 r = \varepsilon - \frac{I_3}{2} r.$$

This follows because, each charge passing through ε is raised in potential an amount ε. However, by Ohm's Law, each charge also loses potential $I_0 r$ by crossing the battery's internal resistance. When we consider the passage of current through the external circuit, then $V_{AB} = I_3 R$, by Ohm's Law. Hence

$$I_3 R = \varepsilon - \frac{I_3 r}{2}$$

or

$$\varepsilon = I_3 \left(R + \frac{r}{2} \right)$$

Rewriting the three equations obtained, we find that

$$R + r = \frac{\varepsilon}{I_1}, \quad R + 2r = \frac{2\varepsilon}{I_2}, \quad \text{and} \quad R + \frac{r}{2} = \frac{\varepsilon}{I_3}$$

We must eliminate all resistance variables to obtain the given formula.

Solving the first equation for r, and substituting this value in the second equation, we obtain

$$r = \frac{\varepsilon}{I_1} - R$$

$$R + 2 \left(\frac{\varepsilon}{I_1} - R \right) = \frac{2\varepsilon}{I_2}$$

or

$$- R = \frac{2\varepsilon}{I_2} - \frac{2\varepsilon}{I_1}$$

$$R = 2\varepsilon \left(\frac{1}{I_1} - \frac{1}{I_2} \right) \qquad\qquad (1)$$

Inserting the calculated value of r in the third equation

$$R + \tfrac{1}{2} \left(\frac{\varepsilon}{I_1} - R \right) = \frac{\varepsilon}{I_3} \qquad \text{or} \qquad \tfrac{1}{2} R = \frac{\varepsilon}{I_3} - \tfrac{1}{2} \frac{\varepsilon}{I_1}$$

$$R = \varepsilon \left(\frac{2}{I_3} - \frac{1}{I_1} \right) \qquad\qquad (2)$$

Dividing equations (1) and (2) gives

266

$$1 = \frac{2[(1/I_1) - (1/I_2)]}{(2/I_3) - (1/I_1)}$$

$$\frac{2}{I_3} - \frac{1}{I_1} = \frac{2}{I_1} - \frac{2}{I_2}$$

or $\quad \dfrac{2}{I_3} = \dfrac{3}{I_1} - \dfrac{2}{I_2}$

Multiplying both sides by $I_1 I_2 I_3$

$$2I_1 I_2 = 3I_2 I_3 - 2I_1 I_3$$

or $\quad 3I_2 I_3 = 2I_1(I_3 + I_2)$

$\therefore 2I_1 I_2 - I_2 I_3 = 2I_2 I_3 - 2I_1 I_3. \quad \therefore 3I_2 I_3 = 2I_1(I_2 + I_3)$

MAGNETIC FORCES

● **PROBLEM** 19-14

A scientifically minded Romeo has found a method of sending secret messages to a beautiful Juliet who is immured in the top floor of a castle 50 ft from the ground. Romeo places two light metal rods (too light to use for climbing up) against her windowsill, and between the rods he mounts a wire 10 cm long, to which is attached the message and a magnet so placed that the wire is permanently in a magnetic field of strength 0.049 Wb · m^{-2}, at right angles to the plane of the rods. When he passes a current of 10 A up one rod, through the connecting wire and back down the other rod, the message,wire, and magnet travel at uniform speed up the rods. The moving assembly weighs 0.25 kg. Neglecting friction, calculate what the length of the rods must be.

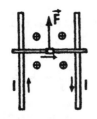

FIGURE A: Front View   FIGURE B: Side View

Solution: From figure A, we see that the magnetic field must be at right angles to the plane of the rods and acting downward. The magnetic field vector is perpendicular to both the direction of current and to the force. The right hand rule determines that the direction is downward. The magnitude of the force experienced by the wire and attachments is

$|\vec{F}| = \ell IB \sin \phi$ where ϕ is the angle between the direction of I and $\vec{B}$ • $\phi = 90°$, and

$F = \ell IB = 0.1 \text{ m} \times 10 \text{ A} \times 0.049 \text{ Wb} \cdot \text{m}^{-2} = 0.049 \text{ N}.$

Considering fig. B, we see that the forces acting on the wire and attachments are three in number: the weight acting vertically downward, the force F acting up the plane of the rods, and N, the normal reaction of the rods on the wire acting at right angles to the plane of the rods. Since the assembly moves up the rods at uniform speed, $F = mg \sin \theta$.

$$\therefore \quad \sin \theta = \frac{0.049 \text{ N}}{0.25 \text{ kg} \times 9.8 \text{ m} \cdot \text{s}^{-2}} = 0.02.$$

From the diagram, $h/L = \sin \theta = 0.02$.

$$\therefore \quad L = \frac{h}{0.02} = \frac{50 \text{ ft}}{0.02} = 2500 \text{ ft}.$$

REFRACTION

● **PROBLEM** 19-15

A flat bottom swimming pool is 8 ft. deep. How deep does it appear to be when filled with water whose refractive index is 4/3?

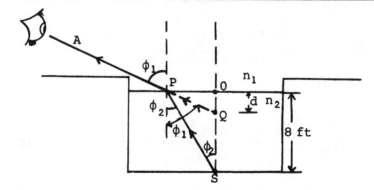

Solution: In order to see why we would expect to observe a different depth for the pool when it is filled with water, examine the figure. If no water is in the pool, light coming from a point S on the bottom of the pool will travel directly to the observer's eye. If the pool is filled with water, light emanating from point S will be refracted at

P, as shown. Upon reaching the observer's eye, the light appears to be coming from Q and he perceives the depth of the pool to be the distance OQ, rather than the actual depth OS. Our problem is to find the distance d.

Note that, from the figure,

$$\tan \varphi_1 = \frac{OP}{d}$$

$$\tan \varphi_2 = \frac{OP}{8} \text{ ft.}$$

Hence

$$\frac{\tan \varphi_1}{\tan \varphi_2} = \frac{OP}{d} \cdot \frac{8 \text{ ft.}}{OP} = \frac{8 \text{ ft.}}{d}$$

and

$$d = \frac{(8 \text{ ft})\tan \varphi_2}{\tan \varphi_1} \tag{1}$$

From Snell's Law,

$$n_1 \sin \varphi_1 = n_2 \sin \varphi_2$$

where n_1 and n_2 are the indices of refraction of air and water, respectively. Therefore

$$\left(\frac{n_1}{n_2}\right) \text{ in } \varphi_1 = \sin \varphi_2 \tag{2}$$

To calculate the tangents in (1), we must also know $\cos \varphi_1$ and $\cos \varphi_2$. These we may find by observing that

$$\cos \varphi = \sqrt{1 - \sin^2 \varphi} \tag{3}$$

Using (2) in (3)

$$\cos \varphi_2 = \sqrt{1 - \sin^2 \varphi_2}$$

$$\cos \varphi_2 = \sqrt{1 - \left(\frac{n_1}{n_2}\right)^2 \sin^2 \varphi_1} \tag{4}$$

$$\cos \varphi_1 = \sqrt{1 - \sin^2 \varphi_1}$$

Hence

$$\tan \varphi_1 = \frac{\sin \varphi_1}{\cos \varphi_1} = \frac{\sin \varphi_1}{\sqrt{1 - \sin^2 \varphi_1}} \tag{5}$$

and using (2) with (4)

$$\tan \varphi_2 = \frac{\sin \varphi_2}{\cos \varphi_2} = \frac{(n_1/n_2) \sin \varphi_1}{\sqrt{1 - (n_1/n_2)^2 \sin^2 \varphi_1}} \tag{6}$$

Substituting (5) and (6) in (1)

$$d = (8 \text{ ft}) \frac{(n_1/n_2) \sin \varphi_1}{\sqrt{1 - (n_1/n_2)^2 \sin^2 \varphi_1}} \cdot \frac{\sqrt{1 - \sin^2 \varphi_1}}{\sin \varphi_1}$$

$$d = (8 \text{ ft})\left(n_1/n_2\right) \sqrt{\frac{1 - \sin^2 \varphi_1}{1 - \left(n_1/n_2\right)^2 \sin^2 \varphi_1}} \tag{7}$$

Now, since we don't know the angle φ_1, we make an approximation. Suppose φ_1 is very small. (This means that the observer is looking almost directly down into the pool.) Then $\sin \varphi_1 \approx 0$ and the square root in (7) becomes 1. Therefore

$$d = (8 \text{ ft})\left(\frac{n_1}{n_2}\right) = (8 \text{ ft})\left(\frac{1}{4/3}\right) = 6 \text{ ft}.$$

The pool appears to be 6 ft. deep.

INDEX

Numbers on this page refer to **PROBLEM NUMBERS**, not page numbers

Numbers on this page refer to **PROBLEM NUMBERS**, not page numbers

Numbers on this page refer to **PROBLEM NUMBERS**, not page numbers

REA's Test Preps
The Best in Test Preparation

- REA "Test Preps" are **far more** comprehensive than any other test preparation series
- Each book contains up to **eight** full-length practice tests based on the most recent exams
- **Every** type of question likely to be given on the exams is included
- Answers are accompanied by **full** and **detailed** explanations

REA publishes over 70 Test Preparation volumes in several series. They include:

Advanced Placement Exams (APs)
Biology
Calculus AB & Calculus BC
Chemistry
Economics
English Language & Composition
English Literature & Composition
European History
French
Government & Politics
Physics B & C
Psychology
Spanish Language
Statistics
United States History
World History

College-Level Examination Program (CLEP)
Analyzing and Interpreting Literature
College Algebra
Freshman College Composition
General Examinations
General Examinations Review
History of the United States I
History of the United States II
Human Growth and Development
Introductory Sociology
Principles of Marketing
Spanish

SAT Subject Tests
Biology E/M
Chemistry
English Language Proficiency Test
French
German

SAT Subject Tests (cont'd)
Literature
Mathematics Level 1, 2
Physics
Spanish
United States History

Graduate Record Exams (GREs)
Biology
Chemistry
Computer Science
General
Literature in English
Mathematics
Physics
Psychology

ACT - ACT Assessment

ASVAB - Armed Services Vocational Aptitude Battery

CBEST - California Basic Educational Skills Test

CDL - Commercial Driver License Exam

CLAST - College Level Academic Skills Test

COOP & HSPT - Catholic High School Admission Tests

ELM - California State University Entry Level Mathematics Exam

FE (EIT) - Fundamentals of Engineering Exams - For both AM & PM Exams

FTCE - Florida Teacher Certification Exam

GED - High School Equivalency Diploma Exam (U.S. & Canadian editions)

GMAT - Graduate Management Admission Test

LSAT - Law School Admission Test

MAT - Miller Analogies Test

MCAT - Medical College Admission Test

MTEL - Massachusetts Tests for Educator Licensure

NJ HSPA - New Jersey High School Proficiency Assessment

NYSTCE: LAST & ATS-W - New York State Teacher Certification

PLT - Principles of Learning & Teaching Tests

PPST - Pre-Professional Skills Tests

PSAT / NMSQT

SAT

TExES - Texas Examinations of Educator Standards

THEA - Texas Higher Education Assessment

TOEFL - Test of English as a Foreign Language

TOEIC - Test of English for International Communication

USMLE Steps 1,2,3 - U.S. Medical Licensing Exams

U.S. Postal Exams 460 & 470

Research & Education Association
61 Ethel Road W., Piscataway, NJ 08854
Phone: (732) 819-8880   **website: www.rea.com**

Please send me more information about your Test Prep books.

Name _____

Address _____

City _____ State _____ Zip _____